Lore of Trout Fishing

A Special Collection of Lessons
From the Pages of
FLY FISHERMAN

Art Lee

Foreword by John Randolph

Human Kinetics

Library of Congress Cataloging-in-Publication Data

Lee, Art.
    Lore of trout fishing : a special collection of lessons from the
pages of Fly fisherman / Art Lee ; foreword by John Randolph.
        p.   cm.
    Includes index.
    ISBN 0-88011-790-7
    1. Trout fishing.   2. Fly fishing.   I. Title.
    SH687.L374   1999   98-47330
    799.1'757--DC21   CIP

ISBN: 0-88011-790-7

Acquisitions Editor: Martin Barnard; **Developmental Editor:** Rebecca Crist; **Assistant Editor:** Chris Enstrom; **Copyeditor:** Jim Burns; **Proofreader:** Myla Smith; **Indexer:** Marie Rizzo; **Graphic Designer:** Robert Reuther; **Graphic Artist:** Yvonne Windsor; **Cover Designer:** Jack Davis; **Photographer:** Kris Lee; **Illustrator:** Galen Mercer; **Printer:** Edwards Brothers (color insert by Original Smith Printing)

Human Kinetics books are available at special discounts for bulk purchase. Special editions or book excerpts can also be created to specification. For details, contact the Special Sales Manager at Human Kinetics.

Printed in the United States of America   10 9 8 7 6 5 4 3 2 1

Human Kinetics
Web site: http://www.humankinetics.com/

United States: Human Kinetics, P.O. Box 5076, Champaign, IL 61825-5076
1-800-747-4457
e-mail: humank@hkusa.com

Canada: Human Kinetics, 475 Devonshire Road Unit 100, Windsor, ON N8Y 2L5
1-800-465-7301 (in Canada only)
e-mail: humank@hkcanada.com

Europe: Human Kinetics, P.O. Box IW14, Leeds LS16 6TR, United Kingdom
+44 (0) 113-278 1708
e-mail: humank@hkeurope.com

Australia: Human Kinetics, 57A Price Avenue, Lower Mitcham, South Australia 5062
(08) 82771555
e-mail: humank@hkaustralia.com

New Zealand: Human Kinetics, P.O. Box 105-231, Auckland Central
09-523-3462
e-mail: humank@hknewz.com

This book is for my Krissy.

Contents

Pursuing
a Vision

The chords that resonate to all fly fishers have *possessed* Art Lee. He has spent his adult life pursuing trout and salmon on a fly. He has devoted himself to those pursuits and to their description in finely crafted essays. Few men have such a clearly defined, and refined, vision of their world. Fewer are capable of describing their passion in a way that speaks compellingly to others.

As the editor of the world's largest and most influential magazine on the sport of fly fishing, I must fish for writers who can speak clearly to my readers with a vision that they can share. Art Lee can do that. He helps me create a magazine where fly fishers meet to share expectations, hopes, dreams, challenges, and explorations—the chords they feel and respond to.

Art has written for *Fly Fisherman* magazine for over two decades, as long as any of our contributing writers. During most of those years I have edited the magazine; thus I have observed his growth as a writer and development as a fly fisher. The two must occur simultaneously, for a fly fishing writer cannot mature without movement upward in both fields.

We fly fishers are a curious hunting fraternity. We separately begin our journeys toward maturity as youths armed with worms and spinners, stalking fish wherever they are found. We try to catch, and kill, everything, and we carry our trophies home to prove and improve our image.

Then—somewhere, sometime—we are introduced to the arts and ethics of fly fishing and the doors begin to open for us, the scales begin to fall. Slowly, in the long trek, we learn of new challenges, new arts, and new visions of an aquatic world where fish are the consummate beatitudes. We begin to cherish them for their inherent value, and we learn to release them as an expression of our concern for their future. Then, like a musician learning the importance of those spaces *between* the notes, we begin to see what connects things, the important subtleties that hold things together. We see a fish's world from within, and the word *ecosystem* takes on a new meaning.

Through his writing, the readers of *Fly Fisherman* and I have watched Art Lee open his doors into this world that so few have the good fortune to enter. He has taken us along with him in his exploration of the web that connects the natural world of trout and salmon, and that connects them to the fly fishers of the world.

I can think of no finer accomplishment in life than that of true vision, for it opens the path to happiness and fulfillment. It makes little difference which road one follows to that vision, but a commitment to understanding and excellence is an essential element of the journey. Art Lee is a *fly fisher* and a *writer*, and in both endeavors he is exceptional. This book offers his mature, clear-eyed vision, that clear-eyed view of a world that non–fly fishers must consider at best arcane and at worst immodestly self-indulgent.

For those of us who find ourselves onstream, this book is an important personal testament of our chosen commitment—our faith. Truly, each step that Art Lee takes and describes here is one he shares with all the true fly fishers of the world.

John Randolph
Editor/Publisher
Fly Fisherman Magazine
Harrisburg, Pennsylvania

And Yet So Far

Time always stood still when you started to cross that field. By midsummer it would be a cornfield, full and green, but now, in April, it looked only huge and brown and bare, except for the files of bleached stalk stubbles—row after row of them—that reminded you, despite yourself, of the gravestones on a historic battlefield. Across the field, the lines of trees that marked the banks of the stream seemed to swim in the morning mist. The sky was low, the faraway trees naked and gray under it, and this somehow made you see the stream as a million miles off.

Chett was very old by then and had to walk slowly. He was tall and lean but walked bent at the waist as though into a wind. By then the corners of his mouth had begun to turn downward so that if you didn't know his eyes, you might have taken him for a dour man. But Chett was never dour. It was just the pain.

I would snatch glances at one of his big hands, and you could see it tremble. The tremble was permanent now and I know he knew he would live with it always. It meant that he could no longer hold his brushes and had turned instead to pallet knives and to painting only out-of-doors. I had watched it come on him little by little over the years, until at last it had become so much a part of him that I had ceased to long so achingly to reach out and stroke his white hair, as you'd stroke the hair of a terrified child just awakened from a nightmare. By then I had come to understand that Chett felt no fear and had learned to abide the trembling and the pain because Chett was Chett and it could be no other way.

"Did you do them for me?" he might ask, turning his head to speak when you were a short distance out into the field.

"Last night," I'd tell him, tapping the Union Leader pipe tobacco tin in my mackinaw and smiling at his eyes. "Enough for a few days, anyway."

"That's my boy," he'd say then, and the corners of his mouth would pitch up as if reaching for a smile, then retreat again. "But don't let me have more than three, maybe four, now will you?"

"Why don't you carry the tin?" I'd ask, knowing we'd be separated for long periods during the day.

"The goat to guard the cabbage patch," he'd chuckle, then cough. "I'd probably just sidle up to one of those big trees and smoke my head off. Then where'd we be?"

This was all just part of a game we'd played countless times since the disease had begun to slowly take him from me. I had to roll all of his cigarettes for him now—he'd never smoke another cigarette if he had to smoke the store-bought kind—and I knew that if he carried the tin himself, he'd be much tougher on himself than if I carried it to dole them out upon request. From me he'd always manage to get the three or four without suffering a lick of guilt.

It was not the only game we played, of course, to try to make the time crossing the field go faster and less painfully. Sometimes we'd promise ourselves not to look up from the ground, not for 50, even a 100 paces. Then you'd stare intently at your feet, determined to concentrate only on them as you tramped along—counting one, two, three, four, in an attempt to corral your anticipation. Not once did either of us ever stick it out through 50, however. Thirty always seemed to be the limit of our endurance. At 30, as if on cue, our heads would pop up simultaneously, only to find that we apparently had gotten nowhere. Often as not, the tree lines would actually appear to have retreated before our advance, as though at any instant they might dissolve into the mist in front of your eyes, a mirage.

"Tell me about ol' George Vanderbilt," I might say to him then. "Was he really such a snob?"

"Oh, ol' George was a snob, all right," he'd answer in the voice of a master bedtime storyteller, one who never betrayed how many times you'd covered the same ground before. "But then, ol' George was really a corker, too."

"But *you* knew how to get to him."

"'Twasn't me so much. No, anybody could get to ol' George, once you found out his weak spot."

"What about his weak spot?"

Chett Osborn

"You got to ol' George through his tackle. Yessir. 'See you got a new pole, George,' you'd say. An' he'd glower at you, his face getting redder than an apple. Then he'd start grumblin' under his breath, 'Hrumpf . . . new pole . . . indeed . . . it's a rod, goddamn it, custom made.' So you'd pretend you'd never heard him and say something like, 'Gee, George, I don't know how you do it. Me, I just can't get used to a new pole. If I ever lost or broke this ol' thing, I guess I'd just hafta quit fishing.' Oh, I tellya, my boy, if looks could kill . . . "

"And wasn't he some kind of a dry fly purist?"

"A purist? Well, I guess he was, *pure* as the driven snow. Dutch an' me, we'd be fishin' wets or streamers, but ol' George he'd sit there on the bank starin' at the surface all day long if need be. Ol' George wouldn't even get his waders wet unless the trout were risin'. Now, Dutch kinda saw ol' George as a rich ol' s.o.b. But George was okay, really, once you toasted him and cut off the crust."

"You and Dutch were partners a long time."

"A long, long time. First got together in nineteen-aught-three."

And that would get me to wondering what Chett must have been like when he was young like me. And I'd wonder if the trout would be rising today and if Chett might be wondering the same thing. Why I never asked him, I'll never know. I tried to imagine him with Dutch, breaking camp and loading gear into a canoe and shoving off downriver. You could picture them breaking her at the tail of a long rapids, then paddling ashore to fish a pool, maybe one where nobody had ever fished before.

And then you finally became entirely unaware of your footfalls under you as you crossed the field, because your mind was far behind you now. And you could see Chett sketching, sitting on a white boulder, the sun streaming through branches of spruce, a whitetail doe drinking in the shallows just off the far shore, raising her head, then turning in silence to signal her fawn, who'd been hidden among the alders, to join her. You could see Dutch at Chett's shoulder, filling his pipe, watching the river and the forest and the doe coming to life on paper. You could see Dutch nod, then reach out gently and touch Chett on the shoulder, whispering, "I'm going to grab my rod and sneak upstream."

Then I might look over at Chett and he might already be looking at me. Our eyes would meet. The field was crossed—actively, passively—and was now something of an abstraction. Chett would nod as we'd stop under the big buttonwood tree, and I'd reach into my mackinaw to fetch the Union Leader tin. You'd have to hold both rods while Chett leaned against the tree to strike a match. By then to light a match had become a terrible effort and it usually took several tries before the tobacco would fire. But this chore he always insisted on doing himself, probably to spare me any further blame as an accessory. "Nice rolling job," or something to that effect, he'd usually say after inhaling deeply and lovingly releasing the smoke through his nose and mouth. "Nice 'n tight, the way they should be."

I felt no guilt then and feel none now, and so I'd smile a smile of genuine gratitude for being appreciated.

"What are you going to try?" Chett would ask softly, the smoke like the low ceiling of clouds around his head.

"Some kind of streamer, I guess. Looks like our only chance. What do you think?"

"I think so," he'd answer after glancing quickly over his shoulder at the stream. "You mind tying one on for me?"

Just behind us now, the stream would be high and gray, still tinged with the milk of spring runoff, and most of the rocks would be buried beneath the icy water. We knew we wouldn't see a trout rise all day, probably wouldn't see a trout at all, although we'd fish the day all the way through.

"Which way you headed?" Chett always asked then.

"Makes no difference. You tell me."

"Then, why don't you sneak upstream for a couple of hours. Maybe there'll be something doin' above the big bend."

And I would start away, leaving him there puffing what in later years might have been called the "roach" of an honest-to-goodness cigarette, aware each time I left that time was no abstraction, that it had begun to move again, wishing against all the realities and abstractions there were some way to freeze it. Now I would listen only to the stream spilling by and would turn back only long enough to throw Chett a wave after the words he *never* forgot to call out had caught up.

"Good luck to you, partner."

Acknowledgments

The years have rushed by so fast and yet I see myself now as having been a part of *Fly Fisherman* magazine forever—living in a rhyme. There have been laughs and cries, the occasional brawl, but all in all, FFM, one of the few acronyms for which I have any toleration whatsoever, has been the center of my professional life for as long as I can remember. (I still wonder—but only occasionally now as I grow younger—what I'm going to do when I grow up.) And even as more people inform me that somehow I'm attaining "elder statesman" status within the fly fishing fraternity, I can only blush, shrug and scratch my head, for frankly I cannot help but continue to feel as though I'm still 25 and the whole thing is just starting. I suppose it's like trying to cure a man from hallucinating by simply telling him to stop hallucinating, as futile as it would seem rational.

What you are about to read is the work of a satisfied man, and satisfied men—if they pause to think—never reach that place alone. It is deeper even than what Donne had to say; though he reflected on the merits of individuals in convocation by conjuring up the island as the potential residence of misanthropy, and by implication, utter failure as a human being, he never put to paper the plain and simple need for *thanks*. My notion is—a hard lesson learned—that if any man is indeed an island, it is because he never learned, or somehow forgot how, to say thank you and mean it.

Christ, what a world, what a life, what folks it has been my honor and joy to know since that day when FFM founder Don Zahner called me and asked me to write for his fledgling magazine and to serve as its Northeast Field Editor. Thank you Don for yesterday, today and tomorrow. Staffs have turned over and over and over, and to protect myself from embarrassing myself by forgetting to name someone out of one of them—to try out an "elder statesman's" prerogative for the first time—I am going to thank them individually *in toto* from the bottom of my heart. I do want to say a special thank-you to "Stick," who always kept me laughing and sat a motorcycle wonderfully. And to the memory of Craig Woods in hopes that he is aware how much I wish I had known and had tried harder. I pray you have found peace, Craig.

What can I say about John Randolph, present editor and publisher of the magazine, who is still a kid like yours truly? I've known John since not too long after he'd been to Williams, did the school, but was never quite talked into buying the T-shirt. We love you, John, which, of course, implies thanks, or having never been to Williams myself, I sure hope it does because it's certainly intended to. John, by the way, was not only delighted to learn that this book was to come, but gladly and promptly wrote his generous and insightful Foreword to it. Then there's Managing Editor Philip Hanyok who listens, and Debra Brehm, assistant to the editor, who does. Never have I asked either of them for anything when they didn't try, and for that I offer a heartfelt thank-you.

To name all the people who live between the covers of this book would take a book in itself, and so to them, too, I'm afraid I'm going to have to say thank you collectively. You know, it wasn't long ago that at the urging of my fishing partner and closest friend Galen Mercer I retired a Richardson's Fye Box which I had worn for years. The box, containing hundreds and hundreds of flies by tyers and anglers at home and abroad who are angling household names from the past and present, was simply too valuable historically (and probably financially). Galen insisted, no doubt correctly, to continue to use its contents on a day-to-day basis, which had been my practice. "For god's sake," Galen reminded me one day, "a lot of these flies were prototypes."

All of which I guess is true—*except* I never thought of those from whom I obtained the flies as legends, or whatever. To me they were, and are, my generous friends, from the late Charlie Ritz and Arnold Gingrich to the living Ed Van Put and Poul Jorgensen, who had simply candied me with their makings the way friends do. Which is the way I know they were thinking as they reached out their hands to me. So many buddies, so much intelligence and skill, so much potential luck in the form of fur and feather affixed to steel. Without you and without the fruits of your brilliance, this book might never have been, or if it came to be, would certainly be a whole lot different than it is. Thank you all.

This is my third book for Human Kinetics and I certainly hope not my last. Only "time and the river" will tell. A couple of years ago, I was contacted by Martin Barnard, acquisitions editor and now friend (he sent me a *personal* Christmas present, not a company-sponsored gift), informing me that the physical fitness and coaching book giant wanted to try its hand in the fly fishing field. Would I write for it and help it to learn the game and the players? I thank Human Kinetics and its large and busy staff for its commitment to me and for following through. Angling will be better for your involvement and growth within the sport. I am sure I have learned better than I've taught, although I will say I do hope Martin will never again "hit" anything over 12 when a blackjack dealer is showing a card 6 or lower and that he will come at last to accept that the odds against a short fighter getting butted and cut *under* the eyelid, not in one fight but in two consecutive fights, by a taller fighter are beyond astronomical, no matter what his feelings about the shorter fighter and his past might be.

Thanks, too, to my editor Rebecca Crist for working on my behalf so deep in the trenches that I am yet to see her face or hear her voice, but without whom this book would and could not be.

And finally to Kris and Galen, who have seen me at my best and at my worst and are still with me making this puss look the best it can look by way of photo and illustration, for making things I scribble all the more clear for the thousand words added inside each of their published frames, and for making the places and conditions we've encountered be as they are, not as someone might like to see them through rose-colored glasses. You are the best. Please consider this *thank-you* a thank-you for all the times I have failed to say thank you in the past. Your work is superb, but as people, friends, loved ones, you mean more to me than words could ever begin to express. Given that there is no word and expression that transcends thank you and God bless, I will leave it at that.

Introduction

At this writing, I am 55 years old. Kris is, well, she'd rather not say, which speaks volumes, doesn't it, for as we began hiking the trail to what you are about to read, age didn't matter, not to me, not to Kris. We had plenty of time, not to mention, in my case anyway, a full head of hair and a waistline I didn't need to watch. (Kris, I'm pleased to report, hasn't changed a bit in either instance.) These were the days during which we began living what we called then, and still do, "the life." And although we'd like to believe that we've worked hard for lo these three decades we've shared, despite that hard work, including several brushes with death, we've never really thought of what we've had as a "career." In other words, two beggars have ridden a single horse the length and breadth of a metaphor, a trillion-to-one shot. A miracle.

How well I recall years ago standing outside the elevators of a posh New York hotel when who happened along but Ernest Schwiebert and company and over-hearing some of that company congratulate—some tease—the once boy prodigy, author of *Matching the Hatch* while still a college sophomore, about having turned 40 the previous June. "Christ," I thought, "Ernest Schwiebert, 40, I've got all the time in the world. Means nothing that I have no entourage, or significant following for that matter, nor that rarely does anybody shake my hand, at least not in connection with what I do in the outdoors world. My time will come."

For the record, I guess that sort of stuff mattered a lot then, but as time passed, it came to matter less and less, until now—though I suppose it's nice to have doors held for you—while I'm eternally grateful to those both within (Ernest is now Ernie to Kris and me) and without the field who have supported us, the rest of it, the "angling celebrity" if you will, doesn't matter a whit to either of us. What does matter is time, how we've spent it, how much more of it we may have left, and how well we will use it from now on in order to prove worthy of the continued faith of what we'd have to be blind not to recognize is today a considerable following.

I've always felt that anthologies were for heirs, part legacy, part closure. Yet, through the years I cannot begin to count the number of anglers, many of whom weren't even born when I began to scribble and Kris began to open and close the shutter, who have asked me when I might "collect" my work for *Fly Fisherman* magazine into a single volume. Though not a humorist, and I pray neither glib nor coy, truth is, my responses have always suggested something akin to taking a peek at my last will and testament, usually addended by a stated wish to outlive everyone named in it, meaning one helluva long time. So, when Human Kinetics contacted me with the request to publish such a collection of trout pieces, I was chary to say the least, and rushed to the sawbones for a checkup.

Truth is, I almost said "no" for a whole host of reasons, virtually all involving my inbred Irish inclination to fear jinxes and a real and continuing desire to lay a bigger *oeuvre*, rather than to crack the one already in straw mid-cluck. Besides, I had generally found anthologies—except some of fiction and the occasional compilation from the war hero or statesman—deadly dull, not to mention largely left unread by the public. The latter, by the way, was and remains of no small concern, since to shore up "the life" requires, as it does for everyone else, that Kris and I "gotta make a living," that truism apparently so old and/or so much taken for granted that not even Mr. Bartlett seems to have dug up its origin. Franz Kafka and J.D. Salinger notwithstanding, most writers write to be read, and I certainly can neither lay claim to being one of those lofty exceptions nor certainly to being by no means a man of means, to turn the lyrics of the late Roger Miller on their ear.

However, across the room from me, even now, there is a long shelf quite literally crammed with one copy of each magazine for which I've written an article or story from the beginning to date. I can hardly believe, for instance, that I've had a feature in the last 54 consecutive issues of *The Atlantic Salmon Journal*, a quarterly. It is certainly true, though, that for all of this other work and whatever implications may be drawn from its numeration, quality, or sometimes lack thereof, I have *belonged* to *Fly Fisherman* magazine quite literally since the day its founder Don Zahner, a brilliant essayist and source of the "Un-cola" advertising campaign that saved a dying soft drink company called 7-Up, asked me to serve as his Northeast field editor. Even as Don's brainchild has grown, flourished and changed hands, until today it is our sport's most widely read and influential medium; it has kept faith with me and I hope I with it. And while it hasn't made me as wealthy as those who have bought and sold it from time to time during my long tenure, even chain owned as it is today, there is little difference, for instance, in the palavers between its present Editor and Publisher, John Randolph, and me and those I had with Don it seems now an eternity ago.

But in and of itself, would, could, should or does this relationship, this affinity, justify the volume you now have in hand? The answer is a resounding no—any more than free fishing trips can ever be seen to justify puffy "payback" articles, which, regrettably, too often find their way to print. Anthologies, collections, call them what you will, will be anthologies or collections on Judgment Day. And so without something more, something to really breathe life into such a thing, something to confirm that the author is still on the hoof, *and kicking*, that what he has had to say, though recycled, true, is worthy of your money, time and attention, the product would be a conceit, a negation of the long-standing relationship between magazine and author from the narrowest perspective; it would be a breach of faith with sport and sportsmanship, and most crucial of all, a repudiation of the respect for those whose respect you have sought and who have favored you with it so openly and so gladly.

This, then, was a hard book to do, no mere assemblage, in some ways harder than it would have been to write a new one. Hard for manifold reasons, not the least of which was that I had to find a way to arrange its contents so to at once instruct, the quiddity of Human Kinetics books, while remaining not only true to the essence of the metaphor, which to me is what angling has been all about from the get-go, but also to somehow convey the wonder of discovery. It is the latter that gives meaning to writing, keeps the book true, and justifies, if any justification beyond the sheer joy of experiencing the instant event and future prospect is necessary, all those days on so many waters in so many places, doing the "research" from which the contents have sprung. If you finish it having learned little or nothing to make you a better angler, then I have failed you in the fundamental sense. But if you finish it void of at least some empathy with one who fishes to live and lives to fish, and in that void find no promise for yourself and others, then I might rightly perceive myself, and be perceived by you, as one who has spent his time wading aimlessly amid the currents of streams of dust.

Writers write. Editors edit. Publishers publish. Most publications have what's called an "editorial budget," although its name is misleading, since the word "budget" here has nothing to do with the expenditure of bread. Rather, what's involved is looking at, say, a year's publishing cycle and seeking to decide what will appear in the magazines individually and collectively, so that the range of subjects covered, the authors assigned to cover them, among countless other concerns, will have the broadest possible appeal to the broadest possible readership. Each issue, then, has what's known as a "feature well," which typically the "editorial side" tries to expand while the "business types" do their damndest to try to keep as tight as they can, in order to maximize advertising revenues and so overall earnings. While often contentious, the system is rooted as far back as Addison and Steele and is, I have to admit grudgingly, a healthy and productive one. Were both sides to search their souls, it can only be hoped that ultimately what each is really after is "balance."

The issues involved, however, ofttimes aren't only departmental. It would be hoped, for instance, that a writer, any writer, would try to deal with his assigned subject both fully and literately. Editors, on the other hand, frequently find that in some areas writers overwrite or, frankly, write badly and so must go to work with the ol' "blue pencil" to make things right. Many of the pieces I have written for *Fly Fisherman* and other publications have benefited immeasurably from the work of skilled editors. But there are times, too, when an editor fully recognizes that the work he must undertake on a given day isn't based on quality or substance, but on the realities of the editorial budget (long-term) and "feature well" (short-term), and so he or she must cut a piece simply to make it "fit" those two priorities, understanding full well that something of value will be lost in the doing. Thus, the mature writer must develop a certain objectivity, an ability to step aside from himself, and so be able recognize the difference between the two scenarios.

I note this by way of explaining why most of the pieces you are about to read will not read exactly as they first appeared in *Fly Fisherman*. In particular, you will find additions, occasionally considerable, which are, for me, the happy consequence of not being bound in the book format by either the "editorial budget" or "feature well" as each of these terms applies to magazine editing and production. Having retained a copy of each issue of the magazine in which the piece originally appeared, as well as one of each original manuscript, what I have done, then, is to juxtapose them, taking from each what it seemed to me would make for the fullest, clearest, most informative and entertaining reading on the subject covered. In a few instances, though only I will know it, there may even be a whole new line or two where I've inevitably slapped myself on the forehead, asking myself, "How could you have ever missed putting in this point, dummy?" In the main, though, what you are about to read you will find to represent what so many of you have so generously asked for through the years.

I'm quite sure I would prefer you see it as a *book*, an independent entity, not really an anthology or collection at all. Despite my eternal gratitude to all those at *Fly Fisherman* past and present, and certainly in no way presuming to diminish the job they have done for me by allotting to me so much of their "budgets" and "wells" through the years, nonetheless I would hope that from the way I've arranged it you may decide it stands on its own, much as the books of Joe Brooks, medleys really of his wonderful work for *Outdoor Life* years ago, scored so that you invariably forgot they were medleys at all. Selfless as they are, I am certain this is the way my good friends at *Fly Fisherman* would have it between us, too.

Finally, a few words about content. Frankly, I had no idea there had been such goings-on, that I'd written so many pieces (trade lingo) for *Fly Fisherman*. Indeed, I soon found that any attempt to reprint them all, even without illustration, would be nothing if not *War and Peace in Waders* as penned by an angling hobo. So, what to include, what to leave out, how to find some measure of symmetry and continuity in order to wind up with anything akin to what I've already protested as my chief concerns? Notwithstanding the occasional tricky current, the river had to flow, be accessible and at least reasonably easy wading on the easy chair. I have, therefore, tossed chronology out the window, presuming you, like me, to be anglers, not historians. I have also stuck pretty much to what I sensed most of you would most like to read, although I must admit I wish I was smart enough when I was holding forth on bonefishing, for example, to have related my experiences in presenting flies gently to trout to those of presenting bonefish flies. Or for that matter, that I had explained the relative universality of reading water, whether a freshwater flat on a favorite stream or saltwater flat where bonefish feed, or how, having learned to spot a mottled brown over a cobbled stream bottom helped to make spotting ghosting bones a relative piece of cake. But, alas, I didn't, and so those stalking bones (such a *kick*) I fear will have to look elsewhere. What I will swear, though, is that *not one piece* was omitted because I wished to save it for another forum. I have to shave every morning—except under the nose and over the upper lip.

I love to fish not one iota less today than on that day—a day so far removed in time I couldn't begin now to pinpoint it—when something occurred somewhere, no doubt astream, which prompted me to believe it might be worth sharing with my fellow anglers by way of an old Royal typewriter. While among other things, I hope I have evolved as an angling technician and have grown as a writer, if the book leaves you with nothing else, I hope you leave it with a recognition of this uninterrupted and unbound affection for "*The Quiet Sport*," *Fly Fisherman*'s motto, by the way, and in some way it helps you to reaffirm your own.

CHAPTER 1

May I Present

I'm not much interested in how many trout dry fly fishermen catch. It's not the braggin' or complainin', understand. Fly fishing would be "incompleat" without that. Rather, it's because numbers out of context are usually meaningless or deceptive. Give me a presentations-per-trout-caught ratio instead. Now, that's angling quantification, no ifs, ands or buts.

Fly fishing is essentially a predatory act, whether or not you kill the catch. Most anglers fish to catch trout. Skillful dry fly fishermen, like all successful predators, are efficient. The trick is to show your fly to each trout as the trout wants to see it. Or put another way, to make each fly presentation count.

Casting a fly is to presenting a fly what hitting a golf ball is to making a shot. Most anglers, I've observed, make too many casts and too few presentations.

Dry fly presentation, besides the casting element, involves numerous preparatory steps: reading water, observing rise forms, approach and positioning, choice of fly pattern and tippet diameter, among others. Then, too, the angler must perfect a wide range of casts in order to be able to vary his presentations, at least subtly, from situation to situation and from trout to trout. Absolute control of line, leader and fly is paramount. Anything less amounts to "chuck and chance it."

I *expect* to hook a trout with every presentation I make. If I didn't, I wouldn't cast. If I don't connect, I've made some mistake that I certainly don't want to repeat. Therefore, my presentations-per-fish-caught ratio measures my effectiveness during a given outing. One-to-one, of course, is the ideal. But getting there—now that's the rub.

The goal should be to limit mistakes by minimizing chance. By exercising patience and self-discipline, I take many more trout now than in the past while making far fewer casts—or presentations. (This is especially true regarding big trout that tend to be intolerant of even little mistakes.) I hook more trout on my first presentation than on my second, my second than my third. The number of fish I hook after three or four presentations represents only a minuscule percentage of my total catch each season.

The strategy is climaxed by showing a fly to a rising trout and is launched long before even hitting the stream. Each tactical element involves preparing for the "moment of truth." Develop a checklist. For instance: Am I comfortably dressed? Will my outer clothes offer adequate camouflage? Are the soles of my boots in keeping with conditions? Felts may be called for, but studs, chains or cleats may make too much noise, particularly in low water. Will I need a wading staff?

The list goes on. Is my rod appropriate for conditions? (I choose one for the lightest line practical.) Is it properly rigged or have I perhaps missed a guide? Do I have extra leaders and plenty of tippet material? Is the tippet material handy? It better be or I may hesitate to make essential repairs. How about clippers, a leader straightener, dry fly floatant, fly-drying powder? Do I have my Polaroids, and is my rain jacket squared away in the back of my jacket or vest?

The process continues as I proceed to the stream. Where is the sun? Will it impact my vision? Will my shadow be a factor? Shadows cost fish. Is there a breeze? Upstream? Downstream? Or perhaps swirling? Should I change rods? If so, no time like the present.

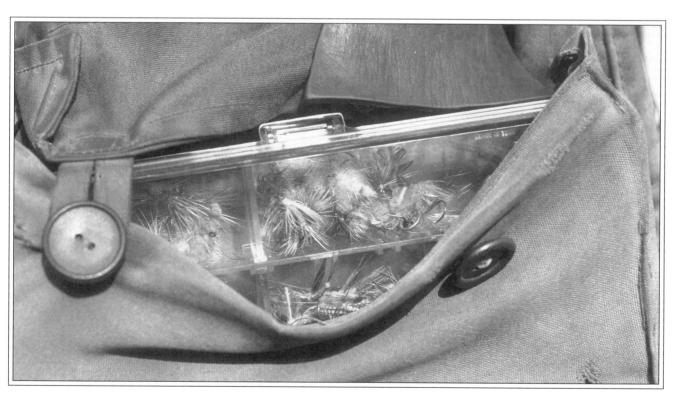

To fish effectively, you must know where everything you might need is at all times. In other words, you have to know your way around your vest (or fishing jacket) *blind-folded.* I had a helluva time finding just the right vest for me, so I asked Elsie Darbee, yup, the legend, to help me out. She helped me in spades by tearing apart a store-bought vest and putting it back together again to create a vest that gave me easy access to just the flies I wanted at any given time.

I see approaching a stream as part of a job, as opposed to a stroll in the woods. To arrive at the stretch I intend to fish, I give other "fishy" stretches a wide berth. I'm particularly careful to stay back from the banks. A high silhouette is easily spotted by trout, and vibrations resound through the water. Where possible, I stay close to a tree line or other dense cover.

If forced to traverse a shore or beach, I try not to grind stones underfoot. I make all stream-crossings above or below productive water that I (or somebody else) may want to fish later. Above all, I never use the stream as a trail.

Having arrived at my destination, I take a *long* look at the stream and ask myself a lot more questions. Are there insects on the water? Emerging mayflies? Ovapositing caddis? Or maybe a spinner fall? Are insects also over the water? If so, what kind? A single species—or perhaps numerous species at various stages between emergence and death?

Do I have the right fly patterns in the right sizes to cover each stage of each insect I see? Mayfly emergers? Low-floating and high-riding duns? Spinners? Caddis larvae and emergers? Adults? Ovapositors and spent-wing patterns? The trout may key back and forth from one to another at intervals throughout the day. Are my fly boxes strategically placed in my vest? I don't want to waste time changing flies. Or, heaven forbid, the right flies will do me no good back in the car.

Now it's time to observe the fish. Assuming that trout are rising, I note their numbers, whereabouts and which of the fish appear to be large and small. Next I locate prime feeding lanes. Are the trout holding to feed, cruising, or perhaps both?

I study the rise forms of numerous fish. Are they pretty much uniform or do they vary from rise to rise and fish to fish? Are the trout keyed to flies on the surface, in the surface film or just beneath the surface? Do the fish appear to be coming all the way from the bottom to take each bug, or are they holding near the top?

Do the rise forms suggest the species of insect or stage of emergence the trout are concentrating on? Dimple rise forms left by gulpers, for instance, may suggest trout feeding on duns. Swirls may point to ovapositing caddis. Splashy rise forms may indicate fast-swimming mayfly or caddis emergers, while sipping rise forms may betray a preference for stillborn duns, spent spinners or midges.

I also monitor the feeding rhythms of several fish. Are the intervals between rises relatively uniform? For instance, one trout's rise rhythm may be as predictable as a rise every 8 or 10 seconds, while another's may only *appear* random—until you really check it out.

Complex rise rhythms—that is, sequential rise repetitions of, say, 5 seconds, 9 seconds, 6 seconds, 10 seconds—are very common, particularly during heavy hatches. Having the rhythm wired tells me *precisely* when and where to pitch my fly.

Now it's time to home on a target trout. Focusing on a single fish, in my opinion, is central to sound, sight-fishing strategy. Usually I base my choice on two criteria: (1) location, and (2) size. I rate location over size because I want each trout to represent an interesting problem. However, unless the fish is holding in an inspiring spot, I seldom choose small trout. The reason is simple. The surest way *not* to catch big, rising trout in a pool is to catch small ones in their vicinity.

My choice of target is also influenced by the relative locations of several interesting or large trout. Normally I hope to take more than one good fish from a stretch of water. And so in choosing my target, I must also consider how my approach and presentation will impact other feeding fish and productive water. Obviously I can't barrel through a host of feeding stations, for instance, without spooking trout. A good analogy is a game of pool wherein you address each ball you play without losing track of the balls that lie ahead.

Unless it's raining, I'm still bone dry at this point. *Most anglers wade too much.* Often I've seen trout 50 yards away react to even careful wading. At worst, excessive wading puts trout down; at best it puts them on guard.

Uneasy fish, I'm convinced, tend to turn selective, or to focus on a particular insect or stage of emergence with which they feel secure. This, in turn, makes your job difficult by forcing you to adjust fly pattern and refine technique. Therefore, I make it a rule *never* to set foot in the water unless I'm sure that doing so is essential to my ultimate goal.

My wading is normally confined to stalking and positioning immediately prior to presenting to each target trout. Before taking my first step, therefore, I weigh a lot of options and ask a lot more questions.

What is the stream like between me and my target? Deep or shallow? Flat or broken? What about the bottom? How many alternative positions are there from which I might present a fly? Which will offer me the best perspective? Which involves the least wading? Which promises the best fly float, drift or swing? How's the light? Will I be troubled by glare? And, lest I forget, will wind be a factor?

Galen Mercer exhibits stalking perfection—rod at the ready, creeping upstream against the current, using a leaning tree for both concealment and to stay any wake he might make. Galen has already chosen his target trout, and nothing at this time will break his concentration or cause him to lose focus. That's one of the reasons that Galen is as good as they get.

Longtime friend and angling companion Jack Manes of North Salem, New York, took the largest brown trout I've ever seen hooked with a dry fly on the Beaverkill because he was savvy enough to stay low, that is, out of the fish's "window," and to present his fly with great delicacy. Moral? *Putting it all together pays dividends.*

I also weigh what will occur *when* (never *if*) I hook the target trout. How is it likely to make its fight? Are there snags or undercut banks about? Will I be able to snake the fish away from trout I've targeted for later? If not, it might be better to try another fish first. If the trout runs downstream, will I be able to follow? By what route? And last, but hardly least, how will my strategy impact the fishing of fellow anglers? My fun for theirs just ain't a fair swap.

Experience has taught me that there's only one ideal position for presenting a dry fly to each target trout. Because style and skill level differ from angler to angler, however, this position varies somewhat from person to person. But if the practiced caster determines it correctly and approaches it with care, his (or her) presentations-per-trout-caught ratio is sure to improve.

When I finally take that first step toward my target, this trout becomes the only trout in the world that matters to me. "Be deliberate," I admonish myself over and over, "stay cool and take your time."

I remind myself not to throw a wake and to be sure that one foot is planted before beginning each step. I also caution myself not to kick stones or drag my feet—anything that may redirect the target trout's attention from feeding to me.

Whenever practical, I wade bent at the waist, thus minimizing my risk of being spotted. Fortunately, a low profile also lowers my center of gravity, which improves my balance by giving me greater stability. A low profile and greater stability can also be attained by wading deep, especially on the flats where heavy current typically isn't a factor.

As I wade, my eyes dart back and forth continually between my target and my ultimate destination. I try never to have to look down at my feet. Each glance at the bottom to me represents a failure to anticipate.

As always, the shortest route to one's ultimate casting position is a straight line. So I try to take it whenever practical. Unfortunately, it is all too easy to confuse the shortest route with the *best* route. The best route is the route that minimizes the risk of spooking either my immediate target or other trout I aim to take later.

I always try to find features of the stream that help cover my movements. For example, it is usually less obtrusive to cross broken water than flat water. Similarly, staying behind a bedrock rib or exposed gravel bar checks your wake.

Fine-tuning position at the last moment often makes the difference between hookup and rejection. A single step upstream, downstream, ahead or back may make or break a fly presentation.

So, again I ask myself a series of questions. Is my target trout within my effective casting range? Is everything between me and my target as expected? How will intervening currents influence my line, leader, tippet and fly? Will drag be a problem? If so, will I be able to prevent it from occurring from this position? And finally the real toughy: am I a proficient enough caster to get the job done? If not, I'm really back at square one.

Now that I'm so close, I take the fish's measure one more time, pinpoint its feeding station and assess the line of drift. I check out the natural insects passing over the trout's lie and observe their behavior. Once again I try to relate insect species to rise form in order to be certain that I understand *precisely* what the fish is doing. I also follow the trout through *at least* a couple of rise repetitions to be certain I have a handle on its rhythm.

With the "moment of truth" at last at hand, a few 11th hour questions still remain to be answered. Am I certain I have chosen the right fly? Will it not only imitate the overall appearance of the key natural, but can I make it create the right behavioral impression? (I like to be *sure*, although occasionally, like all anglers, I do play hunches.) Where do I want my fly to enter the trout's field of vision, or its "window?" Is my fly well tied to my tippet? No pigtail in the tippet, for instance. Is my tippet long enough? Fine enough? These final two questions often turn out to be critical.

Only when I really like what I see, do I begin to cast. There are, of course, dozens of alternative casts to choose from, and it's my responsibility to have learned how to execute each one—the steeple cast, for instance, or left or right curve casts, or the stop-and-drop. Whichever I opt for, given my position, however, my goal is to put all the essential elements of a perfect presentation into the cast, including distance, line mend and drift potential.

My fly should land on the surface *exactly* where I've planned—not feet, or even inches, away. However, if I do make a mistake—and I make lots of them—better to be short than long. A presentation that shows any tippet to a trout more often than not proves *disastrous*.

If the trout doesn't take my fly, I decide quickly whether the fault lies with the trout or with me. More often than not, forced objectivity suggests the fault was mine. So now I must really bear down.

Whether I make a second presentation immediately or wait awhile depends largely on what I perceive to be the ramifications of my first presentation. If the target trout appears to have been undisturbed, I'm inclined to present again right away. This is typically the case if I've missed decidedly short, since the trout may not have seen my first offering at all. However, if I sense anything untoward—say, the trout breaks its feeding rhythm or changes its lie—I wait.

How long I wait also varies markedly from situation to situation. Sometimes I wait no longer than it takes to see the trout rise again and to make any small adjustments I decide may be called for. Other times, though, I may find that I've made a major mistake. I may have made the wrong kind of cast, for instance. That is, I may have made a simple stop-and-drop cast, say, when a steeple cast was called for. This means that I may have to reposition myself entirely, or change my cast, or both.

In sum, then, I do whatever has to be done and wait for as long as it takes—5 minutes, 15 minutes, a half an hour—to make sure my next presentation is right.

I once watched Mike Kimball of Ithaca, New York, by far the best all-round fly fisherman I've ever met, make only three presentations to one target trout in two hours. In the end, however, his rod was bent double, while his reel screamed to the treetops that every sight-fisherman really ought to be following his lead.

The net result of sound strategy is fish like this each and every outing. It all may seem overly technical, even robotic, at first; but in time, virtually each move you make becomes second nature. This, in turn, frees you to delight in the experience of doing a thing well, not to mention time to contemplate the joys of just being astream when between fish.

CHAPTER 2

Besting Bigger and Better Trout

It's one thing for a fly fisherman to locate a truly big trout, another to hook one once you've found it, and yet another to land the fish once you've got it on. These distinct phases can be said to represent the three "principal parts" of trophy trout fishing. Now, I'm not referring to ordinary trout dubbed *big* simply because they've got a couple of inches on a stream's run-of-the-river fish. No, I'm talking about those once-a-season, once-in-five-years, once-in-a-lifetime trout that many anglers never wholly believe exist—until they meet one face-to-face. These trout are freaks, biological exceptions, as uncommon as 600-pound men or women or 20-year-old dogs and cats. Still, there are few rivers or streams where some such fish don't exist—rarely seen, seldom hooked, and almost never landed.

Beyond suggesting that exceptional trout, because of their size, strength and predatory predilections are likely to dominate spots with the best access to food supplies and cover, it would be presumptuous and unrealistic of me to try to tell you precisely where to locate them. That is strictly a river-by-river, stream-by-stream thing to be achieved largely by truly learning the water you fish. Nor can I really fairly generalize about what constitutes *big*, since relative sizes among resident trout vary markedly from fishery to fishery. While a big trout inhabiting a wee brook, for instance, might be only 18 or 20 inches long, perhaps even smaller, on waters that hold numerous large fish, the exceptional specimen could weigh 18 or 20 pounds. On the other hand, don't be surprised to find a 5-pounder in a creek narrow enough to jump across. Such freaks are less rare than you might expect.

Everything had to come together to land this 9.8-pound brown trout on a 6X tippet and size 22 fly. But I'd also like to think it didn't happen by mere happenstance, either. If the mono of my tippet had been weak, my connecting knot iffy, my fly's hook the slightest bit rusty, my reel too stiff, I wouldn't have had a chance. You can never count on exceptions, but you should never count them out.

Likewise, it's irrelevant to say too much about how to hook these fish, because those techniques likely to work on, say, the waters near my Catskills home might waste the time of anglers elsewhere. (Unfortunately, too, the fine points of fly choice and presentation remain largely parochial matters, best gleaned from your own experience and the experience of those who live with a fishery. In other words, seek out the best local advice.) Ultimately, though, neither locating nor tempting big fish to take matters unless the angler knows what to do once the trout is on. So here, "at the beginning of the end," so to speak, there are some rules that almost universally apply.

As noted earlier, like all sound angling strategy, this begins prior to hitting the stream. It begins with understanding—even believing—that *this is going to be my day* and outfitting yourself accordingly.

Toward that goal, each angler must ask himself: "Can I expect the best from my tackle *when* I hook a big trout?" While I oppose using too much rod for typical fish just on the off chance you might strike an exception, you should be satisfied that the rod you choose is in peak condition. Is the shaft sound? Are the guides and tip-top well anchored? Is the grip firmly affixed? Is the reel seat secure and fully functional?

Next, the line, leader and tippet material ought to be inspected before each outing. Fly lines should be clear of weak spots, particularly cuts or abrasions that expose a line's core. (Damaged or rotten fly lines do sometimes break before tippet material against the strain of really big fish.) Leaders in a range of lengths and breaking strengths to meet all eventualities should be stored conveniently in your vest or fishing jacket. Has the monofilament retained maximum breaking strength? This question is particularly relevant to those who fish a lot in hot, dry climates and insist on the most staying power per unit of tippet diameter.

Now to the reel. Is it properly lubricated? No worn parts? Is the drag mechanism functioning correctly? And is the reel outfitted with adequate backing? No angler belongs on the water anywhere without at least 50 yards of 15-pound test backing, even if he fishes most of his lifetime and never sees an inch of it outside his rod's tip-top. Trout that require it, after all, don't come along every day, but seem perversely drawn to poor souls who deem backing unnecessary.

What is more, don't neglect your knots, namely the splices between backing and fly line, the one that joins line to leader, and if the leader is of compound construction, each knot along its length. Pay special attention not only to strength and soundness, but that excess material is trimmed short enough to assure smooth passage back and forth through your rod's guides and tip-top. Conversely, be sure that blood knots used for tying leaders include at least four turns of mono and that there's enough tab outside the knot to ensure against slippage.

And lastly, pore over your flies to be sure that (1) you have at least a few patterns meaty enough to appeal to that eccentric monster that could suddenly materialize before you, and (2) that their hooks, as well as those for your everyday patterns, are in good shape. Be especially alert for rust that ultimately weakens hooks, causing them to break at the barb or bend under the pressure of outsized trout.

A significant percentage of the biggest trout get away because anglers don't expect to hook them in the first place and aren't ready for a real struggle. We've all heard the same "hard luck story" time and again, when in point of fact, luck, good or bad, seldom has anything to do with "the one that got away." Landing or

Big fish tend to be lazy, so slow-moving stretches are likely spots to find them. Experience teaches that they most often live within 15 feet of a bank, especially if it's undercut, and seldom wander far from home, except in some instances late at night. Here Galen Mercer has found such a fish and must now put all the tricks he knows to work to keep it from hanging him up amid all the obstacles that line the shore of this Upper East Branch of the Delaware.

Talk about smart. They don't come much tougher than this spot where Galen Mercer skillfully lands a fine fish. He does so by working himself into the swift current, maneuvering the trout upstream of him, lifting the fish, then by relaxing the pressure ever so slightly, encouraging the trout to slide tail-first into his waiting net. You'll not see it done better.

losing big fish is entirely a product of discipline and tactics, meaning the skillful angler has to be an efficient predator.

It is wise to approach each stretch of water with a big fish in mind, regardless of the odds against such an encounter. Trophy trout sometimes show up in the damndest places. So before making a cast, analyze the situation carefully and never position yourself where you can't handle a horse should one happen to latch hold of your fly.

As noted earlier, playing big trout requires strategy not unlike that you'll observe among the top pool players, all of whom think ahead. Survey the water and try to anticipate each move the trout will make, deciding in advance what you will do to compensate. Where you know such a trout is holding, it's sound strategy for you to forgo one crack at him in order to walk through each maneuver of the anticipated fight in advance. Pay particular attention to obstructions, notably snags in the water and branches, downed trees or roots along the banks. Chances are your quarry will seek to turn them against you. Figure out, too, how to keep your fish clear of sharp rocks or boulders they will probably try to use to foul your line or cut your leader. And above all, be acutely aware that few trophy trout attain such size without having beaten one or more anglers. Most such fish know all the tricks. So *never* underestimate your opponent.

Calculate carefully your potential for mobility along a stretch of river or stream. Will you be able to follow a big trout downstream if you hook it here? Will you be able to get abreast of, or below, a fish to play it? How long is the fight likely to last? Will you be able to cross the stream without drowning if necessary? (This is no joke. A friend of mine drowned probably because he failed to consider this point.) These are a few questions that just must be resolved before you commence fishing. Answer them often enough and planning strategy will become virtually automatic.

Sometimes the answers provide a tip-off as to whether a big trout may be lurking along a given stretch. Although hardly a rule of thumb, the likelihood tends to decrease as conditions become more advantageous to the angler, particularly on heavily fished rivers and streams. Thus, playing large trout frequently comes down to making the best of bad situations, something more readily achieved by those who can predict the pitfalls in advance. Big trout seldom forgive mistakes, and the larger the fish, the more unforgiving they are likely to be.

Big trout, of course, are like fish of every species in that some specimens prove more game than others. Of all the game fish I've taken on over the years, however, trout have shown me more tricks and less quit pound for pound than the best of them, including, for instance, the Atlantic salmon. Most underrated is the fight of the biggest of brown trout. Two years ago I slugged it out with a

The game here was to keep this big fish from racing downstream through the rapids below where even with lots of backing I never could have kept up. So, by suddenly changing pressure points, that is, the angle of pull of the hook in the trout's mouth, I conned the fish into believing that its best chance of escape lie in doing what I wanted it to do. It worked and I soon had the trout on its side in front of me where I could easily net it.

9-pounder and had a tougher time with that fish than I've ever had with a 30-pound salmon. I'm still not sure I should have gotten the decision. Most species, especially salmon, give you an occasional break. But when you've landed a trophy brown, you can be certain *you made the breaks.*

When you hook a big trout, it's crucial to take charge at once. This is hard to accomplish if you're unaware that it's a big fish you're attached to. The only way to be ready is to pay attention every instant your fly is in or on the water. As unoriginal and obvious as this advice may seem, who hasn't permitted his mind to wander and regretted it?

I have read many yarns in which the writers describe fish as being "in control" during the early stages of their confrontations. While in some cases the scribes may have simply been exercising literary license, the outcome of other stories, loss of the fish, was likely not mere coincidence. A skillful angler *never* permits a big trout to get the notion—not for an instant—that it's the boss.

It would be swell to be able to describe accurately the typical take of an exceptional trout. Unfortunately, it's impossible. I've had them take flies with ferocity and delicacy on the same stream. The latter can make it very difficult to assess a fish's size, particularly when the trout doesn't show on top. And even if it does disturb the surface, many big trout leave deceptively small rise forms behind. So watch out.

The single giveaway is weight. Most big trout, that is, all but those suffering from terminal illness, for instance, are heavy. Therefore, discipline yourself to strike no harder than is necessary to set the hook on the largest fish without breaking it off. This is accomplished by rotating the rod upward firmly but smoothly in the manner associated with saluting with a sword. Anglers should also train themselves to approximate fish weight through their rods within seconds of hooking up.

Nor are the initial reactions of big trout to the sting of steel predictable, even to the extent that we know, for example, salmon are likely to go to the bottom where they will shake their heads and try to grind the hook away. Occasional big trout may do just that, while others will make long runs without hesitating a single second. Still others seek cover instantly. Regardless of the trout's reaction, though, the angler must recognize it and make his first move to compensate at once.

For example, a huge trout nails a streamer and shoots for the tail of a pool. What do you do? First you get to a position from which you can move without difficulty, even if it means conceding more line as you retreat ashore. Then, holding your rod high and keeping your line taut, you follow the fish, if possible matching its speed with your own, so the trout won't feel the vibrations of a ratcheting reel through the line. Never should you simply plant your feet and pray the fish will stop before your line and backing are all gone, that is, "cleaned" or "spooled" as we call this ignominious defeat. For even should you luck out, you will be compromised by the fact that each yard of line lost adds weight and resistance between you and your fish, thus increasing the strain on your tippet and hook.

Keep your strategy as simple as possible. Extraneous moves increase the like-lihood of disastrous mistakes. With this in mind, novice flyrodders in particular should learn to reel with the hand opposite that with which they cast. (All big trout, of course, should be played "off the reel.") For a right-handed caster to change to his left hand to play a fish in order to be able to reel with his right—the brainchild, I have to think, of mad King George who lost the New World to a ragtag colonial army—makes no more sense today than to wear a baseball glove on the hand you throw with. Countless big fish are lost during the exchange of hands. Blowing fish aside, though, playing trout with the casting arm is more logical, since that arm is apt to be stronger and thus should hold up best through-out the fight. Further, because the casting arm is normally an angler's dominant one, it will probably prove better coordinated for the fine work essential when the trout is in close.

When playing big trout, don't pussyfoot around. Make your fish work. En-courage them to jump, for instance, remembering to lower your rod tip, which minimizes shock and limits the leverage a fish can exercise to throw your hook. Nothing tires trout faster than jumping.

Given the alternatives, I prefer big trout that run to those that sulk. Sulkers are really dangerous, since most obstructions are found near the bottom. Run-ners should be made to pay for every inch of line, however, preferably by aug-menting a light drag by either thumbing or palming your reel. Remember, too, that a fish running downstream, that is, with the current, can't breathe,which really plays into your hands.

The occasional sulker seems impossible to move, sometimes even convincing you that the fish has broken off, leaving the hook wedged, say, between stones. It is important, therefore, to train yourself to recognize the subtlest throbbing as it's telegraphed back through the rod. Such throbbing, of course, is the tip-off that your fish is still on.

When a big trout sulks, first try changing pressure points, that is, the direction, or angle, of pull against the hook. If you're positioned slightly downstream of the fish—where you ought to be most of the time—edge 10 feet farther down in an attempt to turn the trout's head. If it won't budge, walk upstream until you are abreast of the fish, and if it's still no-go, try moving a short distance upstream. These failing, there are a couple of tricks of last resort: (1) Raise your rod tip high and tap *gently* on the butt with the heel of your hand. Try it once, wait, then try it again. If you get no response, try tapping in coordination with a change of pres-sure points, both by moving upstream and down and altering the pitch of your rod relative to the water's surface and to the fish itself; (2) Clip a short length of key chain around your line and let it slide down into the fish's face by raising your rod high. This maneuver, while risky, is virtually guaranteed to drive big trout wild, which is your goal.

The principle of pressure points is integral to playing big fish and yet isn't widely understood among fly fishermen. All trout (and other game fish, for that matter) react to changes in the angle between hook and rod. Thus, to settle a

Have a gander at the bulge in Galen Mercer's net bag, as well as the darkness surrounding him. Galen hooked this 8-pounder on a dry at dusk on a Catskill stream, proving that played wisely, you can even take them on a "slow" 2-weight rod, Galen's favorite. Unless you know what you're about, as they say, "don't try this at home."

fish, a straight pull is best, while to turn one or to move it up or down in the water column, you merely change your position or that of your rod from left to right, right to left, or higher or lower, depending on what's called for at the moment. With practice, you will find that the movements of even the largest trout can be controlled with relative ease, some to a degree that they quite literally behave like pets on leashes.

It is how we perform when big trout are in close that ultimately decides the outcome of most battles, however. Timing is the key, since you want a fish in the net as soon as possible without courting disaster by bringing it in too green. The balance is delicate, and even experienced fly fishermen are occasionally fooled by trout that play possum or suddenly seem to get their second wind.

Weariness in big trout is frequently manifested by their making tighter and tighter circles in front of you until finally they show their sides when they can no longer maintain equilibrium. At this stage the important thing is to keep the fish moving, reversing the direction of its circles by lifting and turning it to deny it any measure of confidence.

I like to net big trout in waist-deep water if the current is slow, thigh-deep in somewhat stronger currents. (I try never to net fish in very swift water.) In all instances, though, fish should be taken to the gentlest spots possible, even when that necessitates leading them almost ashore to net them in side eddies only a foot or two deep.

There are several schools of thought on netting big trout, the most practical of which, I've found, is to hold the net stationary while drifting the trout downstream into it tail-first. The worst way is certainly to attempt to hold a fish stationary while trying to scoop it up with your net. Whatever method you ultimately adopt, however, you should be certain to carry a net with an opening wide enough and a bag deep enough to accommodate the largest trout your imagination can conjure up for the stream you are fishing. For one day, although only perhaps once in an entire lifetime of angling, you're going to need every cubic inch of it and more.

CHAPTER 3

Too Much for a 2X Tippet

When things go wrong, I can get awful cranky, and it's best to ignore me until the mood passes. Not that I blame anyone for a foul-up, not down deep. But the mood represents some measure of consolation, I suppose, and to snatch it from me by saying something chatty, for instance, makes me feel cheated. Usually I let fly. I don't like this crankiness in myself any better today than yesterday or 20 years ago; but time has made it neither easier to control nor more pleasant to deal with for those who love me. The fact that some people who loved me 20 years ago still love me—that they keep saying chatty things at the worst times—is more consolation than I really have coming.

"Look at the mountains, Art. There's fresh snow," Kris tried, "and a flight of swans. Look, please." Doddi, our Icelandic gillie, smiled, which is more dangerous than being chatty. He understood almost no English and such a person is a perfect target.

"The only mountains I wanna see are the ones back home." I hated myself for giving voice to this sentiment even as it was escaping. But I was rolling now. "At least there's no snow. It's August, for chrissake." Kris said nothing. Doddi's smile died. A big part of me wished that one or the other would tell me to knock it off, not that doing so would have done any good. "I don't believe it," I growled, pressing ever onward. "We're supposed to fish salmon. We wait a year . . . travel 4,000 miles . . . and what happens? It's screwed up."

"Doddi says the trout fishing's really good," Kris tried again.

"Trout good. Very many big trout," the Icelandic guide tried, too, struggling to manufacture an English sentence.

One that *didn't* get away. The trout of Laxá I Laxádalur were believed by the late Dr. Dwight Webster, dean of the fisheries management school, Cornell University (considered by many the world's foremost authority on salmonids), to be the finest examples of the species on earth. He'd get no argument from yours truly.

"You don't come to Iceland to fish trout," I pouted. "If I want to fish trout, all I have to do is cross our front lawn." Still glaring, I thumbed Doddi's way. "Sure, he'd claim there are big trout. He screwed up reserving the salmon fishing."

"That's not fair, love," Kris said in a tone she reserves for those times when I'm acting like the original jerk.

Anyone given to crankiness can testify that each outburst costs you. My tab that morning would be to miss being first to sight Laxá I Laxádalur as our van topped a steep incline on the ground lava road. Kris saw it first, and her expression softened instantly, reflecting its beauty. Her face read like the opening lines of a favorite book, reassuring you that you're safe now from ugliness, even in yourself. "Look." It was an order verily barked as she pointed past my head. Automatically, I turned, then sat in silence.

Long silences come naturally when greeting Laxá I Laxádalur for the first time. The only thing you might want to say is that you've found the most beautiful place on earth. But such a statement is best withheld 'til later. At first it's better to relish a fantasy of this being your place alone to live with every day, until one day, somehow fixed yet nonspecific in the daydream, you die here and are buried deep in a grassy hillside overlooking one of the river's emerald pools.

"I hate you for seeing it first," I whispered finally.

"You hate yourself for making it so I would see it first," Kristin whispered in turn.

Laxá I Laxádalur translates literally into "Salmon River in the Salmon River Valley," although this stretch of river and its valley are situated above a falls impassable to runs of Atlantic salmon that teem into the lower river, called Laxá I Adaldal, or "Salmon River in the Main Valley."

Because Laxá I Adaldal may be the world's most beguiling salmon fishery, sportsmen, both Icelandic and foreign, have singled it out from among Iceland's many *laxás* (*laxá* means "salmon river," *lax* being salmon and *á* meaning "river") as simply "the Laxá." In the northeast of the island nation, the river rises in Myvatn, meaning Gnat Lake—the third largest lake in Iceland—and flows almost due north as a duck flies to saltwater in the form of Skajálfandifloi, or Wide Fjord that Trembles, just west of Húsavík, a fishing port of some 2,000 hearty folk. Within the approximately 20 miles between its source and the North Atlantic, Laxá actually meanders and occasionally tumbles about 35 miles through a route of least resistance cut in ancient lava, the stuff Iceland is really made of. Of this water more than half is located upstream of an impassable falls at Laxávirkjun, the gateway, so to speak, to Laxá I Laxádalur.

At the valley entrance there is a steep slope of several hundred feet on each side of the river. Flat on top, the hills are brown and very rocky near their summits, but about a third of the way down, though still well above the level of the road, the barrenness gives way to blueberry bushes and lush grass embroidered with clusters of windflowers of white and purple and pink. Scattered all about, but particularly near the riverbanks, are natural totems of lava, some tinted gray, bronze or light green by delicate lichens. There are no trees.

High overhead, puffy clouds rush by, pushed by arctic winds that carry clear, dry air to the north of Iceland during its short summer. The winds have flattened the hilltops until they look almost like tables draped with cloths that ripple where erosion has worn narrow burns in the sides to accommodate snow runoff that even the spongy, volcanic soil won't absorb. High on the slopes, you spot dots of white, brown and black, which you soon make out to be sheep let out to pasture by farmers who live on the bottomland farther up the valley. Usually the sheep are in pairs, but occasionally there are three together—a ewe and twin lambs, a sign of a farmer's good fortune, according to Doddi. You seldom see the great rams with their curved horns, however, because they wander off into remote areas to live out their summers in bachelor colonies. Although Doddi doesn't say so, many sheep in this valley belong to his family, which owns several good farms on the west bank of Laxá I Laxádalur.

Thanks to Doddi, whose real name is Thórdur Pétursson, Kris and I had fished salmon many times along the river's lower reaches, and until the previous evening had thought we were to fish there again—10 days on choice beats. For this trip, though, I'd made arrangements with a farmer friend, believing his English and my Icelandic sufficiently fluent to handle them. Doddi, although wondering certainly how I could pull it off when just to get one day's fishing is tricky between speakers of both languages who aren't fudging it, friends or not, nevertheless must have guessed everything was set or was too polite to interfere. Suffice it to say, we ended up with only a few half-days of salmon fishing just before the season closed.

Superior guides everywhere possess a common sense of their sports' priorities, and so it didn't surprise me that when Doddi had begun his van, a custom model built on a Spanish jeep chassis, bouncing along the lava road, he suggested, "We fish brown trout now. Go *veidahús*..." His English failed him at this point, but he compensated beautifully by sticking his wristwatch in front of my nose and describing three clockwise circles in front of its face with his index finger.

"Go *veidahús* later?" I said, responding to the game of charades.

"*Já*," Doddi nodded, using one of two Icelandic words for yes. "We fish brown trout. Go *veidahús*, eat *hádegisverdur*."

"Lunch?" I guessed correctly. Doddi repeated the English word for the midday repast deliberately several times, as if filing it for frequent use. "Eat brown trout for lunch at the fishing house in a few hours," I confirmed. He nodded happily and signaled that he'd like the sentence repeated. We volleyed it back and forth several times until he indicated his satisfaction with a self-assured nod.

Rounding a wide turn in the road, Doddi braked the van, shifted down two gears with practiced efficiency and rolled into an almost imperceptible pull-off backed by lava. The river lay hidden beyond the lava that scientists say was deposited here about 100,000 years ago; but Doddi pointed in its general direction and declared with an authority born of growing up with a fishery: "Plenty good place. Art Lee catch plenty big brown trout." He flashed a knowing look I'd come to recognize as part bighearted smile, part cat-choking-on-canary, and I realized that his singular good humor and confidence were infectious. My petulance had evaporated without my ever being aware of it, replaced by a sense of anticipation, a mood essential to initiating all thoroughly satisfying angling experiences at home or abroad.

To diagnose why I'd rebel at the prospect of Icelandic trout fishing on the one hand, while on the other I'd tote three trout rods, a vest full of trout flies and a laminated-wood landing net to Iceland on what I believed was to be exclusively a salmon fishing trip is probably best reserved for an analyst. But I should point out for purposes of continuity, and perhaps an object lesson of sorts, that it would never occur to one who carries fly rods to marlin grounds and bass bugs on trout fishing trips to leave his trout fishing gear behind, even if in the end its only value proved to be another foothold on the climb to upward mobility for airport baggage handlers who charge by the bag.

Something like 20 minutes were required to rifle through duffles and rod cases before I stood ready to leave the van and follow Doddi along a snarl of paths beaten into the lava by generations of cloven hooves. Never one to push, the gillie paused frequently, stooping to pick handfuls of plump blueberries, which he popped into his mouth like a kid eating popcorn. And producing an empty sandwich bag from his windbreaker, he advised Kris with his remarkable gift for pantomime that lunch at our fishing house on this day and for the days to come would be infinitely more appealing if she considered it part of her daily routine to keep the bag full. Kris accepted the bag and the chore with a grin, and we continued meandering until we reached the crest of a knoll where Doddi suddenly halted, folded his arms across his chest, and announced, "Laxá."

For hundreds of days on scores of rivers, I've sought trout and salmon pools the way some travelers seek cathedrals, and somehow each one I'm shown becomes at once the most splendid of them all for the wonder of knowing I'm yet to explore it. For if it's true that the essence of fishing lies concealed in its endless occasions to exercise hope, then the embodiment of this ideal must swim in the waters that glide by under your gaze, awaiting only your presence in them to begin logging dramas for which nature has rehearsed the waters since before recorded time began.

Laxá I Laxádalur, barely 50 feet below us, shimmered under the climbing sun. Upstream, it swung through a narrows in a sharp bend between bluffs, then flattened out into a broad slick etched with tiny currents that betrayed its uneven bottom of bronze bedrock and black lava sand deposited during spring spates. Only the faintest slithering sound was carried on a breeze that seemed to dip and touch the river's surface. From our vantage on the knoll, we could see serpentine growths of weeds hanging loosely in the flow. These abundant weeds, which reveals the incredible fertility of this river, give Laxá I Laxádalur the look of an emerald chalkstream, or spring creek, unique, as far as I know, among all waters of the arctic region.

What I lacked in grace, I surely made up for with abandon, scrambling down the steep path to the riverbank. Odds are better than even that no Icelandic sheep pursued by arctic foxes could have made better time. Doddi trailed me at his casual pace with Kris in tow, both laughing mightily at how the itch to have at the river had clearly supplanted my better judgment. And by the time they caught up, a big Black Ghost streamer, dug from an old leather fly wallet, was already cinched to my leader tippet. I thought I was ready to go.

"No good," Doddi said soberly after examining my terminal tackle.

"Black Ghost no good?" I asked, throwing Kris a skeptical glance. River by river, everywhere I'd fished brown trout, this pattern of black, yellow and white had proven the most reliable streamer, particularly in large sizes.

"*Nei*, Black Ghost plenty good," Doddi responded, shaking his head impatiently. Then he snatched my 2X leader. "No good," he repeated, indicating the tippet.

Doddi dug into his fishing vest and produced a spool of 15-pound test monofilament spinning line. "Good," he declared, pitching me that same single, self-assured nod he'd shown me a half hour earlier when he meant to convey that further work with my English sentence was neither required nor desired.

Something new to Doddi: the first time he'd ever seen a dry fly fished. Skeptical at first, he quickly changed his mind when several browns up to five pounds ended up in the landing net. The river record brown, incidentally, weighed 21.7 pounds and was caught on a Night Hawk salmon fly by the great guide's father.

"This plenty strong enough for big brown trout," I insisted, flourishing the tippet before him while raising my right arm to mimic a bodybuilder showing off his bicep. Doddi looked cooly at me, kind of like an old farmer being told how to plow his fields by a visiting state agricultural agent. "I ain't about to hunt quail with a goose gun," I said to reinforce my argument by introducing linguistic one-upmanship. And when Doddi's look slowly became somewhat less skeptical, the biggest concession I could have hoped for, I pronounced, "We go. Fish brown trout now," in the most preemptive tone I could muster.

After an instant of mutual indecision, the guide shrugged, and smiling, said something in Icelandic I suspect would relate to losing battles but winning wars. He waited several seconds for sufficient bewilderment to register on my face, then motioned me to follow him up along the bank to where Laxá I Laxádalur emerged from a narrows.

We edged into the water and sloshed side by side through the knee-deep flow toward center stream. Perhaps 20 yards in, the rutty bottom began to slope, until about a half-dozen more strides put us in to our waists. Doddi studied the opposite bank, apparently searching for some special marker known only to him, and when he seemed satisfied that he'd found it, he grunted and leveled his arm in front of me to draw me up. The gillie said nothing but gestured with the same arm that I should pitch my fly across and down and to edge downstream slowly after each presentation.

"Long cast? Short cast?" I asked, stripping fat spirals of line from my reel.

"Long cast," said Doddi, taking the streamer from me momentarily and dunking it in the river to soak the marabou wing. "Okay," he said, releasing the fly.

I twirled the fly into the air with an abbreviated roll cast, and shooting line fore and aft in a couple of false casts, shot the big streamer about 60 feet across the current. The flow bellied the line almost immediately, and the upstream mend I made to compensate served not only to right the drift, but to twitch the Black Ghost like a darting fish. A swirl materialized almost at once behind the fly—a small swirl perhaps by salmon fishing standards, but a suck-in-your-breath swirl certainly by the standards of a trouter accustomed to Catskills streams and Catskills fish. I felt nothing. Doddi shot me a glance, then clucked, "Small."

Responding involuntarily to Doddi's voice, I glanced sideways, and in the instant my attention was drawn off the water, a second swirl had been left behind by a fish that jolted me back to business by picking at the streamer. I measured the trout between disappearing rings, managing to find one word to say over the echo of my pounding heart. "Big."

"Very big," murmured Doddi, screwing up his face like a boy who, while clowning with a friend, had just broken his mother's best vase. He motioned to me to pick up the spent cast and to try again, and when the fly had plunked to the surface and disappeared within inches of where it had touched down the first time, his expression changed and he nodded approvingly. After a line mend, the streamer turned slowly, its wing breathing with little nods telegraphed through the line from my rod tip. An eternity of tension swam through me while the fly described its arc, and I'm not sure how long it was before I realized that Doddi was whistling softly—his way, I would guess, to ventilate the agony of waiting.

The fly reached the tail of its drift unscathed. Except for the pattern of currents and little ripples left by a gentle breeze, the river might have held no living thing. I was preparing to lift my line to begin another cast when Doddi suddenly and firmly laid his hand on the rod, as though a voice carried across a thousand years of living with this river had called out from its depths, *Beddu augnablik*— Wait awhile." The pressure of Doddi's hand held the rod tip close to the surface, and I almost complained. But the stiffness of his body, the intensity of his stare at the spot where my fly hung suspended just inches deep, told me to back off. My eyes passed from Doddi to the line, which I followed downstream to the point where it disappeared. I remember a gust of wind touched down all at once, sending long fingers of pewter chop across the surface. It was gone, though, as quickly as it had come, leaving us surrounded by stillness.

The pool was becalmed—Coleridgean—unnaturally calm for as far as you could see, when the trout's head suddenly burst through the surface, pushing six-inch swells to either side of it. Framed by the swells, the head seemed to me gigantic, dwarfing the wing of marabou that spilled from one side of its open mouth. The inside of the mouth looked white and as smooth as good china, but the head was bronze and appeared suspended above the surface in the beginning of an even, unhurried, unworried and effortless roll that would finally carry its head down-ward again, exposing next broad spotted shoulders and flanks, a long muscular back, and at last a tail as big as a man's hand.

The trout's roll propelled it all the way back down to the bottom. Although gripped in the spell of its roll, as the fish sounded I raised my rod to the center of my face like a saluting officer of the guard—a gesture really unnecessary to set the hook. The force of the strike had no doubt carried more than enough punch to lock the hook into the trout's rubbery cheek, and like a brawler hit a good one, the fish stopped cold with the sting and shook its head violently from side to side.

To play big fish in moving water, it's a mistake for you to remain in deep water where the fish is in its element and you are out of yours. Standing waist-deep or

The real thing—an actual shot captured by Kris in the moments after the huge Laxá trout took my streamer. Though we're edging ashore as we should, doing every-thing right so far, it would be some time yet before we would know the inevitable outcome of this awesome battle.

deeper is to trust Lady Luck, from whom you should presume nothing once she's brought you and your fish together. When a fish has room to run, particularly downstream, to expect to park yourself and to drag it back through the current like a cod is an insult both to a good river and a worthy opponent.

"Ashore," I said to Doddi, turning and pointing toward the bank. The gillie nodded, and we began retreating slowly as we had retreated so many times when attached to salmon. Doddi's arm was across my back to be certain I kept my balance.

For all the movement of the big trout, I might have snagged the bottom. Line droned off the reel, the result only of our withdrawal. The fish was lying virtually motionless, an anomaly for a hooked trout, large or small. Ten feet off the bank the nail knot that spliced my fly line to the backing ticked through the last couple of snake guides and passed the tip-top, and yet, except for the gentle arc in the rod and an occasional thump reported to my hand when the trout moved its head, there might have been no trout attached to me at all.

Aren't you the gallant, I thought, *waiting until the guy you're gonna chew up takes off his tie and hangs up his coat? There you are, shaking your head and saying "Any old time." Oh, you'd like to look bored enough with it to lose your temper without losing your dignity. Yessir, you're a piece of work . . .You really think I need this guy's arm around me to stay out of the drink? Not likely. But if it makes you happy to think you're giving me a break, go right to it. If there were a chance, though, just this much chance, I'd end upside-down tomorrow in Kristjan's smokehouse, you think I wouldn't be kicking your* afterhluti *all the way from here to Myvatn?*

But then, "I'm a trout and he's a man," you're thinking. "Worse yet, he's an American. Fat head like his wallet. Mind turned to mush with too many martinis."

You didn't know great-granddad Billy, did you? Or about the Irish in me? Hear of the fever sheds? Or the signs: "No Irish Need Apply," they told us. Know what Billy used to say? He used to say, "The only thing you can thank luck for is the number of miles you were born from a racetrack." Ran a saloon, Billy did. Never touched a drop himself. Guess what killed him? Fell down an elevator shaft. So whaddaya suppose was chiseled into his tombstone? "Billy Lee," it says, "who was he anyhow?" Not another word. If you ever get to Riverdale in the Bronx, look it up. Can't miss the monument—one of the biggest in the cemetery.

So be complaisant if you want to. But while we've been having this little chat, don't look now, but I've been sneaking downstream . . . The Irish in me . . . Opposite you now, right where I oughta be. Gonna make hors d'oeuvres out of you, Krissy and Doddi and me are, one week from today, after Kristjan's through. Wash you down with good cold mjólk. *Can't afford gin in Iceland. If I could, think you and I would have ever come to this? No. You'd be reading sagas or something, and me, I'd be fishing salmon downriver someplace, maybe Àrnes, at 3,000 bucks a week.*

When the trout finally bolted, its power and speed defied description as a "run." Although it involved flight, only a fool could read any sort of cowardice into it. This fish betrayed no panic, no indecision typical of lesser trout. In terms of human conflict, it seemed as though the fish wasn't in flight at all, but instead that it was coming on, bulling in, determined to give better than it took. Backing seethed off my reel and spit sparkling droplets into the air where it cut the surface. My rod bowed like a sapling in a storm. Doddi whooped. I held on.

"Go Laxávirkjun," Doddi crowed, pointing downriver.

"Gotta chase," I panted. The climbing pitch of my reel warned me that about half my backing was already spent. "Can't turn him, Doddi," I moaned. "Won't stop, the sonofa . . ."

Like two seals trying to run on land, Doddi and I turned and scrambled the rest of the way to shore. At the bank, while still doing my best to keep my rod pointed at the fish, I had to drop to my knees and claw my way up to level ground. Once there, I staggered upright and began running, my legs and lower torso seeming lost in my cavernous waders. About 30 feet downstream, I have been reminded, I collided with Kris but recall neither tossing her aside nor the remarkable expletive she conjured up in keeping with my chivalrousless behavior. All I remember is the hollow sound made by my boots on the turf, furnishing rhythm behind my ratcheting reel and the whine of line taut in the air.

A ridge of lava suddenly materialized before me, and the impact of its presence there to block my way struck me an almost physical blow. The ridge ran all the way to the riverbank in a graceful arc that once, perhaps, was this stretch of the river's high-water mark. At the bank it disappeared into a deep hole eroded by ages of lapping and swirling water. Stymied, I had to stop dead in my tracks, and the gap between the trout and me continued to widen.

I've never boxed, but I've watched the faces of enough boxers in the ring to recognize that there's a look—it's in the eyes—that tells you when a fighter knows he's beaten. It may appear just an instant before he's decked, or he may carry it from the first round to the final bell if he goes the distance. The look washes into the eyes from deep inside, maybe from as deep as the soul, and slowly it spills over the face, then downward until the entire body is bathed in the inevitable. The look represents, I guess, the ultimate truce between intellect and spirit, and when you recognize it in a fighter, it's hard not to look away, embarrassed for intruding into a man's communion with reality.

At the foot of the lava ridge, I inched to the lip of the hole. Mercifully, there was no room beside me for Doddi or Kristin to stand. They stood in silence behind me, seeing only the back of my head. Almost skinned now, the sound of my reel had reached an impossible pitch, a sound as shrill as the scream of ultimate despair, and there I was peering down into that hole, trying to wish away the water that filled it, when suddenly the trout jumped in the tail of the slick. It lugged the fly and the leader, the full weight of the fly line and the backing, and yet it leaped full-body clear of the water. It jumped still going away, cutting the surface with almost no splash on its way back down into Laxá.

And then the big fish broke off.

I stood in silence, mechanically retrieving my line and backing when Doddi whispered with a strange male tenderness, "*Veidahús?*"

"Yeah, sure," I responded, still cranking, searching all the horizons within me for a smile.

Late that night I jotted a postcard to my brother, George . . . "wonderful trout fishing. Took a dozen or so, two to six pounds. Lost a monster this A.M. Had it on just long enough to weigh it . . . Weighed too much for a 2X tippet."

CHAPTER 4

Taking Early Season Trout

Fly fishermen seem prone to a particularly acute strain of cabin fever that compels us to strike out for our favorite fisheries as early in the year as the law will allow, regardless of conditions. Who among us hasn't flirted with hypothermia just for a day on the water, understanding only too well we weren't likely to catch any or many fish?

One group of such hearties, of which I'm a charter member, has been gathering for breakfast each April 1st since 1973, and while we have dined on such "country sport" fare as Irish oatmeal, English sausage and Newfoundland bread, once the food was inside us, we went years before one turncoat finally took a single trout from the always frigid waters of nearby Kinderhook Creek. (Lucky bloke—not being drowned for his transgression.) His saving grace was his obviously guilty conscience and vow to fish hookless the following year.

Most inveterate anglers insist that they hit the water so early each season only because they have to "get out." Catching fish, they maintain, has little or nothing to do with it. It's ritual, like doing the Stations of the Cross during Lent. Most go so far as to be willing to concede the early season to those who dunk bait, believing that for a fly fisherman the prospect of really doing well represents some sort of impossible dream.

The obvious question is, of course, does it really have to be that way? The answer: *No*.

Granted, early season trout fishing on most waters is really tough. It may actually represent the ultimate challenge for fly fishermen and require the greatest amount of discipline and patience, if not skill. The "I just had to get out" approach is singularly self-defeating, as it presumes that one spot or one technique

Trout can often be found in the wake of boulders when rivers are swollen, as the Beaverkill is in this photo. Spots chosen thoughtfully and fished carefully can often lead to tidy yields, such as this nice brown taken at the tail of Hendrickson Pool, which took a weighted stonefly nymph fished slowly just off the bottom.

is as useful (or useless) as another, which is patently untrue. If you plan strategy carefully at the height of the season but ignore planning altogether shortly after the ice goes out, you are beaten before you even wet a line. All you'll catch is the proverbial cold.

That bait fishermen catch so many fish early in the season only serves to underscore that trout are feeding and that it can be done. Natural insect larvae, after all, outnumber night crawlers or worms in most streams during late winter and early spring, just as they do during so-called "prime time." It follows, then, that resident trout will eat more nymphs, for instance, than worms during any given spring. The key, therefore, is to adapt your tackle and technique to prevailing stream and climatic conditions, so you can go the worm dunker one better. Popular myth to the contrary aside, the truth is that we flyrodders may even have the edge.

Advance planning is critical to all early season outings. Be sure to obtain accurate information about current conditions, for instance, on several streams as close as possible to your target date, then keep your travel options open until the very last moment. Frequently, thanks to Alexander Graham Bell, I've been able to take advantage of favorable conditions on one stream when others not far away were entirely unfishable due to flood or some other natural bugaboo.

No two streams are alike, of course, but it's true more often than not that lowland waters in more southerly areas will fish well before more northerly ones at higher altitudes. In New York State, for example, a milder climate usually dictates that the Beaverkill near my home in the Catskills will fish better than the Ausable in the Adirondacks during the month of April, given that localized rains, which occasionally swell our river to awesome levels, don't wash us out. The best bet year after year, though, is unquestionably the spring creek, such as those abounding in the Cumberland Valley of Pennsylvania, since they tend to maintain reasonably constant water temperatures and flows year-round and thus are least susceptible to the vagaries of weather.

While some may yearn to have at big water, small streams are often more manageable for fly fishermen during the early season, because the fish tend to be concentrated in shallow, not-too-swift water where you can reach them effectively. During the early spring, small streams, which are tributaries of large ones, may also hold brown or brook trout that have wintered over in the wake of fall spawning runs. Similarly, some tribs represent the spawning grounds of rainbow trout that run just after ice-out, meaning that a stream that will be narrow enough to hop across in a month or two sometimes is waiting with outsized trout for the knowledgeable early season angler.

Until relatively recently it was rarely recognized that choosing the water you fish on a given stream during the early season is more critical than at any other time of year. It's important to know where fish tend to lie, true, but to know where *fish you can get at* are lying is vital to cold weather (and water) fishing. One error I've observed over and over on Catskills streams in April, for instance, is an inclination for anglers to bunch up along the same stretches of water they favor with good reason later on. No matter, it seems, how deep or turbulent those stretches happen to be. This approach to the early season makes about as much sense for an angler as for a baseball outfielder to position himself identically to defend against every hitter in the league.

The chief concern of early season must be to select water in which *you will be able to show your flies to the trout*, ofttimes no mean feat. Your best bet is usually a relatively gentle stretch of water that gets a lot of sun and isn't too deep. Then fish every inch of it assiduously, bearing in mind that the trout may be holding in the shallowest spots just off the shore, particularly when a stream has significant populations of early dark stoneflies that migrate ashore prior to hatching.

Remember, too, that a trout's metabolic rate is slowed considerably by water temperatures below 50 degrees Fahrenheit, and thus early season fish

Don't be surprised if you sometimes find trout rising even when great chunks of ice can still be found on stream banks. I like to look for risers in shallow water near the shore on the inside of a curl where heavier water enters a pool. Here a good brown succumbed to a size-20 Black Stonefly fished on top. Note the standing ice in the foreground. Man, it was cold.

are likely to be logy. Loginess translates into sluggish feeding behavior which, in turn, commonly dictates that the fly be placed right on a trout's nose, maybe numerous times, before the fish can be induced to strike. If most early season trout have one thing in common, it's that they won't travel far left, right, upstream or down, for their meals.

Any advantage bait fishermen might have over fly fishermen during the early season is one of technique, not menu. A properly presented weighted nymph, such as the Dark Stone, Hare's Ear, Zug Bug, or a caddis larva or pupa, I'm convinced will be at least as effective as garden hackle. Ditto, a bucktail or streamer, such as the Black Ghost, weighted Muddler, Wooly Bugger or one of the Matuka patterns, should produce as well as so-called "live bait," or minnows, provided said imitation is shown to the trout properly. This requires that you follow the old adage, *The Mountain Must Go to Mohammed*, that is, the fly must go to the fish, a precept integral to the technique of generations of successful bait fishermen but too often ignored by past and present fly fishermen.

The fly fisherman who served his apprenticeship fishing bait knows that skilled bait fishermen spend most of their time working water almost at their feet. They have learned that the long cast in high water is the kiss of death. You'll note most of the best of them using fly rods to ply their bait, looking if you didn't know better, as if they were "dapping" a dry fly, a technique popular in Great Britain. Depressed metabolism in trout and high, often colored water actually work in the fly fishermen's favor, too, by permitting you to approach your quarry much closer than you could ever hope to at any other time of year. The trick, then, is to steal a page from the bait fishermen's book and to utilize tackle and modify technique only so you are doing what he does, getting down to the fish.

Toward that end, I like a long rod—a 9-, 9 1/2-, even 10-footer, for a number 4, 5 or 6 full-sinking or sinking-tip line. My concern with the rod is entirely utilitarian, since it's likely to take a pretty good beating and will be subjected to such indignities as having its guides sprayed regularly with deicer. The faster the line I use, I find, the better it seems to sink, a product of diameter, I would say. A section of lead core spliced to the head of a standard sinking line is also sometimes ideal. Since I've seldom encountered early season trout that are line or leader shy, and because I must take full advantage of my sinking line, I use the shortest leader I can get away with, frequently as short as two or three feet. A spool of 8- to 10-pound monofilament spinning line makes dandy "tippet material" under early spring fishing conditions.

Although entirely a subjective matter, I happen to prefer weighted flies to adding lead to the leader, except in rare cases of extreme turbulence when to add lead is the only way to go. Any substantial weight immediately ahead of the fly line is bound to disrupt casting flow, and to be "fly casting," as opposed to "lobbing" is a top priority of mine. Experience teaches that such disruption is minimized when the weight is incorporated into the fly. But probably, given your ultimate presentation goals, fly casting in the purest sense is seldom practiced anyway, and so the argument about where to locate lead is probably moot. Your flies, whether they be nymphs or streamers, should be dressed with various amounts of lead to complement a variety of water conditions. The object is to keep your fly on or near the bottom, dictating that flies of the same pattern but different weights be changed regularly from stretch to stretch, or even from pocket to pocket, in order to be certain that the fly is getting to the trout. Nor should you be concerned about losing a few flies to the bottom. Hangups indicate that your flies are down where they ought to be and so are well worth the price of replacement.

Additional lead can be added to the leader in several ways, notably by winding strips of it above the fly or by pinching on split shot as most bait fishermen do. Of the two, I favor the latter option, as long as the shot is positioned below the fly. This is accomplished by tying an extended blood knot, as when preparing a cast for two wet flies, then placing the shot where the head fly of a cast would go, your fly in the location of the dropper, or about six inches above the shot.

Flies, I've found, are best three-quartered upstream. Hold your rod high and parallel to the water and mend line regularly to assure drag-free drifts. Use no more working line than is required to reach the bottom directly perpendicular to the rod tip when the rod is extended at arm's length. Then fish the same water slowly and meticulously, over and over, permitting your fly to belly around for as long as it can be held on or near the bottom. Your free hand should monitor the line constantly, watching for a telltale sign or feeling for the subtlest strike. (I've never used a strike indicator in my life and never will.) This technique is particularly effective in small pockets and side eddies near streambanks where, incidentally, trout are most likely to be stationed soon after ice-out. Twitching of the fly should be kept to a minimum, since the slightest movement beyond

Galen Mercer was savvy enough to pick a spot where a small tributary ran into a large stream and so found this outsized brown, which no doubt had wintered over in the trib, and ravenous, had just wandered downstream towards its usual habitat. Doping out a plan is often as important to early season fishing—or at any time of year for that matter—as being a beautiful caster or tackle mannequin.

that caused by currents is likely to discourage logy trout from bothering to latch hold.

How slowly you must fish can't be overemphasized. Reassure yourself that you are working over trout even when you can't see them, and keep at it. A small pocket barely large enough to hold one fish, for example, may take a half hour's fishing time. Therefore, if by the end of the day you discover you've covered more than 25 to 50 yards of an average-sized stream, you can be reasonably certain you've been fishing too fast for conditions. More than anything, this kind of fishing requires the patience of a cat at a mouse hole.

Finally, a few words on and of comfort.

An angler who is miserably cold or wet is bound to be less effective than one who stays reasonably warm and dry. (If you're ever totally comfortable, though, you should check your calendar. You're probably not fishing early enough in the year.) When planning early season fishing trips, therefore, always take into account the potential for extreme climatic and water conditions. Pack all the clothing you could possibly need, including backups. A good rule is to take too many clothes, since there's no law to say you have to wear them.

Wear clothing in loose layers, bearing in mind that wool (still my favorite, despite all the breakthroughs in "fleece" and other synthetics in recent years) is the *only* material that retains its capacity to insulate even after it's wet. Of course, to stay dry should be a top priority, and toward that end you'll need reliable rainwear. Since at 40 degrees Fahrenheit, for instance, as much as half of the body's heat is lost through the head, a warm hat is a must. In addition, the avid early season angler would have to be foolish not to invest in the best waders money can buy to stay both warm and dry. Generally speaking, boot foot waders are warmer than stocking foots worn with wading shoes. You should always carry a pair of heavy gloves in your pocket, as well as a pair made without fingertips for fine work, such as tying knots, while on the stream. Nor is a hand-warmer of the sort used by deer hunters, kept constantly fired up, a bad idea, notwithstanding the razzing you'll probably get from your cronies who have failed to take theirs along.

The early season also calls for extreme caution astream, since a dunking in frigid, high water is potentially deadly. Hobs or stream cleats are very helpful if the bottom is composed mostly of soft rock, such as shale. The same hobs or cleats are absolutely useless, even dangerous, though, on hard rock surfaces, such as granite. For wading all rocky streams, therefore, I'd recommend wearing felt soles at the least and, for added insurance, using a stout wading staff.

Here, I suppose, I should be able to come up with an appropriate ending for this chapter. Teachers of creative writing and journalism would no doubt suggest something that at once sums up the points I've made, is inspirational about the subject to boot, and if possible, is cute. To save my life, though, I can't think of such an ending. So I'll simply tell you that yesterday I took a trout from the Beaverkill. Yesterday was February 18, 1981. The trout was small and ate a dark Stonefly Nymph (size 18).

CHAPTER 5

Spring Training

Dry fly fishing is the only sport I know in which the World Series is played *at the beginning of the season*. That is, the best hatches, those you really want to be ready for—the Quill Gordon, Hendrickson, Shad Fly, March Brown, Green Drake, etc., where I live—come off early rather than late. No wonder then, given a long winter layoff, many anglers find themselves too rusty to make the most of "prime time."

But it doesn't have to be that way. Many streams (those in New York's Catskills, for instance) have profuse hatches each year *before* most anglers even dig out their tackle. While the remnants of ice floes still litter the streambanks, millions of tiny bugs, mostly *Diptera*, come off each day.

Like the mayflies and caddis that will grab our attention soon enough, most midges struggle on or near the surface before taking off. They hatch, mate, deposit their eggs on the water and finish their lives as the equivalent of spent spinners. So, dry fly fishermen who want to hone their skills can approach these hatches as "spring training."

Not that it's easy fishing. It can, in fact, be very tough. But that's all to the good, since once mastered—that is, if you learn to spot the flies and rises, approach the trout correctly and present your fly well enough to hook the fish—you should be ready for anything prime time dishes out.

So why is this fishing such a well-kept secret?

Historically, relatively few anglers fished so early in the year, and most who did, including myself, were absolutely wedded to the adage, *The Mountain Must Go to Mohammed*. While sinking-tip lines, split shot, weighted nymphs and strike indicators do produce trout, to many this now seems a relatively uninteresting way to fish, especially for the dry fly fanatic. Moreover, fishing deep, with its repetitive lobbing (as opposed usually to true casting), probably does more to dull than hone the essential skills of dry fly fishing that you'll be needing all too soon.

I might never have taken this rainbow at all were I not midging in mid March in 43-degree water. The fish was no doubt returning to its regular home far down river after spawning when I discovered it sticking its nose up near the bank of a long eddy on Willowemoc Creek near my home in the Catskills. Having had my fun, of course, I sent the fish on its way again.

Then, too, there's climatic change, or a recent trend toward mild winters, at least here in the Northeast. Though of questionable benefit to the overall welfare of this region's streams, most anglers who must travel to fish haven't recognized yet that mild winters mean less in-stream ice, earlier and gentler ice-outs and minimal runoff, a situation clearly kind to midge populations, as their burgeoning numbers beginning in later winter illustrate.

As E. Neale Streeks, an extremely knowledgeable streamcraftsman and writer, has pointed out, midges have always represented a major food source for trout not only during the so-called pre- and post-seasons, but throughout the year. Thus, it's only natural that, given substantially increased numbers of midges in and on the water, this dependency would be reinforced, but that it would only become apparent at first to those ideally positioned to monitor trout behavior day in and day out.

There's also the matter of tackle, particularly terminal tackle. Not so long ago, midge tackle we now take for granted simply didn't exist. A 9- or 12-foot leader was thought long, a 5X tippet light, and a size 20 dry (ofttimes shamelessly overhackled) a small fly. Today, thanks mainly to the work of spring creek specialists, long, supple 6X, 7X, even 8X, leaders, tippet material strong enough to hang a horse and flies so small as to virtually disappear in your hand, are available everywhere.

So that leaves only the long-standing reticence of some to fish midges, regardless of the time of year. The most common complaint I hear is: "I can't see my fly"—a curious concern since it often issues from the same folks who think nothing of fishing weighted nymphs upstream. I usually can't see my midge either. The trick is to know where it is in or on the stream at all times.

"Spring training" begins with locating midge feeders. Best bets are relatively slow-moving pools, flats and eddies, as opposed to swifter pockets or riffs (see illustration 1). Watch: (1) tight to undercut banks; (2) the lees, or inside curls, created when fast water enters pools obliquely; (3) over jabble on a stream's shallow side (if the water isn't too swift); (4) in back bays, along secondary channels and sloughs (including some that may dry up later); (5) in small, revolving side eddies next to streambanks; and (6) in shallows immediately adjacent to sudden drop-offs, usually toward the heads of pools.

Sometimes you'll also find pods of trout midging over the deepest holes in pools. When bunched up like this, the fish are especially vulnerable to well-presented midges—although why I'm not sure. Security in numbers, perhaps, or some kind of competitive urge. Never, however, do I recall having spotted a singleton midger over water so deep so early in the year.

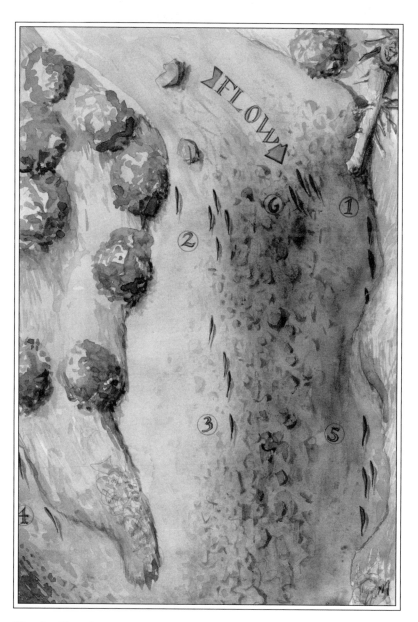

Illustration 1

Although clearer is better, the water needn't be more than translucent for trout to rise. In fact, a little murkiness can make catching fish easier. A good yardstick seems to be the ability to see your boots in water about two and one half feet deep.

Note my get-up in this photo: a wool scarf, fingerless gloves, and the heavy sweater peeking out from under the cuffs of the fishing jacket, which is tucked into my waders and under my vest. Turned out like this, I'm good for the whole day.

Surprisingly, stream temperature has little impact on either the number of hatching midges or the inclination of trout to eat them. (I've done well with water temperatures in the mid-30s.) Perhaps this is because when water is cold, flies take longer to get off the surface, and so they are more vulnerable to trout.

Atmospheric conditions, though, do affect both hatches and feeding behavior. Warm, calm days are better than cold, windy ones. A bitter wind is usually murder, although occasionally, given a cross-stream wind, a few trout will work to the lee-side bank.

A correlation also exists between what meteorologists call the "windchill factor," the water temperature and the trout's willingness to come up. When the windchill falls below the actual water temperature, even by a degree or two, trout tend not to rise in numbers, no matter how many midges are hatching. The only exception seems to be when there is an abrupt dip in the air temperature at sunset following a warm afternoon.

Although high barometric pressure is demonstrably preferable to low pressure, bright sun tends to suppress, if not midge hatches themselves, then the inclination of trout to surface-feed during them. (Active feeding does occur underwater, however.) But be on the lookout for clouds. A single cloud passing in front of the sun often sparks a sudden flurry of feeding on top.

The ideal pre-season midging day is unseasonably warm but overcast, with a rising barometer and no wind.

Given late winter, early spring conditions, preparation for the stream can make or break a day. Always dress warmly, bearing in mind that standing in frigid water for long periods, even on warmish days, can be a chilly experience. A chilled angler tends to be an antsy angler, and an antsy angler is seldom effective.

Neoprene waders (5-mm. are ideal) over polarfleece (or comparably warm) pants, and *warm socks* will take care of your lower half nicely. Clothing above your waist should be drab-colored to avoid spooking fish, and layered, so you can take it off and put it on as needed.

A couple of cold weather hints from one who's done his share of shivering. An old-fashioned wool scarf wrapped around your neck is like wearing an extra sweater, and a pair of fingerless wool gloves, though probably best removed and stuck down the front of your waders when casting, are a godsend while standing belly-deep waiting for trout to rise.

The fishing itself can be approached from two slightly different perspectives. One is to see it as pure midging, and so to stick strictly to midge fishing tackle and technique. The other involves adjusting midge fishing strategy just enough so this fishing also serves as a tune-up for attacking prime-time hatches.

Ask yourself a question: "Am I catching as many trout during late April or May as I might if their hatches occurred in September?" If not, choose option two.

Use a rod with power yet which is tapered for accurate and delicate presentations, a light line (number 4 or number 5), and a long, fine leader, and you'll really be getting the best of both worlds. Generally speaking, the closer you can come to making delicate midgelike presentations, including controlling long leaders (15-20 ft.), when you present, say, Hendricksons later, the better off you'll be.

Post–ice-out midge rises are typically the subtlest of the year, and thus the toughest for many anglers to see. Rise forms to floating adults usually appear as mere pinpricks on the surface, whether the surface is broken or flat. The rise forms to emergers are even more subtle, and the higher the water, certainly, the tougher they are to spot. But take heart. Learning to spot (and interpret) these rises makes spotting trout rising to mayflies or caddis later a relative piece of cake.

You should spend lots of time looking for fish, as "chuck and chance it," "prospecting" or "blind casting" with midges is virtually useless.

The key to spotting midge rises is to confine your attention only to those places where rising trout are most likely to be, then to discipline yourself to separate the extraordinary from the routine—in other words, to concentrate only on those surface features which would seem not to conform to the natural flow.

Remember, only the forward momentum of a living thing, i.e., a rising fish, can reverse the direction of surface flow abruptly against itself. So, since rough fish seldom start surface

I hooked this trout on a size 22 midge though fishing much the same way I would later during, say, a Hendrickson hatch. Could I see my fly? Not to save my life. The trick was to spot the rise, present the fly exactly where I wanted it, and monitor its progress toward the riser by coordinating its drift in my head with the speed of flow of the stream.

feeding until the water is warmer, if you are able to perceive this subtle manifestation of the midger's rise form, you've got it licked.

Approaching surface midgers is both easier and harder than approaching conventional risers later in the season. On one hand, since the fish usually haven't been pressured for months, they tend to become *uneasy* rather than *frightened* by your presence. On the other, since they require relatively little food early in the year, it doesn't take much to cause them to lose interest in eating altogether.

You'll find that trout often go down as you approach, perhaps because they "feel" your wake or "hear" you grinding gravel underfoot. But once you're positioned, just stand still a few minutes and they'll usually show again.

And don't be surprised (or discouraged) when all midging ceases at intervals throughout the day. My theory is that this is a predictable component of the normal feeding and digestion process of trout during periods of slow metabolic rate. Don't move around and they'll start feeding again soon enough.

Take a gander at just how prolific midge hatches can be. Everywhere along the shore on this not uncommon day, we found millions of shucks, stillborns and drowned midges. Such is probably also the case on your favorite stream, but you'll never find out at home watching TV. On the streams near my home, I like to say I can take a trout any day when the rivers aren't iced over. Try it where you live, and you'll experience the same thing.

Metabolism, I believe, is also the key to why this fishing is so exacting—and so represents the ideal tune-up for prime time. Because the trout require so little food, and the insects are so plentiful, the trout needn't, and so won't, move very far in any direction to take a fly—natural or artificial.

It's really a game of inches and instants. An inch or two one way or the other usually makes or breaks a presentation. The object is to dead drift your midge (drag is death) smack down the feeding lane of your target trout. Moreover, each drift should coincide with the precise instant when your fish should be ready to sip a natural. So be sure you have a handle on its feeding rhythm before beginning to cast.

Being able to put your fly in the right place at the right time takes a lot of the worry out of choosing the right midge pattern. Midging trout can be awfully finicky, particularly with regard to what stage of emergence they home on. In other words, some fish may feed only on emergers or crippled adults in the film, while others may clearly prefer healthy adults free of their shucks and almost ready to fly.

Given these parameters, though, whether your imitation must replicate the prevailing naturals or simply create a reasonable impression often depends on your ability to place your imitation exactly where you want it, when you want it there. Being able to do so seems to minimize the instinctive inclination of most trout to become suspicious when something doesn't look "quite right."

I've found, for instance, that a simple Griffith's Gnat works far better when I'm "on" than when I'm "off," which suggests that the fly's effectiveness depends more on presentation than on pattern. Conversely, when I'm "off"—particularly when I miss "long" and hence leader fish—I'm usually forced to turn to more realistic midge patterns, which I hate to do because they're a bitch to tie.

Whereas a properly presented midge is usually taken without ceremony, a sign you may be getting in trouble—even though you're catching some fish—is when trout begin "drifting with the fly," that is, backing downstream under your fly before finally deciding to take.

But none of this is really so different, is it, from the prime-time experience? Although some anglers seem determined not to believe it, the biggest problems they have catching more fish (particularly big fish) during prime-time hatches are self-created. They cast too much, they pay little attention to feeding lanes or rise rhythms, their presentations are inaccurate and ofttimes too long, and their leaders and tippets are too short, too stiff and too heavy. As you resolve each of these problems, you tend to become commensurately less fly pattern dependent at any time of year.

The principal difference between fishing larger flies during prime-time and early season midging is that in midging everything is scaled down. But that's all to the good, since by becoming comfortable with making do in miniature—spotting small rises, tying on tiny flies, fishing long, fine leaders, confining presentations to narrow lanes, sensing subtle takes, etc.—you are making it all easier on yourself as the time arrives when you can scale back up again. In other words, if you become sufficiently nimble to tie size 24 flies to 7X tippets, tying size 12s to 5X tippets is certainly no sweat. And so it goes throughout the process.

Here I'm using a long 7X tippet, and as you can see from the swirl, playing a pretty good fish. Learning to scale down and maneuver trout effectively gives you added confidence when fishing the major hatches later. Unless for the purpose of building or rebuilding a leader, I carry nothing with me these days heavier than 6X. Advances in the breaking strengths of leader and tippet materials vis-à-vis its diameter have made this possible.

Success during "spring training" also helps build the confidence to integrate many of the fine points of midge fishing into your day-to-day angling strategy. Having mastered longer, lighter tippets, for instance, you're more apt to try light tippets when fishing larger flies. And make no mistake: a long 6X tippet, say, behind a size 12 or 14 Hendrickson dry, will help you raise countless trout that would surely ignore the same fly lashed to a short 3X or 4X tippet.

Similarly, learning to use midges that are difficult (or impossible) to see on the surface helps instill the confidence to fish the low-floating dries that we now know attract more prime-time trout, particularly on flat waters, than traditional high-floating, easy-to-see dry flies do.

Sensing the exact whereabouts of your fly, as opposed to actually seeing it, is a skill acquired only over time. But here are a few hints to help speed up the process.

- Make time to practice casting to precise spots in all kinds of conditions, and keep at it until the ability to put your fly exactly where you want it becomes second nature to you.

- Learn to measure precise distances "in the air," that is, to know not only how far across the surface a rising trout is from you, but also how much leader and line you'll have to false cast and shoot in order to "lead" the fish and put your fly smack-dab in the middle of its feeding lane.

- Practice drifting clearly visible flies on the surface of as many different kinds of water as you can find. Watch what the fly does, how it behaves, from the time it contacts the surface until it's time for each pickup. Now make a cast, then close your eyes, visualizing in your mind's eye the progress of the fly along its lane of drift. Open your eyes only when you feel the fly should have reached the pickup point. If you've gotten it right, it'll be there.

- Learn to recognize the relative speed of stream flow and fly drift on each piece of water you fish. By telling you how long it will take your fly to get from Point A (where it lights on the surface) to Point B (where a target trout is rising), you'll be able to literally "count" your fly through its drift and so suggest whether or not to "strike the rise," even when you can't actually see your fly.

- When in doubt, strike, just as you do when fishing nymphs upstream. More often than not, your instinct will be right.

- Finally, getting the most out of "spring training" requires up-to-date information from streamside. Ice-out and runoff vary markedly from year to year in most places, as might be evidenced by the fact we were knocking them dead on the Beaverkill by early March in 1991 and '92, while it seemed the ice would never go out as the winter of '92-'93 supposedly gave way to spring.

In most cases, however, it isn't worth the trouble to ask whether fish are rising, as very few sources will be likely to know. Rather, find out whether most of the in-stream ice is gone, if the level is fishable and whether the water is at least moderately clear for a couple of hours each day. If so, play ball.

CHAPTER 6

Diptera: The Fly for All Seasons

What follows here is some *practical information* about fishing flies to represent Diptera, those wee, two-winged insects found balling up by the trillions year-round along trout streams from coast to coast. Excluded is the entomology of Diptera, which is so complex that I gave up trying to fathom it long ago, at the loss of not a single fish, I'll wager. In fact, I'd been fishing Diptera imitations, simply calling them "midges," for a long, long time before I was even aware they'd gotten the going-over from a handful of erudite anglers determined to dabble in advanced science and a dead language. Blissfully I fished them and continue to do so now, knowing little more about their body segments or wing veins, for instance, than I did the day I discovered that trout like to eat them.

For clarity, I will say that the tiny bugs of the Diptera family, including mosquitoes, craneflies and a host of midges (gnats, no-see-ums, black flies, snow flies, and on and on) all have a common Latin derivation: *di*, meaning *two*, and *ptera*, meaning *winged*. Unlike mayflies, caddis or stoneflies, Diptera have no secondary sets of wings. But, then, the Diptera that interest me most as an angler are so small that secondary wings would be hard to spot anyway.

Many anglers don't like to fish midges, as already noted. They view flies smaller than a number 18 with a disdain akin to that I have for the deromanticizing of fly fishing with too much science and its wicked stepsister, verification. Nonetheless, fishing experience at home and abroad has afforded me some insights into fishing midges worthy of all, I'd like to think, but perhaps the ultimate purist and the incurable romantic.

First: Diptera constitute a kind of common denominator among the world's trout fisheries. I've never struck a trout stream where I didn't find these insects, usually in abundance. For example, while scouting for fins in the Middle Atlas

Go West. I have many times with boxes full of Diptera imitations and have found that the same ones that work in my backyard do the job beautifully against a backdrop of snow-capped peaks. In this photo I'm landing a dandy rainbow from a stretch of Idaho's Silver Creek, which was a favorite of Ernest Hemingway's for jump-shooting ducks.

Mountains of Morocco, I discovered a lovely spring creek where plump browns were sipping emerging Diptera, just as browns sip Diptera on the Letort of Pennsylvania, Nelson's Spring Creek of Montana, and the Test, Itchen and Avon of Great Britain. Similarly, clouds of Diptera shade feeding trout on the Beaverkill, the Delaware, the Madison, the Big Horn, eastern and western American rivers, and on the Risle of Normandy, the Elle of Brittany, both in France, and Laxá I Laxádalur, the magnificent river of northern Iceland where they actually represent the staple of the brown trout diet. Thus, it is fair to suppose that when encountering an unfamiliar trout fishery, you won't go entirely wrong when you carry Diptera imitations and know how to fish them.

Second: Diptera tend to abound along trout streams, at least the streams I know best, for longer sustained periods each year than all other aquatic insects. Fishing the Beaverkill near my home, for example, I've taken trout on the surface or in the surface film using Diptera imitations during every month of the year. And these small flies have proven notably effective in the late fall, winter and early spring when the only viable alternative was to fish down, dirty and slow. According to my stream notes, I hooked 32 trout on March 19, 1982, for instance, 29 on a surface midge and but 3 while probing the bottom with a small dark stonefly nymph. Reliability, then, would seem to demand that you pay attention to Diptera's potential.

A typical angler prejudice against fishing midges issues from a sense of insecurity born of the inability to see his fly on the water. As noted earlier, why some anglers confidently fish nymphs upstream while distrusting midges, I'm not certain, but the root of this prejudice represents the perfect starting point from which to discuss techniques to enhance Diptera fishing.

To the angler, the most important stage in the life cycle of a typical Diptera (i.e., the egg, larva, pupa and adult) is the pupal stage. Even fished on the surface, a pupal imitation that represents a helpless insect struggling in the film to free itself from its shuck prior to flight has proven considerably more effective than a dry midge that floats high on the water. However, the dries you do opt to fish from time to time will likely be so small (my favorite is nothing more than clipped hackle wound on a short-shank number 26 or number 28 hook) that the best pair of eyes seldom will see them on the surface, except when fishing the shortest of lines.

The kicker, then, isn't to be able to see your fly at all, any more than it is to be able to see a nymph as it dead drifts downstream toward you underwater. Instead, the trick (as emphasized in the previous chapter) is *to know precisely where the fly is at all times*, so that when a trout rises for it, you are prepared to set the hook. Certainly it requires considerable practice to develop this skill, but with time most anglers can learn to monitor fly drift without actually seeing their flies, to sense the speed and direction of drift by relating stream velocity and bearing of current to the ability to put their flies exactly where they want them in the first place. With no arrogance intended, I respectfully suggest that an angler's time is much more productively given to mastering this skill than to mastering complex data attendant to Diptera entomology.

Through the years, I've had minimal success trying to fish Diptera larva or pupa imitations deep. This does not imply that trout don't feed on these midges nearer the bottom, but rather serves to illustrate that trout are reticent to move far up, down or to the left or right to take tiny insects. Thus, unless you've spotted a fish feeding in deep water and are able to put a Diptera imitation on its nose, you are, in effect, relegating fly presentation entirely to chance, like trying

I'd rather be doing this than just about anything else in the world of fishing—presenting Diptera emergers to pods of rising trout on the Upper Main Stem of the Delaware in the fall. If you can master taking these fish, you can catch trout anywhere in the world. *They're that tough.*

to sink a long birdie putt while wearing a blindfold. No, Diptera are not the flies for "prospecting."

Happily, Diptera imitations are best fished to rising trout whose feeding rhythms you've carefully monitored in advance. Wiring the feeding rhythm is essential, because the typical abundance of natural insects dictates that you ensure that your target fish spots your offering among the multitudes. To accomplish this, you must time your presentation so your fly passes over the trout's feeding station at precisely the instant the fish is prepared to sip a natural. Ideally, then, by means of meticulous timing, your fly must be the only fly the target trout sees as the fish opens its mouth to take.

To show your fly correctly to the rising trout requires that you be positioned to get an *absolutely drag-free drift*. Although your midge pattern may be no more than a wisp of dubbed fur on a number 28 hook, if it drags the trout will usually reject it and the trout will likely spook. Your task is facilitated by planting yourself across and somewhat downstream of your target trout, then three-quartering

Here I hook a good fall trout on a Diptera larval pattern on the Upper Main Stem of the Delaware River. Big rivers are best fished with Diptera patterns, as pictured here, when the water is low because you can get closer to the fish than when levels are up. Remember, never cross a stream with line when a pair of waders will do just fine.

the fly upstream, casting either a right or left curve into your line and leader, depending on whether the stream flows from right to left or left to right.

Long, fine leader tippets are generally essential to Diptera fishing, because (1) typical Diptera water is flat and clear, (2) heavy tippets will just not pass through the hook eyes of such tiny flies, and (3) a fine tippet enhances the impression of a free-floating insect to most trout. Frequently I opt for eight feet of 7X or 8X tippet material, which ironically makes presenting the midge a more manageable challenge than trying to do so while using conventional tippet lengths of two or three feet.

When presenting the midge, try dropping your casting hand to your waist immediately in the wake of your power stroke, while maintaining the rod tip pitch high over the water. This casting technique will cause your leader tippet to tumble and bunch up ahead of your target trout's feeding station. The current, then, will catch your midge and carry it downstream toward the feeding fish as the coils and "S's" in your tippet slowly straighten out behind the fly.

The trick, of course, is to ascertain your fly's probable line of drift before initiating each presentation. This is made easier, incidentally, when you discover that Diptera-feeders seldom need to be led by more than a foot. My rule is to lead a trout not one inch more than I perceive as essential to get the job done.

Despite contrary claims, fishing Diptera imitations requires no special equipment. In competent hands the same rod with which you'd fish a standard number 14 dry and 5X tippet will handle light tippets and tiny flies nicely with a light (but not tentative) touch. When choosing a rod specifically for midging, however, consider perhaps a 9-footer for a number 4 or 5 line for big waters, and an 8- to 8 1/2- footer for a number 4 or 5 line for midsized streams, or a 7 1/2- to 8 1/2-footer for a number 3 or number 4 line for small waters and extreme low water conditions.

Effective Diptera imitations run the gamut from number 20 through number 28 and in colors from black to cream. Among wets, I like a simple pattern tied with a stripped peacock quill body and a bit of fur dubbed as a collar. The dry I use most often is an emerging pupal pattern developed by Mike Kimball of Ithaca, New York, unquestionably among the world's most skilled midge fishermen.

Diptera fishing is usually associated with the sipping rise on flat water, especially spring creeks, limestoners and chalk streams. However, most surface water streams also abound with Diptera species largely ignored by the majority of anglers. When you see trout sipping on a flat stretch along your favorite stream, odds are excellent they are working on Diptera.

Lastly, there's the ultimate challenge: *fishing Diptera in or on fast water*. Although not widely perceived, some prolific Diptera hatches occur on pocket water, riffs and even the most turbulent of rapids. That dusting of minuscule bugs you observed over the river last season was probably one Diptera species or another, and those trout you were so proud to have spotted sipping amid all that turbulence were probably filling up on Diptera pupae.

Next time, why not test yourself? Put away the standard wets or dries, add a long, fine tippet, cinch on a size 28 pupa and find out how good you really are. The fish may give you fits at first. But, ultimately, you're going to be glad you allowed yourself to go a little bit "Dippy."

KIMBALL'S DIPTERA EMERGER

As simple as the pattern appears, hundreds, perhaps thousands, of hours of Mike Kimball's matchless skill and expertise went into the research and development of his Diptera emerging pupa, shown in the accompanying photograph as dressed by Galen Mercer (see also color insert, figure 2). This pattern has proven itself uniformly and remarkably effective on rivers and streams across America, as well as abroad. It is, by the way, the fly with which Mike created quite a stir when he was observed solving the apparent enigma of those evening rises on Armonstrong's Spring Creek in Paradise Valley of Montana.

Here's how it's tied:

Hook:	Number 20-28, Mustad 94833 (TDE, 3X fine)
Head:	Black, brown or cream midge thread, depending on the body shade chosen
Tail:	Several fibers of teal flank feather, tied long and splayed to represent the pupa's body shuck trailing behind the emerging insect prior to falling away
Abdomen:	None
Thorax:	Dubbed fur or poly in black, brown, rusty brown, olive, pale yellow or cream
Wing Case:	A small section of white or light gray poly yarn tied in so there's an exaggerated hump at the rear of the case and a gradual slope toward the eye of the hook

CHAPTER 7

A Toast to Sippers

Since the mid-1950s, our more orthodox fly fishing strategists have insisted that we ought to focus on exploiting predominant feeding characteristics of trout, particularly during periods of insect availability loosely characterized as "the hatches." What angler of today whose top priority is catching lots of trout would challenge such thinking as *the* means to that end? The prevailing insect, after all, is the "glue" of matching the hatch which, it's absolutely clear, is a darned effective method.

Actually I have enormous respect for the anglers who pioneered hatch-matching, for as surely as I know (and knew) many of them well, I know that to catch fish for its own sake, while it may turn out to be their principal legacy, was never their top priority. Indeed, more often than not these pioneer anglers forsook catching trout by then tried-and-true methods in favor of the challenge of distilling fact from fancy for us to chug-a-lug later. And so their satisfaction was derived, not from the trout they caught per se, but from evolving new tactics by which to catch them.

Who am I to decide that one fly fishing technique is intrinsically better than another—any more than I can determine that to sip good whisky straight while alone is a "better" experience than to enjoy a Scotch and soda with cronies at your favorite watering hole? By the same token, no one should really suggest that you match the hatch rather than prospect, for instance, or fish nymphs rather than wets or streamers, unless he's made his own priorities evident for purposes of perspective.

My personal inclination at this writing is to be more concerned with tactics, or how to fool trout largely by means of carefully calculated presentations, than

Live and learn. Here I take a good trout, but by being overanxious, blow another. Had I been more patient, I would have spotted the second good trout rising inside the one I've hooked, adjusted my position by circling downstream, and had my shot at that other trout first. As it turned out, the commotion made by the trout I hooked put the inside trout down for good. I call bungles like this "throwing to the wrong base."

with fly pattern or precise and specific insect representation, although I'm also very concerned with that as you'll discover farther along in this book. Though this is always changing, I'm not particularly interested in how many trout I can catch, or how big they are, but in the problem catching each one represents and whether or not I'm prepared to solve it. To date, by the way, I'm delighted to say the fish are still winning.

Specifically, *sipping rises* and *sipping risers* really engross me, for I'm convinced you can derive the most exacting and potentially instructive lessons to be learned from a piece of water by paying special attention to this aspect of streamlore. What's more, although such fishing is specialized, and somewhat more difficult than more traditional and conventional techniques, happily it tends to support season-through continuity not generally associated with fishing for trout, especially when you are overly preoccupied with hatches. Thus, while the principles I describe here may dictate at least temporary adjustments to your day-to-day strategy, once you've become intrigued, you'll have few outings that won't encourage further practice.

The sipping rise is characterized by the nearly imperceptible rise form left when a trout's mass displaces a small quantity of water and thus breaks or disturbs the tension of the stream's surface only slightly. When the riser sips insects out of the surface film, or drifting larvae, say, an inch or two beneath the surface, the surface tension may not be broken at all. Sipping rises are usually difficult to spot, therefore, especially on broken water common along freestone streams. Nevertheless, learning to pick them up, regardless of a stream's character, is the first prerequisite for mastering the techniques of this aspect of angling.

Being able to visualize a sipping riser at work is indispensable to this end. As shown in position 1 of the illustration below, typically the trout is stationed just below the surface in a direct line with, and no more than two inches downstream from, the precise point at which it will intercept virtually *all* insects it will consume for a period of time. (Lateral adjustments of feeding stations are normally made under the water, thus out of your sight.) Now, to dispose of the bug, the fish simply opens its mouth, and while inclining its head upward ever so slightly, and inhales (see position 2). The trout then closes its mouth and levels off before doing the same thing again. Hence, a sipping rise is completed with little or no forward motion, thereby denying you a look at any part of the fish, except perhaps the very tip of its nose.

There's no way to shortcut the time to acquire a knack for distinguishing sipping rises from all the natural goings-on atop a stream. You'll find it helpful, though, to study the natural elements until you can recognize them at a glance. Then you can dismiss them instantly and move on to differentiating between the extraordinary and the routine. With experience, your mind's eye should be able to visualize the surface of the most turbulent stretch as sufficiently smooth,

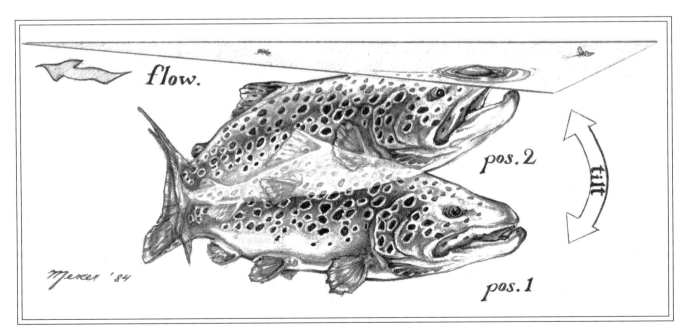

Illustration 1

Illustration 2 This single trout pool offers a host of distinctly different surface variations from which you have to be able to pick up the rise forms of sipping trout. Those in figure 1, for instance, could well be found in the chop at the head of the pool, while figure 2, the classic sipping rise, might correspond to the fish stationed near either bank or over the marl and weedbed beginning about halfway down the pool. But those over the marl and weedbed might also demonstrate rises as shown in figure 3, while the fish near the tail of the pool are apt to show themselves as pictured either in figure 4, the most likely option, or in figure 1, given some large stones and a real tightening up of the flow. Successful fishing for sipping trout, then, begins with honing one's observation skills.

that is, uncomplicated, to make even the subtlest rise form there relatively easy to discern.

Historically, sipping rises have been identified with flat waters, i.e., spring creeks, and small flies. Moreover, we've reserved the kind of fishing generally associated with the rise primarily for periods lacking major mayfly or caddis emergences, or those reckoned outside so-called "prime time." While to link, for instance, Diptera, or midge, feeding, as I've already done, with the sipping rise is certainly accurate, to infer exclusivity in this linkage risks neglecting legions of sippers that decline to conform to the stereotype of the hungry trout.

Look hard enough and you're likely to discover busy sippers along any stream on any given day, prime time notwithstanding, from the opening to the close of the season. Too, like me you'll no doubt be astonished by the variety of the sipping trout's menu which might include, among other delights: emergers of all sizes and descriptions, which for one reason or another, croak and thus fail to make it off the water; wee mayfly duns that sometimes aren't even cataloged in angler entomology texts for a given period of the year; drowned duns of easily recognizable species; caddis larvae swept from their chambers by acts of God; low-floating terrestrials with no business on the water in the first place—not to mention a smorgasbord of mayfly spinners from large to tiny just waiting to be devoured by opportunistic fish.

So, with all this sipping going on, why have so few anglers tuned into it? Reasons are manifold. One is surely unawareness of its existence as a consequence of unfamiliarity with the rise form. Then, too, sipping often occurs along overlooked snatches of stream. Side eddies and shallows are good examples. Thirdly, fly fishermen as a troop tend to hound the more-publicized, sequential emergences each season, as though to forgo but one Hendrickson hatch might

Kris was standing with camera by the tailgate of the car when I found a lovely brown sipping on the shallow side of Cairns Eddy on the Beaverkill. It was garbage feeding but ultimately fell to a well-placed Isonychia spinner. Moral? Wade carefully even when on the way home to supper.

court a permanent jinx. But most significant has to be an unmistakable reluctance to commit the amount of time and attention required to make this way of fishing pay off when conventional methods yield greater tangible results, particularly in the short term.

The skills demanded to catch sippers systematically won't be mastered overnight, even given undivided attention. Since each fish is apt to represent a different problem, seasoning yourself to the overall challenge is a cumulative thing, requiring that you define and redefine, refine and re-refine strategy and technique dozens of times each day and hundreds of times each season. Then, though no doubt you'll wind up a better and more confident angler for your trouble, you're still likely to undergo at least one season, and perhaps two or three, of fewer total trout taken than you'd net fishing conventionally. Though I'm convinced the end does justify the means, many anglers simply can't handle that consequence.

Assuming you're willing to go along with me, though, let's look first at strategy and then at technique.

Somewhat paradoxically, the chief strategy concern is to reconcile *concentration* and *discipline* with *flexibility*. First, forcing yourself to disregard all other feeding activity, you must establish whether sippers are working and if so, which fish suggest the most interesting challenges. You may opt to try only big trout, for instance, or maybe to ignore size altogether in favor of working to difficult lies.

Now, no matter how tricky, you must evolve an advance plan for stalking each target trout in its turn with minimum risk of spooking other fish that might be feeding. (Consider each spooked target a *significant failure*.) Forget your habitual practices, such as proceeding generally up- or downstream, adjusting instead to position yourself optimally for each trout and each fly presentation, even if to do so means considerable hopscotching from place to place. To be effective, you must become an "Artful Dodger" in both the *specific* and the *general*: the specific because you'll learn that there's only one *ideal* location from which to present a fly to a sipping trout and it varies somewhat from angler to angler, the general because you must so situate yourself again and again without compromise to your overall plan.

For best results, it's invaluable to ascertain *exactly* what each sipper is doing, although individual behavior may vary markedly from trout to trout. You need to know precisely where, relative to the surface, each sipper is intercepting its food and, if possible, what insect species it is feeding on. Sippers tend to establish fixed feeding rhythms, which though personal, are calculable with observation and should be gauged before any fly presentations are made. Additionally, faithful observation of your target trout's behavior will enable you in time to anticipate and identify any number of nuances and details—a forthcoming change of feeding lanes, for example—which will prove useful to you time and again as you attack tougher and tougher fish.

Because problems presented by sippers are so diverse, generalities concerning how to approach single fish would be purposeless here. The first rule, in fact, is to accept that there are really no rules, except always to try to give yourself an edge. Even your stream dress, for instance, should meet the best standards for stealth essential to reach that optimal spot from which to present a fly without detection. Don't make your task more difficult than it already is by playing it too cute, however. You'll only outsmart yourself. If pocket water trout appear most approachable from directly downstream, say, go for it. If you like pitching to trout sipping on flats by three-quartering across and downstream, give it your best shot. But before doing anything, always pause to consider whether your first presentation is going to count. If not, you've fouled up somewhere, probably by putting yourself in the wrong place to make your presentation.

Delicacy is the key to each and every technique component involved in this arena, which in part anyway, explains your forgoing the usual means of exploitation of predominant rises in favor of working exclusively to sippers. In most hands, tackle used for presenting, for instance, Green Drake or Hendrickson dries, much less bushy bucktails, just won't do for this game. Nor have I found gear that has completely satisfied me as compatible with everything I'd really like to be able to do, given, say, both a major hatch and lots of sippers during a single afternoon. (Huge strides, thanks to rod designers and new leader and tippet materials, have closed the gap in recent years, however.)

Rods, lines, and particularly leaders and tippets for this kind of fishing are decidedly specialized, although you can get away with your everyday rod *if* you work long and hard enough at it. I like a nine-foot rod tapered for the lightest possible touch and gentlest short- to mid-range presentations when coupled with number 3, 4 or 5 lines. Experience indicates that double-taper lines outperform weight-forwards hands down where delicacy is concerned, and thus I use DTs a good deal of the time for sippers, despite some potential for loss of distance.

Leaders and tippets ought to be tapered to *behave*. Control of your leader must be absolute, and whether it's in the air or on the water, the entire length has to respond to all the signals from your hand, no matter how subtle. Toward this end, my leaders, which are generally from 14 to 25 feet long depending on conditions, are built with stiff butts (one-third the length) to maximize power transfer, and supple midsections and tippets (two-thirds of the leader length) for ease of manipulation. In addition, I recommend the longest (6 to 15 feet) and finest (6X, 7X, 8X) tippets even marginally compatible with the flies you'll be using.

The dead drift presentation is the one constant in fishing the sipping rise and thus should constitute the cornerstone of your technique. Bearing in mind that significant action on the part of either insect or fish is inconsistent with the sipping rise form, your job becomes getting a fly to a trout without the kind of fuss that might cause your fly to be rejected. This is a very unforgiving business, usually requiring absolutely drag-free drifts. Even so-called "micro-drag," you're sure to learn the hard way, is disastrous.

Simply put, a drag-free drift occurs when the float of a fly is dictated entirely by the velocity and direction of the flow of the water with which the fly comes in contact. The effects of all other water, including that which alters currents between angler and fly, must be compensated for by calculating the exact configuration of your line and leader on the water throughout the course of each presentation. Accomplishing this, of course, is much easier said than done, although with practice any angler should be able to master the pertinent maneuvers.

The fundamental thing to remember is that to straighten your leader out while in the early stages of getting your fly to a sipper is wrong—a difficult concept to appreciate for many anglers used to conventional methods. In some situations the ideal presentation incorporates a measured "S" or line, leader or tippet to absorb the potential stress exerted by each intervening current likely to cause drag. The key, then, is to learn to put those "S's" right where you want them, a skill acquired only in time. Other problems are solved by curve casts, steeple or puddle casts, or my personal favorite, the stop-and-drop which I developed and featured in my first book, *Fishing Dry Flies for Trout on Rivers and Streams*.

Once again, the stop-and-drop is executed as follows:

fig.1   *fig.2*

Illustration 3

Positioning yourself across and somewhat upstream of your target, false cast until you've built considerable line speed. Now make a short power-stroke, lean forward into the cast and lower your rod tip until your rod is almost parallel to the surface as shown in figure 1. Then, when most of the working line has passed through the guides, raise your rod tip abruptly again as shown in figure 2. At this point you will feel a jolt as the pitching rod stops the forward momentum of your line. In the wake of this jolt, the "stop", your line, leader and tippet will "drop" to the surface in a series of "S's," which in turn will straighten out as your fly proceeds downstream along the line of fly drift you've chosen.

Whether or not this exacting game with sippers is for you is a question which only you can ultimately answer. Seldom, if ever, will you catch as many sippers as you could take fish by going after conventional feeders by conventional means. Even now, sometimes I wonder what possesses me to subject myself time and again to what can be a very humbling experience. But then my answer, I suppose, like your own, is neither simpler nor more complicated than what each angler expects from a day on a trout stream.

CHAPTER 8

Getting Sharp About the Flats

Many streams, even the most turbulent, have quiet stretches I like to call "the flats." Frequently dubbed "stillwaters," excellent examples abound on such northeastern streams as the Beaverkill, Willowemoc and the Ausable, all in New York State. Western waters—oh, the Henry's Fork, the Big Horn and the Madison come quickly to mind—probably have even more. Regardless what you call this water, though, historically it got less attention from anglers than swifter stretches, usually because few anglers mastered the techniques essential to handling it effectively.

The principal characteristics of a flat are its glassy surface and slow flow. A flat, therefore, differs from a pool, for instance, in that a pool, although usually smooth on top, quite clearly moves along at a considerable clip.

Among the finest flats in America is Cairns Eddy on the Beaverkill near my home, a popular (sometimes too popular) piece of water that paradoxically also illustrates the dearth of interest among anglers in still stretches. While Cairns receives heavy fishing pressure on an almost daily basis, it is unmistakable that the bulk of it centers on the eddy's upper quarter where the water is broken by a rush from Horse Brook Run above. Anglers indicate that they concentrate on the head because that's where they have succeeded in the past and therefore believe that is where most of the stretch's trout must hold.

On the latter point—except during stress periods when water temperatures rise exceedingly—they are wrong.

Trout, like most fish, are lazy by nature. Of all the trouts, the brown is the laziest. If there's suitable cover, water temperatures congenial to their metabolism and a reliable food source, they'll generally opt to live where they must

Particularly when levels get down, almost nobody bothers with the lower two-thirds of Cairns, plied above with picture-perfect style by Galen Mercer. Fishing the flats generically differs markedly from, say, Diptera fishing, in that the trout may exhibit all kinds of maddening behavior, including cruising, which makes it tough to execute bang-on presentations. But this is just one of the challenges that also makes stalking the flats my favorite aspect of trout fishing.

expend only minimum energy to maintain the holding positions. This is particularly in evidence among large trout that require more and more food just to survive as they grow old and so are programmed by nature to choose spots where the living is easy. To that end, flats are ideal.

Creeping along the rocks on the south bank of Cairns late one summer afternoon, I spotted eight fish larger than any I had heard of being caught at the head of the eddy all season long. Two I would have estimated in the five- to eight-pound class, while the remaining six were 20- to 24-inchers. On two successive days, a friend and I took two, 22 and 20 inches respectively (by the tape measure, incidentally, not by the eye), on small dry flies. Those are fine trout for any eastern river and not bad on most waters in the West.

Yet, resistance by some against fishing flats has always persisted, even among very fine anglers.

Friend Francis Betters, resident expert on the West Branch of the Ausable in the Adirondacks, and I have fought a running battle over the years concerning what kind of water offers the best fishing. He says pockets. The flats, I insist.

Now, I'd be the last person to deny Francis's expertise for wrestling big trout from some of the river's roughest water, but I still contend he'd do just as well were he to devote more time to the Ausable's flats, among the most beautiful and challenging anywhere.

Fact is that when you come upon a flat, you can seldom perceive its potential simply by looking at the surface. Typically, unless there's a major hatch or spinner fall in progress, there will be little surface activity, and the fish that are rising will likely be small. Yet, when you consider the usual depths of flat water, the undercut banks, the debris that's apt to accumulate because the flow is inadequate to push it on through, an experienced angler ought to get that "fishy feeling." Note, too, that a flat is liable to represent a perfect nursery environment for a host of aquatic insect species, not to mention a variety of rough fish, such as chubs and dace, that seldom inhabit swifter water in great numbers. Thus, while the surface may be still, you can assume there's plenty going on underneath.

To take advantage of these goings-on, however, you have to learn to do it right.

Flats are unpredictable, and therefore in anticipation of fishing them, it's important to prepare in advance for every conceivable contingency. Ideally, it would be wonderful to have access to a couple of rods, for instance, but that aside, you should choose one that will permit you to present both large dry flies and midges as effectively as possible, as well as wets, nymphs, bucktails and streamers, whether these subsurface flies be large or small. A nine-footer for a number 4 line is my "gamer." I carry two reels, one with a floating line, one with a sinking-tip. The length of backing, of course, depends on the dimensions of the flat and the size of the trout you feel you may encounter. Always have enough backing, though, to handle the *biggest fish* and the *longest runs* you conceive as possible on the flat.

Since the nature of slow water of flats tends to encourage trout to look their food over carefully before committing to eating, and because available food is likely to be diverse, you should carry a more varied assortment of flies than you would usually need to tackle broken waters. You should have dries from the largest attractors (sizes 8-12) down to the tiniest midges (sizes 20-28). In

This ol' brute of a brown, tough as he was when I got him on, was really a lazy fella, long ago having kissed rapid water goodbye in favor of dwelling under a bank adjacent to a flat. Every now and then he'd venture out to feed. I caught him on a Black Ghost streamer, which I sent knocking on his door.

between, you should be prepared for prevailing hatches and spinner falls with a supply of both traditional and hackleless dressings. And for prospecting, you should also have at least one all-around pattern, such as the Adams (sizes 14-18).

Terrestrial insect imitations work especially well on flat waters, notably black and cinnamon ants (sizes 14-22), black, brown and tan Beetles (sizes 12-16), Jassids (sizes 14-20) and Leaf Hoppers (sizes 20-22). Nor should you discount Black Crickets (sizes 12-14) or Grasshoppers (sizes 10-14), even when the time of year doesn't seem exactly right. Frequently, a hopper plopped against an undercut bank in May will bring you one helluva surprise.

For nymphs, to augment your usual supply of conventional dressings, don't hesitate to take along and try the biggest and scruffiest creations you can find. The more you can make them "breathe" in the still water, the better. The same goes for caddis pupae, for instance. For fishing flats, try to tie or buy nymphs and pupae made only with materials that give the most lifelike impressions in the water. A selection of wet flies in standard patterns and some soft-hackle flies are also a good idea to have along. Probably the most important flies you can carry for probing the depths of flats, however, are bucktails and streamers, such as the Black Ghost (sizes 2-12, 8X long), the Muddler Minnow (sizes 4-12), black and olive Wooly Buggers and Matukas (sizes 2-10) and a good Sculpin imitation (sizes 2-8).

In all instances, of course, patterns will vary according to region and water. In general, though, when it comes to fishing beneath the surface of flats, the key is likely to be size. Experience teaches that when fishing a flat, unless a hatch is on, a larger fly handled imaginatively will outfish a small one almost every time.

Varying techniques so radically dictates that you be ready with a wide range of leader lengths and tippet strengths. Your leader wallet should be stocked with wet fly and dry fly leaders from 5 to 12 feet long in tippet strengths from 12 pounds down to 8X. Remember, on the lighter side a 12-foot leader can easily become a 20-foot leader with a minimum of snipping and bloodknotting. Some wet fly leaders made to accommodate as many as three dropper flies should also be in your kit.

On the water, a meticulous battle plan is essential. Its elements, of course, will depend to some degree on what you observe when you get there, but generally speaking, you will have to make some tough decisions. It's not unusual, for example, to find quite a few trout surface feeding, particularly near the banks. Unless it is clear that they are big fish, however, you have to determine whether they are worth the chance of spooking larger trout that may be lying (and feeding) between you and them. Since small trout tend to resume feeding reasonably soon after being disturbed, it's likely you may want to opt to leave them until you've at least a go at the flat's heftier residents.

Regardless, to get the most from a flat, you should plan to stick with a single, short stretch of water throughout the day. A stretch, say, 50 yards long is more than adequate to occupy the careful angler from dawn to dark.

Giving a flat a wide berth in order not to be spotted approaching, walk to the upper reaches and fish downstream using a large bucktail, streamer or weighted nymph or, perhaps, a wet fly with a dropper. Soft-hackle wets, I've found, make ideal dropper flies for fishing flats. Fish slowly. Disturb the surface as little as possible. Never throw a wake that may be detected by the fish. And above all, keep a low profile and don't drag your feet, particularly if you're wearing hobnails or metal cleats. Trout will "hear" them grinding and spook for sure.

If the flat is wide, divide it in two and make your first pass fishing only to midstream. Presentations should be long enough, however, to assure that trout won't see you before they see your fly. When you've reached the lower limit of your water, return to the head and fish the flat through again, this time wading at about midstream and casting tight to the far bank.

Cover for trout along a flat is likely to be located near the banks, and so it is crucial to fish them carefully. Pay particular attention to small side eddies, undercut banks, holes under overhanging trees and areas around big rocks. Vary presentation. Try dead drift first and if it doesn't work, try slapping your fly against the bank and drawing it back, at first smoothly, then with short jerks. Finally, pull out all the stops and bring your fly streaking out from the bank, as if to imitate a natural panicked by impending death.

I frequently devote several hours to this kind of prospecting, changing flies from bucktail to nymph, nymph to streamer, large fly to smaller one, using first a floating line and long leader, then a sinking-tip line and short one. With experience you'll get hunches, and it's always best to go with them.

Galen Mercer has found a pod of big trout feeding in a depression in a flat during a Hendrickson hatch. Now the game gets really tricky, as he must present his fly so that he can take each fish in order without spooking the others. (Trout, if disturbed, *will* spook like bonefish off a flat.) It's best, usually, to try the "tail" fish closest to you first, hook it and lead it away from the others, being certain not to permit it to make any surface commotion. The others, then, become like balls in the proverbial pool game, each a matter of thinking ahead.

If these tactics come to nothing, it's time to reassess your situation. Are there still fish rising? If so, maybe you'll want to give them a shot. When there are natural flies around, your choice of pattern won't be too difficult. However, when there are none, try to choose a fly that looks like nothing but looks like everything, such as an Adams, a Usual or a Comparadun. If the rising fish are close to a bank, though, a terrestrial, such as an ant, may prove to be the best choice. Ants, I've discovered, fished to bank feeders on flats, frequently outperform mayfly and caddis imitations, even during periods when the trout have been working on natural aquatics.

In any event, choose the smallest pattern you are confident will do the job, if only to enable you to use the finest leader tippet you can. On most flats there's no such thing as a tippet that's too fine.

Approach target fish carefully in an upstream direction when dry fly fishing on flats, even if it means having to circle the flat back from the bank over and over again. Stalk your fish, trying to create little or no wake. Then, once positioned, wait several moments for your wake to dissipate before presenting your fly.

Presentation is critical because the slow flow guarantees the quarry a long look at your fly. Therefore, never show a trout any leader. Lead each fish unless the behavior of the naturals on the water and the trout feeding on them dictate otherwise, and always try to provide plenty of drag-free drift behind the trout so that (1) the fish can follow the fly downstream and (2) you will create minimum commotion when picking up your line to make another presentation. I'm convinced that more trout are spooked on flats by drag and premature pickup than all other blunders combined. It is critical, therefore, to take your time.

Large attractor dries are seldom tried by most anglers who fish the flats. It's a specialized business that's probably best saved for a last resort. Like standard patterns, attractors such as the White Wulff, Ausable Wulff, Hornburg or Skater, should be fished ahead of the lightest tippets manageable, but unlike the more traditional dressings, they normally shouldn't be shown to the trout so the fish can look them over very thoroughly. Working a size 10 White Wulff to a riser, for instance, I don't lead the fish at all. Instead, I put the fly right on the trout's nose. If after two or three such repetitions the trout refuses to take, I skitter the fly. A skittering attractor, you should know, however, is likely to do one of two things. It will either raise a fish or scare it to death. So, the technique is best used only when all else has failed.

Large dries, including attractors and terrestrials, are sometimes effective when fished upstream just as you fish a large streamer downstream. With a minimum of false casting, pop the large dry over the likeliest spots big trout would hold. Move carefully and quietly, but don't waste time. In and out, in and out, three or four casts, and move on. Permit the fly to rest only seconds before picking it up to make another presentation.

There is no kind of trout water I don't like to fish. But there's something special about fishing the flats—an ever-present element of mystery, perhaps. Whereas when fishing broken water I sometimes get the feeling I'm cupped in the hands of Lady Luck, no such feeling ever occurs to me when I'm on the

Do flats hold good fish. I'm not a numbers guy and rarely keep score. I had to one year, however, as part of a special writing project I was involved in. During that season I caught and released 86 trout of more than 16 inches from the lower end of one Beaverkill flat alone. Now that's fishin' "to write home about."

flats. There's too much to know, too much to learn, too many things to do wrong, any of which can blow it for you. So when I bring a good fish to the net and watch the evidence of our confrontation slowly dissolve into the face of a flat's expressionless surface upon releasing the trout, I know I'm not really a lucky guy at all. Instead, I'm a guy who has done his best, and having caught a fish, has earned it.

CHAPTER 9

Once Upon a Catskills Stream

Earlier it had rained and now you could feel a hatch coming on. The rain was gentle, had drizzled down from a soft cloud cover that took up the morning sky. There was no breeze, and the rain had shined the stones on shore before drifting on with the clouds over the ridges to the north.

Everything shone in the wake of the rain. Everything looked yellow and green except the sky, which was very clear now and very blue. The sun had approached at midday and with it the young leaves, new grass and the ferns—especially the ferns—looked all the more like spring.

Couldn't you just feel that hatch coming on, though?

We were sitting cross-legged on the bank overlooking the tail of the flat. The water of the tail was smooth and slow for that time of year and passed silently before us. It too looked yellowish green, reflecting the spring foliage. The sun was warm. Far above us near the bend, the river slid to either side of a great stone, and behind the stone there was a calm spot where flies collected when they were hatching. A very big trout always took that spot during a hatch, and we had already decided that David should have a crack at it today.

We had matted the grass on the bank as deer do when they sleep. David had a new rod and line and we looked them over while we ate and drank and palavered. Nearby were three poplars freshly downed by beavers and the air held the scent of the new grass. A lot of birds were singing. On the flat in front of us, the surface bulged with occasional risers, and we would look up after spotting a rise and watch it in silence until all of the rings were washed away.

"You've got to see her sometime when the ice goes out," I told David.

That's me with angling partner, the late Dave Danzig of Schenectady, New York. I was (and remain) proud that David, a real loner, chose me as the first regular fishing companion of his life. He's been gone, though, for some years, but I'm proud to say that I was able to help him fish until just three days before his passing, and that I still think of him, and miss him, every day of my life.

David smiled and nodded. "Maybe when I retire," he said. "You don't know how damned lucky you are to live here." He picked a single blade of grass and smelled it.

I looked across the flat to the opposite bank. That bank is different, bedrock mostly with beds of moss, old trees that hang onto the rock, some with roots exposed almost like veins. Some of the trees were dead but standing, gray and full of holes. Some were young and full of life, proud, or so it seemed, of their new buds and leaves. Closer to the ground were growths of rhododendron with polished leaves. Soon they would be in bloom with white flowers as shiny as porcelain against the dark green leaves.

Nobody really had to tell me how lucky I was and still am.

We stood up together. David leaned on his wading staff. There was a rise near midstream. The trout had missed the emerging fly. I lit a cigarette and picked up my rod.

"You know, you really ought to give those up," said David, sniffing the air. Like so many former smokers he still loved the smell.

"You've said. You die your way, I'll live mine." I didn't mention Dave's rantings against the humorless zealousness of the converted in all areas of life when he was still smoking. I drew and inhaled. It was too nice a day.

We walked the crest of the bank until we reached the first cutoff. David kept to the path while I turned off and started down the bank. Glancing to my left, I caught glimpses of him in the broken light through the underbrush. Once ready to fish, David hated to miss a second of it and now he had increased his pace. The hatch was coming, and man, could you ever feel it.

You feel a hatch all through you. At least that's what we who fish in the Catskills say. The cynic and the stranger sometimes attribute this feeling to chauvinism or biological predictability, but it just isn't that way. The feeling is internal, comes from your gut, and I have felt it from the first day I ever fished here and have never felt it more surely in any other place. I am certain that Theodore Gordon had felt it almost a century earlier exactly as David and I did that day.

Already the occasional fly was showing. These were the first to come off and you could still count them—one, two, three—drifting with the flow or kicking off the water and making for one bank or the other even as swallows swooped and dived to pick most of them off. The sight is bittersweet. The flies emerge as though by sleight of hand, and when there are so few, they are particularly charming to see. You spot one and follow its course downstream, first toward you, then in front of you, then by you, and finally off the water and away. You cannot but root for the first of them. They are so fragile and so vulnerable and it seems to take them forever first to dry their wings and to leap into our world, then to make it ashore against such odds.

I have always liked to stick with the first I spot all the way ashore, believing maybe that by sticking with it, its safety will be assured. Why can't the birds wait? I've always wondered. The time will come soon enough when the air will be dusty with flies. In the meantime the flies are individuals, fragile lives beginning a journey. They climb and circle, swimming through air, until they become smaller and smaller to the eye. If luck is with them (and you) finally they are only specks and at last they are gone altogether, safe on branches or under leaves or on blades of grass.

I turned and looked upstream. David was positioned and poised for a drift in the wake of the stone. Bent at the waist, waiting, he was wearing his favorite fishing cap, the one he had thought was lost until I found it in the cookie jar. I smiled. But had I known the implications of my discovery, I wouldn't have smiled at all, for the cap in the jar was just one of the first signs of the disease that would soon kill him. A good friend who deserved to live to be a hundred. You had to see his profile. David had a magnificent nose.

The river boiled around my legs and it felt good to lean into it. I was in thigh-deep and the current was stronger than you might have thought by just assessing the surface. The water was clear but appeared tinted slightly ocher because of the winter algae that dies off but remains on the trap-rock bottom until it totally degrades. During this degrading process,

There's nothing quite like fishing through a hatch. It defines trout fishing to my mind. So I was more than content with the tail of the flat while David gave the wake of the big rock his best shot.

though, it becomes gritty, and when you wade, it grinds under your boots and billows in your wake like dust in the water.

A trout rose in front of me. I didn't see the fly it took. But now suddenly flies were bobbing up all around me and the trout rose again. This time I saw it take a fly and saw the fish clearly. It was a small fish. I glanced to the left and right and saw that the surface had come alive with emerging mayflies. Some drifted motionless. Others kneaded the river's surface as they dried their wings. Still others, struggling awkwardly to rid themselves of their nymphal shucks, seemed in a special hurry to take their chances in the air.

A good trout showed just off the far bank, leaving a bubble that drifted downstream. Another rose below me, another between the two. Carpeted with flies now, the flat was coming to a boil, and I found myself a touch giddy as always when I have to decide which way to go.

There is always more river, and less you, when a big hatch is on. It is hard to imagine so many trout pushing the surface of a river apart. The river seems to swell with them, and only then does it appear permanently uncompromised by time or the insensitivity of man's enterprises. Maybe more than anything else, that's why I love our hatches so.

I chose a fish just downstream of me and halfway to the bank. I had watched it rise twice, nice leisurely rises, perfectly timed. The trout wasn't particularly large but it had the kind of rhythm I like best to fish to, starting up slowly when it had picked a target insect, ascending and adjusting as need be as the fly drifted along on the surface, then butting its head through the surface, mouth open and waiting until the fly arrived.

The angle of the sun couldn't have been better and I stayed with the trout until it had returned to its lie near the bottom. There I could pick it up lying over the stones despite one of nature's better efforts at camouflage. Blowing on my fly, I edged downstream. The trout rose again to take another fly, then tipped downward once more, driven by its tail. This rise had barely disturbed the surface.

They look golden in this water, I thought, and so small when they are down there, even the big ones. The trout, I could see, was fanning now over a flat rock and appeared almost translucent and very streamlined. To see your fish really makes a hatch, I thought.

My fly touched down ahead of the trout after whistling back and forth high over the water several times. I could see that the fly had cocked up just right. I watched the trout and the trout watched the fly. The fly floated slowly toward the trout. It was sparkling in the sun. Then I saw the trout begin to rise and I looked from the trout to the fly, then from the fly to the trout, again and again. There was just enough time.

Then, for some reason I'll never fathom, I glanced at David.

David had "whooped." And I had lost focus and glanced at him. *Stupid*.

And it was just at that instant, of course, that the trout took my fly. In fact, I knew at once that it had quite literally taken my fly. All that remained where my eyes should have been all along was a ruined splash that threatened to capsize a couple of naturals that happened to be floating by at the time.

Then David "whooped" again.

Planted toward the middle of the river and well below the stone now, David looked like some kind of distorted figure in bronze as he tried to net a fish, because even as he was doing his job, he was also waving his rod overhead, beckoning to me, his left arm buried to the elbow in the river.

"Odd time to be doing your laundry," I shouted, squaring around to face him. My hands were on my hips. "Whatcha got?"

"Come and see," he called back, obviously bound and determined not to look my way.

"Only if you promise to hold that pose 'til I get there," I said.

Funny, but he never would repeat exactly what he had shouted next.

You learn a lot about the condition you're in when traveling against a river in the springtime, even a flat. It is like pushing through a gale with lead weights on your feet. Why didn't I go ashore, you might wonder, and just walk up the bank? I don't know for sure, for it is certainly the best move strategically. But in those days, I suppose that to leave a river once beyond halfway across represented some kind of retreat.

Illustration 1   Regrettably, I have no photos of these treasured moments of my angling life. But Galen Mercer has done an excellent job of rendering not only the action, but the ambience of the scene as David and I lived it.

"This had better be good," I told him when I finally reached his side. My line and leader were trailing me.

"You're puffing," he snorted. He was still bent over and when he looked up at me, the sun suddenly lit his face. The light was warm.

A mayfly flew in front of me and I jabbed at it like a boxer. "Please don't carp at me again about smoking," I said.

"You could've gone ashore," said David.

"As you can see, I wanted to troll," I shot back. I turned slowly and examined my trailing line. The flyless tippet had sunk.

"What fly you got on?" he asked.

"None."

"Hell, any fool can catch them with a fly on," said David with a smile.

"So I see," I countered. This kind of banter would continue all day and has often made me think that there's truly nothing better in this world than having a regular fishing partner.

David straightened up and I leaned over, and up with his arm came his landing net. Water flushed off the net and his hand glistened with water and the sleeve of his shirt was dark because it was wet. The net was verily full of trout.

It was a brown trout, long and deep with yellow fins and orange and black spots haloed by pale blue. The trout shook in the net as if to let you know it wasn't really through, and David's wrist sloped downward under its weight.

This ain't the critter, but it was a trout similar to this, positioned much like this in David's net bag, that I had the joy of sharing with him.

"Behind the big stone?" I asked the unnecessary question.

"Behind the big stone," he said.

I nodded.

David lowered the net into the water and snatched it from around the fish. The big trout swam down and away with the current, then turned sharply near the bottom and faced upstream. A mayfly drifted over the trout and I followed it downstream until it disappeared in a swirl. There were still lots of flies on the surface. Two anglers walked side by side into the tail of the flat far below us. You could see them pointing here and there and hear their laughter.

"I was sure you'd want to see that fish," said David.

I looked at his eyes and nodded again.

CHAPTER 10

Coping With the Ultimate Blanking

Dry fly fishing for trout can abound in frustrations, chief among them are persistent risers that do everything imaginable on or near the surface around your flies but get down to business and eat them. They rise and refuse them, bulge under them, splash in front of them, just behind them, swat them with their tails and, of course, drown them. I've even had trout come up with their mouths closed and gently touch my flies as though testing, then slowly sink to the bottom again. The upshot of such antics is likely to be to raise 40 fish in an afternoon, foul hook one or two by the tail or dorsal fin, then go home skunked with a terrible urge to break your rod over your knee.

Trout of all species have given me this kind of going-over more times than I care to relate. But the most memorable (and excruciating) episode occurred some years ago when I was fishing Wagon Track Pool on the Beaverkill with Ed Van Put, a fellow local who is among the best dry fly anglers I've ever met. It was an evening in May, one of those rare, midweek evenings when you can call Wagon Track your own.

Early on there was little surface activity, but in the half hour before dark, the entire pool suddenly erupted. When they came, the flies were a mixed bag of leftover Hendrickson spinners, a caddis we call the shad fly, and the omnipresent midges which are, as already noted, largely overlooked by anglers during the peak season.

Under more favorable circumstances, I might just have cut this trout off. But so frustrating was this day that when I hooked the fish, I was willing to tear an entire brush pile apart just to possess it for a few moments. Perhaps the problem really was that I wasn't wearing my lucky hat.

Prior to the eruption, I'd been working a pair of shad fly wets dressed by the late Walt Dette of Roscoe, while Ed prospected with his ubiquitous Adams, the only fly he used most of the time. Undisturbed by tromping feet for some time, the fish in the pool seemed at ease and had been reasonably responsive. We both had some trout, Ed, as usual, a couple more than my few.

When the action really began, I cut off my wet fly cast, rebuilt several leader sections including the tippet, and tied on a number 14 Adams, the same size Ed had been fishing. Soon I was making good presentations, or so I thought, to free-rising trout. Yes, the trout rose to my fly well enough. In fact, ofttimes exploded on it would be a more accurate description. Up they'd come again and again, shoving water in all directions. I'd set the hook—and *nothing*, *nada*, *rien*, squat. In minutes, I was talking to myself, at times I probably shouldn't admit, at the top of my voice. The substance of that diatribe, however, would get this book an R rating and so will be forgone for the sake of sales, if not morality.

Nor was Ed silent upstream. To say he was holding forth with a few colorful "blankety-blanks" of his own should be sufficient. Suffice it to report that Wagon Track that evening gave us the *ultimate blanking*.

Such treatment from trout certainly isn't peculiar to the Beaverkill, or for that matter, eastern surface water streams. I remember all too well, for instance, a similar splashy afternoon on the Henry's Fork in Idaho. Nor are false-rising fish given to inhabiting only one kind of water, pockets or rapids, for example. You're just as likely to encounter them—maybe more so—on flats as on broken water.

So, what to do?

Your first item of business is to check the rising fish against the prevailing insects very carefully to pinpoint with absolute accuracy what they're feeding on. Noting the rises themselves and rise forms left in their wakes helps you to present your flies so they accurately imitate the behavior of the right insect or insects. This, in turn, should help you to entice the trout to take your flies in the same manner they are taking the real ones.

You want to know, for example, whether the trout are concentrating on duns at rest on the surface, for which their rises would generally be lazy rolls, or on duns trying to get off the water, which might spark more splashy rises. Or are the fish taking duns at all? Are they perhaps working only on emergers and seldom breaking the surface tension? During spinner falls, observe whether the trout are taking mostly the spent fly or attacking the more active ones as they deposit their eggs on the surface.

That done, choose a fly that best represents the natural—or more precisely, stage of the natural—on which the trout seem to be homing. Pay particular attention to size and silhouette. (Color is a less important criterion.) Then attempt to show your artificial to the fish in exactly the same way the naturals are showing themselves to the trout. For instance, if you notice that the naturals are floating into a trout's window, allow for enough lead when presenting your fly to ensure that yours likewise floats realistically into this oval of trout vision. Moreover, if you happen to notice trout taking naturals in a downstream direction, plan to drift your imitation so it will float drag-free for up to 10 feet below the lie of the target trout.

Now, if none of this works, consider the following.

It just may be that a trout to which you're fishing is leaving the bottom intent on taking your fly, but when it gets within inches of the fly, it spots your tippet. This is likely to spark one of two responses. The first is classic rejection, that is, the trout will simply turn away at the last instant, either making no surface disturbance at all or creating a small bulge of water just under your fly. If, however, the trout is moving fast toward the fly, the fish, being unable to turn away in time due to its momentum, will make a major splash on top. In either case, try switching to a lighter tippet, the lightest you feel you can get away with without spinning your leader up, while making certain your fly will still drift directly over the trout's nose. A presentation just an inch or two

Sometimes trout feeding just off banks or shores will be somewhat more forgiving than those feeding at mid stream. This is because the fish are inclined to "garbage feeding," that is, taking pretty much anything that floats over their lies. Also, by casting straight upstream to the fish, you are draping your line and leader over a trout's one blind spot and so may be spared being detected as described in the text.

Over the years I've learned that the surest dries to spark unconditional takes are those that float low to the surface. Here a Beaverkill brown has a no-hackle fly, called a Sidewinder, right where it ought to be, in the maxillary, the corner of the jaw. Other excellent dressings for this kind of response are the Usuals about which you'll read more further along in this book, and the Compara duns.

long is usually what gives trout that disastrous look at your tippet.

Next, observe your imitation's speed of drift relative to that of the naturals. A fly drifting too fast can cause a trout to have "second thoughts" about it, evoking a response not unlike the checked swing in baseball. Similarly, a fly floating too slowly (1) sometimes offers the target trout too long a look at the fly or (2) throws the trout's timing off so, like the hitter out in front of a change-up when expecting a fastball, the fish misses the fly altogether. Interestingly, in the latter instance the fish often spooks itself, sometimes to the extent that it will stop feeding altogether for some time.

Experience teaches that if there's one factor that will cause the false rise, it's a fly that's too large for prevailing conditions. Large attractor patterns are so good at this that we frequently use them to spot fish we take later with more conventional offerings. Be certain, therefore, that the fly you use isn't oversized for the naturals present and that when fish begin splashing on, or dunking your flies, you switch to a smaller one, even if your eye suggests that your chosen alternative is actually smaller than the prevailing naturals.

Another problem seems sometimes to be bushy flies. Traditional dries have worked well for generations, but their high-riding quality will at times work against their effectiveness, I suspect because they create an impression of the imminent escape of the fly and so rush the trout into missing altogether, or alternatively they occasionally spark that weird, typically short-term quirk of trout to become inexplicably playful or totally brutal rather than to simply fill their stomachs.

In either event, here are several ways to compensate.

First: Try using traditional dries tied with softer hackles that will collapse when wet, thus floating the flies lower in the water.

Second: Soak up standard dries and open your casting loops so all the excess water isn't snapped out of the fly during false casting. Added water means weight, which controlled with practice, enables you to float your flies as low in the water as you please at any given time.

Third: Perform surgery on traditional dries. Using a pair of sharp scissors, snip the hackle straight across the bottom of the collar of each fly, taking off about one-third of the length of the hackle fibers. If that doesn't work, try another cut that shortens the fibers to about one-half of their original length. Such alteration won't compromise the buoyancy of your flies but will make them float closer to the surface.

And finally: Purchase or tie some no-hackle dries in patterns that coincide with those that predominate on streams that you fish. Being a dyed-in-the-wool northeasterner, I still concede a weak spot for the traditional dressing but know full well that under many conditions there's no question that no-hackles are far more effective. One of those times is to false risers, especially on flat water, and even more especially if those false rises are splashy. The Sidewinder patterns popularized by Idaho's Mike Lawson are, in my opinion, the most effective alternatives to traditionals I've ever used.

CHAPTER 11

Selective Selectivity

Kibitz your way down the bank of any "in" trout stream and you're bound to get an earful on *selective trout*. Over the years, the term "selectivity" has taken on a nigh mystical meaning all its own, quite independent of its intended job as a word to describe the eating habits and table manners of certain fussy fish.

Let's face it. "Selectivity" has a nice ring. Whether in the noun or adjectival form, it is the sort of word an awful lot of anglers—although not necessarily the most skillful anglers—feel they can really *use*. Can you conceive of a better alibi for a skunking than to transfer the blame from yourself to the finicky tastes of your quarry, or perhaps by implication, even to the tyer of flies who somehow failed to accurately "match the hatch?" Then, conversely, what better gimmick to enhance the aura about you when you have succeeded when others have failed? It's one thing to have caught a whole passel of trout, after all, quite another to have caught a passel that was feeding "selectively."

But what is trout selectivity, really, and is it fact or myth? Do trout habitually shun all but a single insect species, or putting a finer point on it, a single stage of a single insect species? Or is the concept bunk? If it is valid, why is it valid, and how far should you take the concept as a skilled angler? Should you accept, for instance, that there are periods when trout feed selectively on worms, or on night crawlers if you really want to dig into it? How about rough fish? Will a trout pass up a sucker at a given time on a given day because it only has eyes for chub?

I raise these questions in hopes you may have all the answers, because, alas, I do not. Like most writers who would like to speak with authority, I must confess that I'm sorely tempted here to support one point of view or the other by means

This Henry's Fork rainbow took a bogus beetle at the height of a Pseudocloeon hatch, a regular occurrence on this Idaho spring creek. A good thing, too, because when these tiny olives are on in real numbers, most of the time your imitation gets lost in the crowd of naturals on the surface. I guess we'll only understand this lucky happenstance if we come back as fish.

of the illustrative anecdote. Yet, I've had a boodle of fish refuse what I offered and cannot claim to be sufficiently self-assured to presume that my flies were at fault or the techniques I may have used to purvey them. Fact is, too, I've caught an awful lot of trout generally judged selective, and even "ultraselective," on patterns which likely would have prompted the arbiters of such matters to swoon.

Regular readers of my work know that after fishing scores of rivers and streams I'm prone to refer to trout as *opportunistic* rather than *selective* feeders. This means that my experience indicates the fish are most likely to eat all readily available food so long as it provides maximum nourishment for minimum effort. Thus, while I've seen trout inhale everything from pieces of pinecone to cigarette filters, that doesn't contradict the principle that, given a carpet of one fly species on the surface of a stream, it shouldn't be upon those flies that the trout would concentrate their attention. Unfortunately, though, this does little or nothing to support the selectivity concept, since it certainly doesn't deny that each of the same trout might take something decidedly different should it pass directly over its nose at the precise instant it was ready to gulp. The doubter might try slapping a streamer on the button of a big trout he observes feeding on midges to see what happens.

Some time ago, I received a letter from my late friend and fishing companion Ken Miyata that started me wondering if the selectivity issue didn't really turn in great measure on semantics. Ken, who wrote an interesting article on fishing ant imitations through hatches, reported being charged with a student team whose task it was to run hourly drift net samples on the Henry's Fork in Idaho, in order to catalog insect species available to that river's trout during different periods. The samples, then, were compared to the contents of pumped stomachs of fly-caught trout.

According to Ken, the students learned that the fish did feed selectively in an *ecological sense*. During heavy Trico hatches, for example, the typical rainbow contained a higher percentage of *Callibaetis* spinners relative to Tricos than showed up in their nets, although the fish, of course, contained more Tricos than *Callibaetis*, since the Trico was far more abundant. Ken interpreted this to mean that the trout showed a "selective preference" for *Callibaetis* over Tricos when they were available simultaneously, adding candidly, if without interpretive comment, that he had caught most of the fish for the study on ant or beetle imitations.

Some writers—myself included—are often charged with trying to make chaos out of order, while scientists such as Ken try to find order in chaos. Be that as it may, Ken's letter suggested to this writer that the trout of the Henry's Fork weren't actually being selective at all, but were really feeding eclectically. Given their willingness to take *Callibaetis*, ants and beetles, as well as Tricos, might not these fish have gobbled up all manner of other bugs with equal relish? And, should we not interpret the team's data to indicate a preference for insects in short supply, though various, over ones that were plentiful? If this represents selectivity in an ecological sense, then ecological selectivity sure contradicts the concept of pure and simple selectivity so widely revered among the present generation of erudite fly fishermen.

Skillful anglers try to interpret and utilize trout behavior to their own ends, thereby minimizing time spent on extraneous matters. This is not to say that

Regardless of the time of year—this photo is all the more emphatic for how early in the spring Kris took it—a crowd of anglers is likely to put trout on guard and thus cause them to become "selective." Here at the head of Cairns Eddy on the Beaverkill, midge feeders may go so far as to key on only one aspect of the hatch, such as the sub-surface emerger. Were no one but you to be in the water, however, I'll wager, the trout would pretty much take an old boot.

nonessential goings-on in and about trout streams aren't interesting, but rather that you ought to be aware that concern with them may distract you from the job at hand. Thus, when trout *appear* to be eating just one species of fly—one perhaps for which you lack a suitable imitation—the point isn't to assume you're stumped, but perhaps to meet the challenge by coming up with a wrinkle to bring the fish around, say, to an alternative fly pattern, or better still, a technique adjustment that redirects the trout's attention in your favor.

The more I fish, the less I'm inclined to deny that periods of true hard-core selectivity *do* exist on many waters. However, I'm not convinced that such periods aren't initiated at least as much by the presence of fishermen as by the natural inclination for selectivity on the part of the feeding fish. More often than not, I've found that selectivity represents a response to angling pressure and that it evolves in direct proportion to increasing pressure, particularly when said pressure is exerted by careless or inept wading.

On the rare occasions that I've had the head of busy Cairns Eddy on the Beaverkill all to myself, for instance, its normally wary trout have proven receptive to all manner of fly patterns, including some that did not even come close to approximating the prevailing naturals in size, silhouette or color. Let me fish badly, however, or let several additional anglers begin beating the water to my left and right, and the fish can be depended on absolutely to home on one insect species and to stick with it at least until we pack it in and leave them alone again for awhile.

Don't fancy that fish ignore you just because they happen to feed at your feet. Trout have wonderful eyesight and highly refined instincts for recognizing danger. Having been pricked several times by a hook, once they become aware of your presence, either by seeing you or as a consequence of some badly botched fly presentations, they are likely to react by eating only what they reckon is safe. Note, too, how the fish generally adjust their feeding behavior as well as their choices of food. Feeding rhythms are likely to change dramatically, as the same fish you observed bolting all manner of bugs that passed over their lies suddenly begin looking over every fly carefully before deciding whether the flies will help keep them fit or make them sorry they indulged.

If selectivity is perceived as a response or reaction, clearly the issue you face becomes how to anticipate its potential and how to compensate to avert it. Your ounce of prevention may not be as simple as considering only whether your pet stretch is already occupied when you arrive, though, but may require critical analysis of the angling techniques of those there before you. A critical eye is essential, since the more clumsy or indifferent the performance of those anglers happened to be, the greater the chances the fish will already be spooked. It is untrue that the propensity of fishermen to pile up on prime pieces of water doesn't undermine sport. Suffice it to point out that it is around such spots that most of the grousing about trout selectivity usually occurs.

Unless my aim is to take on selective trout—a tilt I do genuinely enjoy often—I avoid the busiest water, opting instead for stretches where the fish have likely gotten no going-over prior to my approach. I like feeling I'm the master of my fate. Then, upon choosing a spot, I follow a ritual that's served me well for many years and may help you as well.

- First I reconnoiter the overall scene, trying to get a handle on how things stand. Are fish rising? If so, where? Are insects on or over the water? Is there a hatch or spinner fall in progress? I note the water level, its velocity, the position of the sun and direction of the breeze, if any.

- Next I consider specifics. Sizing up each moving fish and studying its rise forms tells me what the trout are doing, and now and then how large each fish is. Rechecking prevailing natural insects ascertains whether multiple hatches, a so-called veiling hatch, or a simultaneous hatch and spinner fall might be transpiring. And analyzing the feeding rhythms of at least some trout and relating these to the behavior of the insects on the surface helps dope out in advance what presentation technique or techniques should serve me best when the time comes to show a fly to the trout.

- Then I make a plan, calculating the precise approach that bodes for the best shot at the best fish with minimum risk of spooking the others. This step is critical, since experience has shown that a turn toward selectivity is sometimes transmitted among trout as if by telegraph, beginning with those you've dismissed as unimportant or have failed to consider at all in formulating your strategy and thus may have spooked into bolting past other fish, which are now set on guard.

Given space, trout will not only take a wider range of fly patterns and thus be somewhat easier to catch, but they're much more apt to wander a pool, either in search of food or, I guess, just for the fun of it. Although I can't frankly remember what fly pattern I had on, I can see that I'm about to land this trout hooked nowhere near what would be considered a feeding station when the pool was chock-a-block full of fellow anglers.

- Now I ready my tackle to work my plan as best I can in light of conditions. As I never fail to note, I question does the rod I've chosen have the right action? What line taper is going to prove best for the job? Is my leader the correct length, my tippet long enough, fine enough or strong enough? And lastly, what fly shall I try? Spare no pains here. It's how well you fish your tackle in the end that will probably determine whether ultimately the trout play your game or you are obliged to play theirs.

• Finally, I embark to execute my plan *exactly* as I conceived it. Generally, the best approach is careful but deliberate, pausing only to make certain there's no apparent uneasiness among the feeding fish. If any changes in feeding rhythms are exhibited, it's wise to wait until normalcy returns. Here you make the fine adjustments. Am I in the ideal location to present my fly as I want my target trout to see it? Do I have its feeding rhythm down? And, above all, can I make my first presentation count? When the answer to all these questions is yes, I know it's time to let fly.

Regardless of your care and skill, however, its usually but a matter of time before trout wise up to your doings and take remedial action. Whether or not they continue to feed at all, selectively or otherwise, once they've become at best aware that something isn't quite right, at worst aware of you, is testimony to how well or how badly you've been fishing. When all of them go down and stay there, you can be reasonably sure that you've really blown it.

To every rule there are exceptions, and here's one—Falling Spring Run in the Cumberland Valley of Pennsylvania. A wee limestoner, or spring creek, back in the good old days it held a whopping head of trout, none of which seemed to give a damn about how many anglers were fishing for them. They would drive you crazy *until* you hit upon precisely the right fly pattern, many of which, incidentally, were originated by the guy in the foreground, Poul Jorgensen, one of the greatest and most innovative fly dressers of all time. Once you found that pattern, though, you could quite literally move from fish to fish, hooking, landing and releasing one after another. A mystery, yes, but one that drew me back to that little stream year after year for a couple of decades.

But, given the transition from random to selective feeding, what can you do? You could move to another spot, of course, or rest the one you've been fishing. Or you can do what many anglers do, consume considerable time and patience coming up with a pattern that looks just like the fly the trout have turned to. Unfortunately, though, you'll sometimes discover that even it isn't good enough, meaning that you've exhausted your day for a cop-out.

A trout feeding selectively for whatever reason demands that you observe in the minutest detail how the naturals it is taking behave while within the fish's range of vision. Then a fly that represents a *reasonable facsimile* of the natural can be chosen promptly and with minimum hassle and be fished to imitate that insect behavior down to the slightest nuance. Though to accomplish that may require that you master a few subtle presentation refinements you never knew you had in you, ultimately you'll probably discover that even the most selective of trout is really just a glutton for gourmet technique.

CHAPTER 12

When Perfect Isn't Good Enough

It's a living hell to step onto a trout stream and find everything just right—lots of hatching flies and lots of feeding fish—and then not be able to buy a fin. North, East, South, West. It has happened to you. It has happened to me. And until we are able to dope out what the trouble is and how to compensate for it effectively, it's going to go right on happening.

Ironically, I've discovered that very often the trouble is that we are victims of *too much of a good thing*. That is, too many flies.

First a couple of examples.

One September on Silver Creek in Idaho, Kris and I arrived on a secluded stretch of water just in time to hit among the heaviest Trico hatches I've ever witnessed. Typically, the tiny mayflies began coming off by the millions and immediately began their transformation into spinners, to mate and to fall onto the slick surface of this glorious spring creek. On cue, scores of big and not-too-big Silver Creek rainbows started working on the spent flies, at first tearing into them somewhat unevenly, but soon enough establishing easy rhythms—as predictable as those of a waltz or a fox trot. (Exchange the analogy for rap if you fear "dating yourself.")

It would be impossible to estimate the number of spinners that were passing over each square yard of river per minute. Suffice it to say that a trout, even the biggest, hungriest, most gluttonous trout downing them as fast as he (or she) could, wouldn't have had a chance in the world of eating a 10th the number

There I am, being humiliated by those rainbows during that very same Trico hatch on that very same day on Idaho's Silver Creek described in the text. The first person I heard say that sometimes "perfect isn't good enough" was René Harrop, an Idaho fly tyer of extraordinary skill and one helluva nice guy who has been haunting Silver Creek for decades.

drifting over its nose. The flies were tiny, true, but still it was an awesome sight.

Having a plentiful supply of Trico spinner imitations in a range of sizes from 20 through 28, I began fishing with confidence. I carried neat, little poly-wings tied by Walt Dette, feather-wings by Poul Jorgensen, and most reassuring of all to my mind that morning, I had some more local dressings by Mike Lawson and Jack Hemingway. If I fished confidently, I also fished carefully, and right away, the second or third cast, I hooked a nice 13- or 14-inch rainbow. It was going to be a piece of cake, I thought then, so decided to work only to the bigger fish bulging at intervals the length and breadth of the stretch I was fishing.

Well, the long and short of it is that I got a real lesson in humility that morning. Try as I might, and did, I never hooked another trout that morning on a Trico, not with all my precise imitations, not using long 6X or 7X, not with six feet of 8X tippet. Later, several anglers, some pilgrims from the East like me, others locals who looked and talked, anyway, as if they knew what they were doing, told me they hadn't done a bit better.

Then there was that afternoon during that spring our Beaverkill hatches were all out of whack. I was in the tail of Barnhart's Eddy when the whole mess broke loose at once. Within minutes the river was alive with Quill Gordons, Hendricksons, Red Quills, Blue-winged Olives and that little fly commonly known as the Blue Quill, which because its body is actually rusty-colored, is one of the few flies best identified by its Latin name, *paraleptophlebia*, or Paralep for short. Amid all this confusion, there were also at least a couple of species of caddis dancing over and on the water. For sheer number of variety of flies, it was something to behold.

Bet you can guess what's coming. Yup, I fished standard imitations of everything I saw, all to free-rising fish that were eating as if this were to be their last meal. Did I draw a blank? Yup again. I couldn't even sting the "village idiot," not on one of my standard dries.

These examples having been cited, before moving on, I have to say that when I go fishing it's usually to catch fish. In fact, I can be darned competitive about it—not against other anglers, but certainly against the fish. Ideally, I'd like to take trout on dries that create an impression of the prevailing insect, or by matching the hatch if necessary, but finding that impossible, or nigh impossible, after a lot of work I'll do pretty much whatever it takes not to blow the day. Most anglers, I believe, would stipulate feeling the same way, although some find it necessary to stick by the traditional techniques simply because they don't know what else to do.

So, for them, regardless of stream or region, here are a few suggestions worthy of a try.

Before giving up on impressionistic patterns- or strict hatch-matching, first look the situation over broadly and carefully to be sure (1) you have the hatch(es) pinpointed, that you know the species and size of the fly, or flies emerging in case of a hatch or falling in case of a spinner fall, and (2) there isn't a so-called "masking hatch," a secondary hatch (or spinner fall) that the fish are homing in on when they would *seem* to be working on the predominate fly(ies). Next, check rise forms so you'll know the trout are taking the flies, thus enabling you to present your imitations to correspond with the behavior of the naturals. Now choose a pattern, style and size of fly you feel will work best, using the finest leader tippet compatible with the size of fly you have chosen.

Position yourself ideally relative to a feeding fish

Sometimes the problem isn't fly pattern at all, but *where a fish is feeding*. This is among the toughest angling situations I've ever faced—a big trout rising regularly back underneath overhanging willows. To even hook a fish such as this is a real confidence builder. I did and it did, although the trout subsequently broke off.

and present your fly so the trout sees it precisely as it is seeing the naturals. Be absolutely certain you are making no mistakes. Be sure, for example, that your fly is drifting right on the trout's feeding lane, not an inch one way or the other. Make sure there is no leader drag ahead of, over, or behind the target trout. Try your target fish several times, and if it doesn't take, leave it and go on to another. After a half-dozen refusals, you will be correct in suspecting that you are in *big trouble*.

Now you've got a couple of options. The first is to check the stretch you're fishing and to locate one where there are fewer flies. There, the chances are the fish won't be so fussy. But that's really a cop-out, isn't it? Your second option is to move to a different character of water nearby, from a slick, for instance, where you've been busting your hump without success, to some pocket water which may prove more forgiving, or vise versa, from pockets that have been giving you fits to a slick where you'll have a better vantage of what's going on, both on the surface and if the light is right, underneath.

If none of this works, consider the following.

• Try a fly that looks nothing like the prevailing hatch or spinner fall, notably a large attractor, such as a Hornburg, Royal, White or Ausable Wulff, or a Skater. At first, try presenting the big bug so it will behave on the water much the same way as the predominating natural. If that doesn't work—as it's likely not to—don't be afraid to vary your presentations dramatically, as in hitting the trout right on the nose or skittering the fly at various speeds over the trout's feeding station.

This technique works in some instances because the fly undoubtedly appeals to a trout's opportunistic nature, that is, the fish jumps at a chance to get a real mouthful when all it had been getting was small bites. Other times, the attractor, as mentioned earlier, must trigger the fish's impulse to destroy anything that is disrupting its regular feeding rhythm. In the latter case, then, success is based on excitement or rage rather than ordinary feeding behavior. I suspect that attractors also sometimes raise fish which hadn't been feeding on the prevailing hatch or spinner fall at all, and interestingly, these trout are often significantly larger than those that had been feeding on the surface before your eccentric offering appeared.

• Don't be afraid to dig into boxes that contain other than aquatic insect imitations. Terrestrials, notably ants, can be particularly effective when standard patterns fail. (The McMurray Ant, by the way, is the best imitation I know for this purpose.) Ants appeal to trout even when mayflies, stoneflies and caddis are abundant, and thus a well-presented ant, or beetle for that matter, will sometimes take fish that have been feeding on the hatching or falling aquatics. Trout near streambanks, you should know, are unquestionably the best targets for this wrinkle.

In its heyday, trout didn't come any tougher than those on the Letort in the Cumberland Valley of Pennsylvania. Here I worked to what appeared to be a rising fish for heaven knows how long before it finally dawned on me that what I thought were rises weren't rises at all, that the trout was actually taking Sulfur nymphs some ways beneath the surface, and what I was seeing as rise forms were the consequence of the trout's tail sticking through the surface of the shallow water.

• Another effective method is to choose an artificial that "looks like nothing but looks like everything." The best example I know is still the Adams in sizes 10-20, although a standard Usual in the same sizes is a closer-than-close second. First try the fly in the same size as the prevailing hatch when other, more precise imitations you are carrying have failed. Why trout will take the Adams during Sulphur hatches, for instance, I cannot say for sure. What I can say, though, is that they frequently *will*, and knowing this, no more need be said.

• Try fishing a small spinner pattern during a hatch of larger mayfly duns or caddis. Choose a working trout and put the spinner over it time and again until, in effect, you have created a spinner fall of your own which may break the trout's concentration on the predominant hatch. Frequently you will find that a trout, given the alternatives of emerging duns that just might get away and spinners that cannot, will opt for the sure thing.

• The larger a natural insect is, the more difficult it can be to imitate, the reason, I'm sure, being that no one has ever devised a really effective Coffin Fly pattern. During periods when large flies predominate, then, always try to use the smallest imitation you feel you may get away with. Note a trout's feeding rhythm and attempt to place your fly over the fish's nose at the precise instant you would expect the fish to inhale a natural. Should this fail after several repetitions, switch to a small mayfly or caddis imitation, such as an Adams or Henryville Special and go at the fish again. *Time is the key.* Ideally, you want your target trout to spot your fly only after the fish has already started for the surface.

• During heavy spinner falls, perhaps more than at any other time, imitations "get lost in the crowd" on the water. To make yours stand out without abandoning the prevailing species altogether, try tying some of your spent and upright spinner imitations with large egg sacs of yellow, orange or green spun fur, depending on the insect species your dressings are supposed to imitate. When spinners are abundant, trout seem to favor naturals carrying sacs to eggless males or females that have already deposited their eggs. Egg sacs also make effective additions to standard spent caddis patterns.

• When fishing spinner falls, try intentionally dragging your spent poly-winged imitations across the surface of a pool, thus imitating a last-gasp effort of the natural to get off the water before expiring. Like cats with mice, it seems, feeding trout can't seem to resist these frantic but doomed spinners and will take them when the fish wouldn't look at skittering upright dries or even wet flies fished across and downstream in the traditional manner.

This trout just wouldn't take even though it was rising regularly to small duns. So I switched to a McMurray Ant (size 22), and *bingo*. Good bit of strategy, I thought, even though I ended up losing the fish.

But what of the two examples cited at the beginning of this chapter? How did I ultimately make out during those two days in two very different parts of the country? With perhaps a bit of luck and some knowledge, I'm pleased to report, just fine.

After half an hour on Silver Creek that morning, I put away my Tricos and tried a small caddis known as the Hemingway Special, or Hemingway Caddis. Moving from trout to trout, I showed each one the caddis about a dozen times, and while most refused to budge from their Trico fixation, about a half-dozen, including one beauty that broke me off in the weeds, decided to vary their diet a little at just the right time. Then, after going through two tippets because I changed flies so many times that day on the Beaverkill, I finally threw up my hands, cinched on a size 14 Adams and enjoyed one of the most productive afternoons of fishing my home river that I've had in many a year.

CHAPTER 13

Fishing Streamers During Hatches

When you fish every day, you become more inclined to risk your time. You try something new and if it bombs, well, there's always tomorrow. Not so when your fishing is limited to weekends, days off or brief vacations. Those with little time to fish are more apt to play it safe—to stick to the tried and true—especially if they measure success in numbers of fish caught. This chapter is for trout fishermen to whom the fish count isn't important. Rather it's for anglers concerned, as the French say, *à fond*, to the hilt, with the big ones. If you covet big trout, read on. If not, read on anyway. The day is sure to come.

Hooking big trout, or for that matter, trout during overly heavy hatches as discussed in the last chapter, in the East where I live isn't easy. Luck plays little or no part in it. The more you fish, the better your chances, but consistent success requires undivided attention. You must forget many things you like to do best and throw away the old rules you find most comfortable. Big trout seldom play by them.

Some big trout, notably browns, feed exclusively at night, and if you want to catch them, you won't learn much about it from me. Staggering around in the dark after fish I can't see once they're hooked is my idea of doing nothing. I have better things to do with my "wee small hours"—if you get my drift. Many big trout, however, including browns, are also daytime feeders. The big ones feed underneath while our attention is taken up with smaller ones sucking at the

Jack Gartside is among the most innovative streamer tyers, and has made an art of fishing streamers through hatches. Jack dresses the ultimate in impressionist streamers, flies that breathe, and so cannot help but get the attention of trout, even when said trout are keyed to different things, such as hatches or spinner falls. I believe it was Jack more than anybody else who wised me up to the area of strategy you are reading about in this chapter, and for that I'm eternally grateful.

surface. If you could get a cutaway view of each pool you fish regularly, you'd be surprised at what goes on beneath the surface at the height of a hatch.

Time on the water has taught me that dry fly fishing is essentially an inefficient means of catching the biggest trout, like drawing manure to your fields in tablespoons. I fish just enough, both on the surface and underneath, to disbelieve all portrayals of most big trout as predominantly insect eaters. These fish are absolute masters of their living space and will take the most food, which is plenty, at the least expense of effort or energy possible. In most situations that translates into eating other fish.

When we were kids growing up on little Indian Creek, we let the pools tell us where the biggest trout held. Even if the big ones seldom showed by day, we knew where they were, because few minnows, suckers or other trout would be found nearby. One way or another the big trout usually ended up on the banks, then in our wicker creels, and smaller fish would fill the void until another big trout staked its claim. I saw the drama repeated perhaps a dozen times and learned to apply its lesson to seeking the biggest fish a stream has to offer by showing them flies to represent what they should want to eat most.

It helps to understand everything that develops in a pool while all that's apparent is surface feeding. Feeding begins underwater prior to a hatch. Nymphs and emergers drift through, enough to trigger interest among small trout and so-called rough fish. By the time a hatch begins, many fish have already claimed regular feeding stations fixed by the pool's established pecking order. Trout and other species jockey for the first flies to come off, but as the emergence strengthens, they settle into feeding, not unlike livestock at a trough. Even the rhythm becomes predictable as the fish are preoccupied by the hatch, and it is then that they are easiest to approach and to catch if the size, pattern and presentation of your fly is correct. Thus distracted, however, you are not the only predator to which the surface feeding fish are vulnerable.

(Chapter continues after color insert.)

GUIDE TO THIS SECTION

Midges on tippet spool: *Figure 1*
An assortment of midge larvae to be fished in the surface film or just below the surface. Note bodies made of quill, pheasant tail, clipped hackle, ribbed silk, and fur.

Kimball Diptera Emerger: *Figure 2*
See pages 54 and 55 in the text for a brief history of this fly and for materials and tying instructions.

Black Ghost: *Figure 3*
A quartet of Black Ghost streamers every angler should carry in his box or fly wallet. See chapters 13 and 19 for more on Black Ghosts.

Egg Flies on egg: *Figure 4*
Match the egg—yellow for Hendrickson, for instance, green for Shad fly. For further discussion on egg flies, see chapter 16.

March Brown wets: *Figure 5*
See chapter 17 for more on March Brown wets.

Large Gray Ghost Streamer surrounded by Young-of-the-Year imitations: *Figure 6*
Turn to chapter 19 for a detailed discussion of Young-of-the-Year imitations.

Hendrickson dun (natural): *Figure 7*
See chapter 20 for more on the Hendrickson.

Green Drake dun (natural): *Figure 8*
Turn to chapter 21 for a thorough discussion of the Green Drake.

Green Drake Emergers: *Figure 9*
Kimball High-Wing Emerger (left), Trailing Shuck Emerger (right). See pages 188-190 for materials and tying instructions for these flies.

Coffin Fly (natural): *Figure 10*
See chapter 21 for more on the Coffin Fly.

Walt Dette Coffin fly: *Figure 11*
This is the updated version of the fly shown in the text on page 186. Note the teal wings.

Usuals: *Figure 12*
Surrounding the original Usual are (clockwise from top) the Hendrickson Usual, Red Quill Usual, March Brown Usual, Olive Usual, and Sulphur Usual. See pages 202 and 203 for materials and tying instructions for the Original Usual. See chapter 22 for more on Usual variations.

Usuals: *Figure 13*
Surrounding the March Brown Usual featured in the text on page 204 are (clockwise from right) Hendrickson Usual (note split tails), Red Quill Usual (note wood duck fronting wing and in tail), Sulphur Usual, and Olive Usual (note wood duck mixed into wing and tail).

Sulphur Usuals: *Figure 14*
Variation for a variety of purposes as pointed out in chapter 22. (Top row) Sulphur Usual with split tail, Sulphur Usual with wood duck fronting wing and rabbit's foot tail, Sulphur Emerger topped by suggestion of yellow fly bursting forth, and Sulphur Usual Nymph Emerger.

Figure 1

Figure 2

Figure 3

Figure 4

Figure 5

Figure 6

Figure 7

Figure 8

Figure 9

Figure 10

Figure 11

Figure 12

Figure 13

Figure 14

Until the full arrangement of feeding is composed, a big trout may lie under a bank apparently unconcerned. But now it slides into the current and holds near the bottom, gently fanning. Small fish nearby move away but soon take up new feeding stations, perhaps just a yard or so farther off. The big fish rests as still as possible. It has learned to be patient like a cat, and before long it is ignored by the fish now gorging themselves on the drifting duns. The big trout pays no attention to the flies floating by overhead. It has been a long time since it bothered with them, although once upon a time it rose to the flies with the carelessness of a fat chub like the one that is now bobbing up and down, drifting closer to the big trout by inches with each return from the surface to the bottom. The big trout betrays no excitement, but is watching the chub, measuring the decreasing distance with a

practiced eye, always patient, certain and fixed on what it will ultimately do. Soon, in one rush that will take only seconds, the chub will die, first impaled on the teeth of the big trout and crushed by its jaws, and finally turned indifferently in the big trout's mouth and swallowed in the darkness back under the bank.

Unless you swim with the fish, you seldom see such predatory incidents, although they are likely more routine than even creel census takers could guess. Few big fish rise, and those that show just once to take your breath away and then vanish for good probably don't usually come to floating flies at all, but for fish feeding on the flies. So, when feeding to a hatch peaks, you must decide which way you want to go—after the many you know are there because you see them, or the few whose existence you must take on faith. If you like trout that advertise, stick to dries at the height of a hatch. But if you *believe*, switch to streamers.

I've caught many more big trout fishing streamers during hatches than with dries cast to occasional risers, which should be proof enough the technique

No question that this trout, hooked on a small Black Ghost during a Beaverkill Sulphur hatch, was feeding on small fish which were feeding on the Sulphurs. Before hooking it, I had seen it waking back and forth through the shallows at the tail of a flat, as if searching for something, when there were plenty of natural insects both on and in the water and thus if it wanted them, it could have taken up a fixed feeding station.

works, given, that is, you trust my word. Indeed, it has worked for me on numerous eastern rivers and streams and elsewhere, including a couple of spots where I might have gotten the boot if the regulars had doped out the depths of my "research." The technique was inspired by youthful observation, a little logic, some chubs I hooked that big trout thumped before I could shag them, and ultimately, when friend Keith Gardner first wrote a line I've used so often that it's regularly and unfairly attributed to me: "I am supposed to be a trout's nemesis, after all, not its butler." To those sure to challenge the theory, I'll concede skipping all scientific papers whatsoever. Instead, I've relied on experience, which when all the pages of all the world's scientific journals have faded, is the best teacher anyway.

The feeding habits of big trout relative to smaller ones seem to depend on the average size of fish supported by individual rivers and streams. There is no rule that trout of a certain size suddenly turn from easy rising to killing other fish. A big cannibal brown on little Indian Creek might have been stretched to 15 inches against a stock average of, say, 7 or 8 inches. However, I was shown a river one summer where 15-inch fish were small, browns averaged at least 4 pounds, big fish 8 to 10. The 4-pounders of this river rose easily to an Adams, properly presented, but to hook the really big ones you had to offer them something fit for their size, like a Black Ghost streamer on a number 2 or number 4 hook, 8X long.

As a boy with a lot of time to fish, I was taught the pattern of fly or streamer was not as important as knowing how to fish it. Later, when my work limited my fishing for a time, I slid into biologizing and was converted to precise representation, complete with Latin

A quartet of Black Ghost variations, my favorite brown trout streamer (also see color insert, figure 3). From upper left they include, hair wing with yellow hackle tyed as a collar; traditional Black Ghost (note I like long throat hackle); marabou over bucktail wing with a chenille body, and embossed silver body with alternating white, black and white bucktail wing. (Flies dressed by the author—a rare thing to be shown in public.)

names and a supply of urine-strained fox underbelly fur for Hendrickson dun bodies. Now that I'm fishing 200 days or so a year again, I'm back to where I began—although my vest is still heavier, without question, than it ought to be.

Developing precise imitations can be satisfying. And they work. To catch big trout, though, matching the minnow is no more necessary than matching the hatch most of the time, and you can get into trouble when you start to confuse creativity at the fly tying vise with technique on the river. A streamer must behave like a fish—a feeding fish, a distracted fish, a frightened fish, a wounded fish or a just-plain-stupid fish that gets too close to a big trout that is out to eat it. Your first concern, therefore, should be proper presentation, followed by streamer size and silhouette, and finally, if you have the time to fool around, artistry at the vise. A well-fished Mickey Finn, you will learn, hooks more big trout than a poorly fished Black Nose Dace sporting gills and lacquer eyeballs.

If I could fish only one streamer pattern to big brown trout, give me the Black Ghost on size 1/0 to size 14 hooks. I use it now almost exclusively because the late Walt Dette, the legendary Catskills fly tyer, always liked it best and I had absolute faith in him and his judgment. The pattern works well for me, better than any other I've tried on a day-to-day basis, although I won't push it too hard, because my respect for it, like respect for most flies, is largely a subjective thing. (I have no doubt that Wooly Bugger fanciers are tearing their hair out at this instant.) Other patterns I'm sure would work just as well for me, given equal water time. I dress numerous variations of the fly, but mostly because repetitive fly tying bores my butt off. All variations, however, maintain the black, white and yellow mix of the traditional Black Ghost. If I had to give any variation an edge for effectiveness, it would probably be one with a marabou wing, but that, too, may be because my faith in it gives it more river time when conditions are right.

You can't see most big trout working on fish distracted by a hatch, so you will often have to sacrifice the ease of fishing a floating line if you want to get down to them. Except in very high water when fast-sinking lines help, a sinking-tip performs best behind leaders no longer than seven and a half feet, shorter when practical, and flies weighted for conditions. Big trout aren't leader shy when they have such an enticing prospect as a streamer to home on, even in waters noted for fidgety trout. To ensure a straight pull, absorb shock and to minimize breakoffs, streamers should be tied to tippets as heavy as 0X and 1X with double turle knots. Rods should be long and powerful enough to present large streamers long distances without false casting, and of course to bull big trout once you get them on.

To hunt up big trout, the more time your streamer spends in the water the better. It will hook no fish in the air, before or behind you. Try to pick it up and lay it down without false casting. False casts only dry flies off and waste valuable fishing time. Probe places experience teaches you that big trout lie when feeding deep—the edges of eddies with good cover nearby, pockets tight to banks,

Big brown, but no big surprise, really, that this nice brown was lying tight to this grassy bank, ignoring an incredible number of midges floating over its head. Just one look at the ol' Black Ghost, though, began its ultimate trip to my net. Before I had reached the end of the bank, I had hooked or caught four more trout of similar size, all on the Black Ghost.

areas where concentrations of small fish rise during hatches, spots like underwater box canyons where big trout might trap smaller ones. Mark places you see big fish rise for special attention. Big trout tend to be creatures of habit.

Vary your presentations, fly speed and depth of retrieve. Slap streamers tight to banks. Mend line often and permit flies to hang carelessly in the current. Twitch them. Back them off. Tumble them through likely spots, dead drift. Whistle them across the surface. If you turn a big fish that doesn't take, rest it before giving it another look. Even try riffle hitching your largest streamers. Fish through pools with small streamers, then back through them with large ones. When a big trout rolls, go right for it. Offer a trout a long look first, then just a quick peekaboo. If it won't play, bonk the fish right on the head with your streamer. Big trout don't like little fish on their turf.

If a stream holds trout, it holds some big ones, no matter how heavy the angling pressure may be. In the end it becomes a matter of fishing hard and long, covering as much water as you can, meticulously, with a plan. Then if you can resist playing follow-the-leader when most leaders are tipped with dry flies, your day will arrive with a stunning jolt just as surely as the big ones keep making meals out of the little ones.

Pulling a Bank Job

The most fascinating trout to stalk along many rivers and streams are those eccentrics given to feeding almost exclusively from established lies tight to banks, or "bankers" as we like to call them. The bona fide banker seldom if ever alters its feeding position more than a few yards the way most trout do in order to take advantage of prevailing hatches. Nor should a fish that happens to be seen feeding close to a streambank only occasionally be mistaken for a true bank feeder. The genuine article is a total nonconformist to which a commitment to the security of a certain spot would seem so absolute and enduring that the fish becomes at once easy to locate but difficult to catch.

Most anglers seem to associate bank feeders with spring creeks, limestoners and meadow streams that meander along for long distances, retained by obviously definable banks. My experiences suggests, however, that the prevalence of bankers on a given stream depends not so much on the general character of the stream itself, as on the location and architecture of specific banks from stretch to stretch along the stream's full course. Thus, a typical surface water stream, although a preponderance of its flow may lie between shores and beaches rather than banks, will nevertheless hold an appreciable number of confirmed bank feeders, as long as there is an occasional bank to be found somewhere attractive to their type. Interestingly, too, the true bank feeders of most rivers and streams seem to be large fish, at least to the extent that you can expect them to average a few inches longer than the run of trout that inhabits a fishery.

Studies have shown, or so I'm told, that a substantial majority of the biggest trout to inhabit many waters live within 8 to 10 feet of a bank. Now, I'm not certain of the methodology behind obtaining the data to draw such a

See the rise form off the point of rocks upstream of me? Along this stretch, I work my way all the way upstream looking for bankers, which commonly drop back somewhat from the bedrock banks to be seen at the top of the picture. Now having wired the trout's feeding rhythm, I prepare to put my dry just in front of the trout's nose, being careful to drape my leader over its back, a blind spot for the fish.

There he is. Note the direct line between me and the taking fish, which demonstrates that the fly was just where it was supposed to be. This may not square with the apparent side-arm motion in the top photo. The reason is that I was making my false casts toward center stream to be sure I didn't spook the fish during the false casting process. When the moment of truth came, though, my casting stroke was precise and vertical.

conclusion—it would seem to me that a veritable army of monitors would be required to do such a demographic study with any kind of accuracy—but if it is so, then this finding alone might seem adequate to explain to an unsuspecting angler's satisfaction why a representative banker is likely to be larger than its cousins which prefer to feed at midstream.

The trouble is that the fine points of understanding trout behavior as they apply to practical fly fishing frequently defy the logic or perspective prevalent among biologists or professional fisheries managers, particularly those obsessed with demographics. (Regrettably, I guess, there are too few of them and of the too few, too many are forced to spend too much time behind desks doing paper-work.) But if you're out on the rivers day after day, you learn soon enough that the bank feeder is *different*, and that you must approach it almost as if it were one of a mutant strain, unrelated to the other trout in the stream and unconcerned with where the other trout around it choose to live and work. To be effective, too, dictates that you recognize and accept this fish for what it is, an eccentric, and in human terms, a sort of paranoid loner driven by who-knows-what misadventures in the past to alter, and indeed sometimes forsake entirely, numerous elements of fundamental trout feeding behavior in favor of ensuring its safety against all predators, including you.

The banks ideally suited to their tastes are undercut, thereby maximizing security potential, and are situated where sufficient stream flows deliver adequate food, both on and beneath the surface, to sustain a comfortable life throughout the year. Other desirable touches include: (1) overhead foliage, i.e., trees and/or tall grasses to shade their lies, as well as to supply terrestrial insects when times are tough; (2) underwater spring seepages that sustain comfortable water temperatures all year round; and (3) the presence of nearby side eddies, or backwaters, where food becomes trapped, but more important yet, where the fish can lie out of a stream's currents between feeding sessions or when the day's feeding is done. Given such secure, relaxed and bountiful settings, little wonder, isn't it, that some bank feeders would appear to possess a special talent for putting on weight.

More than anything, though, I believe that their large average size usually relates directly to longevity, which in turn is really a manifestation of their extraordinary wariness, or viewed yet another way, their preoccupation with the safety of the chosen lies over all other issues involved in day-to-day life. Indeed, most big bank feeders I've taken over the years have been older fish, virtually all of

Galen Mercer nails a big bank feeder on the spring creek-like East Branch of the Delaware River, a stream of many mysteries and many more big trout than most anglers realize. It was sometimes 15 minutes between rises for this fish and Galen had to have the patience to wait the fish out. Reason? If the fish moved a couple of feet forward or backwards, Galen's entire upstream presentation goal would have been undone.

Ofttimes fishing to bank feeders requires great patience. It helps to be sure within yourself that a fish *is* going to show in a particular spot. I waited more than an hour for this trout to show. But I think you can tell by the size of the rings that the wait was well worth it.

The really important thing to note here is that the position from which I am casting is virtually the same as that which I held for all the time I was waiting for the trout to show. Uncomfortable? You bet. But you have to discipline yourself to withstand discomfort, since if you should move, you're apt either to push a wake or grind gravel, either of which will keep your trout down.

which exhibited a singularly wary nature. Oddly enough, however, I've seldom known a confirmed bank feeder to bolt when spooked, that is, to wave good-bye with its tail as it streaked toward midstream or other parts unknown. Instead, the bank feeder is likely to simply disappear as if by magic, the consequence, I'm certain, of sliding under its favorite bank without haste or commotion and remaining there out of danger until convinced once again that the coast is clear, if you'll forgive the pun.

But the banker's life ofttimes has its inconveniences, too. Not the least of these can turn out to be the occasional burden of obtaining enough to eat with such a restricted zone to which the fish are characteristically disposed to limiting their prowl. While frankly I can't be sure, this may account for the fact that bankers are typically among a trout stream's most eclectic feeders. (It could just as well be, of course, that their predisposition to eclectic feeding issues from seeing a wider variety of foods in the course of each season than more conventionally behaving trout, and thus that their inclination to feed opportunistically, as opposed to selectively, is reinforced.) Be this as it may, however, there is no doubt of a bank feeder's inclination to so-called "garbage feeding" nor its proclivity to continuous feeding for protracted periods, often including those times during which every other trout in a stream seems to be down. These two characteristics, it's clear, serve to make the bank feeder a particularly attractive target to pursue.

The short end of the stick is that to approach bank feeders is usually a mighty tricky business. Then, once in range, to show your fly to such a customer as "His Wariness" in a way that "His Wariness" wants to see it is bound to be no piece of cake either. By carefully considering the approach, though, and with properly conceived fly presentations, I've found few bank feeders that you can't take sooner or later.

There are four fundamental routes for approaching the majority of bank feeders effectively: (1) to creep in an upstream direction on the bank, (2) to wade slowly upstream just off the bank, (3) to wade upstream well out from the bank, and (4) to wade downstream far from the bank. Before taking up the alternatives, I hasten to stress that there are also two courses of approach that ought not be taken, given any viable alternative. To wit: (1) to head in a downstream direction on the bank, and (2) to wade downstream just off the bank. The reasons why both usually prove ill-advised should become apparent with the following discussion of those I've suggested as viable.

Of the various approaches I use from time to time, I prefer the ones that call for upstream movement. The principle is fundamental. I want to sneak up on a wary bank feeder from behind when feasible. (To wade downstream well off the bank, is okay, I suppose, although to do so dictates that you be willing to spook, and so forgo, a shot at most trout either already rising or preparing to rise within several rod-lengths to your left, right or in front of you, no matter how lightly you tread as you progress along. Therefore, I opt for this approach when I perceive no workable alternative, or when I'm concerned with but a single bank feeder that I've already deemed well worth the sacrifice.)

Then, of the stream approaches I've listed, given my druthers I generally remain on the bank as much of the time as possible, for the advantage of its added height over the water affords me better vantage to succeed in my initial

On rivers like the Henry's Fork, there are miles and miles of bank to split up and so to fish alone. However, even there the "buddy system" is fun, and two sets of eyes, to quote the phrase, are better than one. In this photo, Galen Mercer and I switch off, that is, I cast, he helps spot, then next time, he casts, I help spot. This can also be done by the so-called spotter remaining on the bank for a higher vantage while the caster stays in the water to take instant action when a trout is seen.

goal of spotting feeding fish. Even the softest footfalls on a streambank cause vibrations, however, which can, and frequently do, telegraph your presence to nearby bankers. It is essential, therefore, at least on most of the waters I fish, to be able to recognize the telltale signs of the feeding banker from a considerable distance below the trout's lie.

The difficulty herein is, though, that the rise of the banker is typically more subtle, and thus harder to spot, than those of other trout. Why this is so I'm not certain, but I do know all too well that a delicate rise form, particularly if it is left deep in a bank's shadow, makes sighting feeding fish from any vantage low to the water an exceedingly tricky and frustrating affair. Its degree of difficulty, I've discovered, by the way, usually increases in direct proportion to the distance out from the bank you decide to wade. Hence, I generally choose the option listed above as number 2 only on those rare occasions when bankers are rising with a vengeance.

Quite often, in fact, the rises of bank feeders impart no discernible rise forms, or rings, as we have to come to expect from normal rises. Sometimes the banker's rise is marked only by the slightest swelling of the water, a hump of surface water tension. Then at other times, its rise seems but to push a negligible quantity of water inboard against the bank. Of more conventional rise forms, the best you can usually hope for is one left in the wake of the sipping rise, which is so fine that it disturbs the surface no more than had the water been pricked by a pin. The need for vigilance and concentration on your part, then, cannot be overstressed.

Another reason why I like to stick to the banks when hunting these difficult fish is that when the sun is overhead, to your back or to the streamside of the bank you are on, you can sometimes spy bankers that will eventually take, although when you first observe them they aren't feeding at all. Such fish, of course, would prove nigh impossible to locate from any other vantage point.

Once you've sighted a banker, basically there are two ways to go about positioning yourself to have at it. Assuming that you've been stalking up the bank, the first involves sliding quietly off the bank and into the water and then presenting a fly to the fish directly upstream. Or you can enter the water, then circle the fish until when properly positioned, you make your offering inboard to the trout which, of course, is still tight to the bank. Note that I do not advocate presenting flies to bankers from the banks beneath which they feed. My reasons are manifold. Chief among them, though, is that (1) the chances of being able to approach closely enough to execute a reliable presentation without being sensed, heard, or perhaps even seen, are slim; and (2) most streambanks veritably bristle with potential snags, including trees that eat backcasts and tall grasses that muddle up lines.

Because I really prefer the former strategy, that is, to present the fly upstream, I'll touch on the latter only briefly here before dealing with the former in some depth.

A bank alive with bank feeders, but clearly one impossible to walk up or wade adjacent to. So in this case I had to wade upstream somewhat outboard of the bank, watching the bank as usual for risers, then having spotted one, by choice circling around it and presenting my fly inboard to it. The result—an excellent hookup, evidence that the strategy worked.

When you "surround" a banker, as I call the latter positioning plan, it is essential first to wade very carefully so you create no swells to disturb the fish as your wake dissipates outward from your body. Then, I suggest you home on an ultimate position slightly upstream and within comfortable casting distance of your quarry. Next, be certain you know how to compensate for all currents intervening between you and your target, as handling them adroitly will represent the key to the drag-free drift demanded by most bank feeders.

Now, present your fly so that it lights softly in a direct line with the trout's feeding station but just outside the trout's window, or cone of vision. Accomplishing this, I've found, is facilitated by using the longest, lightest tippet you can manage without losing control of the fly's course of drift. Be certain, too, to throw sufficient "S's" into your line, leader and tippet to minimize the potential for drag. Should your fly begin to drag, however, do not pick it up while it can be observed by the trout, as to do so is virtually sure to spook the typical banker. Instead, bite your lip and allow the fly to drift out of harm's way as unobtrusively as possible. Then rest the trout for several moments, or until you see it rise once more, before you chance trying it again.

While I don't really dislike the above strategy and so use it from time to time, it's the *upstream delivery* that really represents for me the ultimate challenge in bank feeder fishing. Handled correctly, it is both lots of fun and extremely productive, although when fudged, it proves disastrous almost every time.

To perfect this technique demands you recognize that from a perspective downstream of, and in line with, a trout, each trout that's lying in about three feet of water has a "blind spot," or more precisely, a "blind line," which is located directly over its back from the tip of its tail forward to the point of its nose. Thus, theoretically at least, assuming that the trout were to face with its nose straight into the stream's flow, one could drape a bright red ribbon over its back for its entire length with absolute confidence that the fish couldn't see it and so wouldn't spook. Your job when presenting a fly upstream to a bank feeder is, then, to square this principle with the practical business of shooting fly line, leader, tippet material and fly over each trout's back in a fashion that the fly at the end of the tippet will be the only item of tackle the fish ever gets to see.

But why not simply make a left or a right curve cast? many anglers will no doubt ask. The answer is a simple matter of not outsmarting yourself. A curve cast by definition places a substantial length of working fly line, and sometimes leader, to the outboard side of your target fish and thereby creates a paradox. To wit, by seeking to avoid the fish with the line, what you ultimately do is to plop the line right where the trout is most apt to see it. The rule in casting straight upstream to trout, therefore, is: *the closer your line comes to the fish, the better, while right over the fish is ideal.*

All of this would be jim-dandy were your object simply to lay out line, leader and fly as straight as a die. Unfortunately, though, the contrary is the case. To ensure against that old demon drag, to which it may seem to some I'm obsessively referring, dictates that enough slack be present in each cast to absorb the pull of whatever erratic currents occur between you and your target trout directly upstream. The number of currents, and hence the potential for trouble with them, of course, diminishes as you shorten the distance between you and the fish. Luckily, trial and error has taught me over the years that by moving slowly and softly and by staying low, it is seldom that you can't approach within 30, or perhaps even 20, feet of all but the very wariest bankers. Having stalked to a position as near as possible to your target trout, pause for several moments to: (1) measure the distance between you and a point *no more than* eight inches upstream of the fish; (2) check your fly and tippet to be certain they are appropriate for your impending presentation problems; (3) strip sufficient line from your reel to reach the spot you have pinpointed, including enough line to create the "S's" essential for adequate slack. Next: (1) align yourself directly with the fish; (2) analyze the velocity of flow, as well as each of the currents that might modify that flow between you and the trout; and (3) reevaluate your position and prospective presentation until you assuage all doubt that you can make your first presentation count.

With this accomplished, now observe the trout through at least three, and maybe four, rising repetitions. Were each of its rises true to a single feeding lane and station? you ask yourself, among numerous other questions. Did the fish arch its body either to the left or right during any of its rises? If so, was the arch so dramatic that it might alter the fish's blind line when you seek to drape your line directly over the trout's back? And finally, what is the trout's precise feeding rhythm? Only when you have answered all of these questions and are prepared to reconcile your upcoming presentation to them, should you deem the time right to let fly.

Now, just how effective can this technique be when it's meticulously managed? One bright September afternoon, friend Mike Kimball and I, alternating trout, hooked, landed and released 17 bankers of between 16 and 21 inches. At midday from a long single stretch of bank on the Railroad Ranch of Idaho's famed Henry's Fork, that's plenty effective enough for me—with interest.

Here is Galen Mercer playing it *really smart*. Along this particularly productive stretch he's waded upstream somewhat off the bank so he can carefully watch the bank, yes, but so he's also perfectly positioned to present to good fish feeding directly above him. The take of a trout well off the bank demonstrates the canniness of his approach.

CHAPTER 15

Spent Spinners— Your Carrion Angels

For as long as I can remember, I've been fascinated by the behavior of aquatic insects along trout streams. Ditto, of course, how trout act and react during evolving insect life cycles. Although I've been governed by no rigid scientific principles, I'd like to believe that such observation has represented the cornerstone of a simple yet effective fly fishing strategy: I seek to show each trout a fly precisely as the trout would want to see it. For, ultimately, perfect renderings of natural insects from the vise are nigh useless unless you know how to make them behave like real bugs.

I'm particularly taken with the doings of mayfly spinners, which stir both the romantic and practical sides of my character. Their gauzy flights over the water, all that uninhibited dancing, their lust, the inevitability of the eventual fall and the finality of so many lifeless bodies swept away by the currents, isn't that the stuff of real tragic theater? You bet. And yet I can also perceive in this drama a clear opportunity to act the predator, as my quarry, the trout, single-mindedly indulges its opportunistic nature.

Absolutes have no place in fly fishing. Therefore, neat as it might be, I cannot declare that *all* trout on *all* streams have a decided penchant for spinners. I can say, though, that the appearance of spinners on the surface of a trout stream usually promises its inhabitants a welcome chance to play scavenger, a role easily reconciled to their self-image, if not to our lofty image of them.

The gauzy mayfly spinner is one of the world's loveliest creatures and at the same time represents a principal food source for trout and other species of game and nongame fish, for that matter. 'Tis certainly true that the life of the mayfly is short but sweet, for all it will do in the short time after it emerges from the river or stream, is rest, mate, then die. Prone upon the water, lifeless, its greatest appeal to trout is that it is a "sure thing."

Time and again I've witnessed trout, especially large trout, snubbing profuse mayfly hatches in favor of foraging on spent spinners, although the spinners may be present in lesser numbers than the emerging insects. Nor does the relative sizes of the flies seem to alter this behavior significantly, since more often than not, I've found that trout tend to opt for small spinners over larger duns. And why not? To a trout, after all, a spinner represents a *sure thing.*

To attempt to catalog even approximate periods during which every mayfly species will return as a spinner would require volumes. (Such volumes exist and may appeal to those willing to invest plenty of time in the reading and memorization of inexact science.) The best teacher, though, is going to be your own experience, just as the best investment of time overall is that time spent observing insects on waters you fish and making notes, mental or otherwise, as your insects progress from stage to stage along their way toward the jaws of trout.

Such observation is invaluable because it serves to teach more than demographics. You will soon discover, for instance, that not only have you become adept at predicting spinner falls to within minutes, but that you have gained countless insights into the behavior of insects during metamorphosis—from start to finish. Thus, when it comes time to put these new perceptions into practice, you'll find yourself able to catch more trout, as if by turning a key in a lock.

There was a time when I identified fishing spinners exclusively with dead drifting hackleless, spent imitations over slick water where trout tended to sip the naturals rhythmically. I tended, too, to think of spinner falls as early morning and dusk phenomena, entirely unrelated to major hatches that consumed my attention during most of the day. I shudder now at how many trout my ignorance must have cost, when all those times I shuffled home convinced I'd been whipped by fish that simply wouldn't get with the program.

It never occurred to me then, for example, that the spent dressing that knocked 'em out on the flats during the hour before dark might be equally effective for prospecting pockets at midday. I'd like to recall what finally rang the bell; but I cannot. Suffice it to say that one day I woke up to the obvious. Trout are prone to bolt spent spinner patterns on fast water because these low-floating flies represent tidbits that simply can't get away. The fish are programmed with the surety of a computer to obtain maximum food for minimum effort, and toward that end, regardless of the hour, there is no better target for them than the obviously helpless spent spinner.

Once the season gets rolling, it is seldom that some spinners aren't around trout waters that host mayfly populations. Seine the surface film of your favorite stream sometime when spinners aren't obvious and you'll probably be startled by the number that drift into the mesh. The gamut of sizes and shades will likely strike you, too, particularly if you've failed to notice lesser hatches that typically occur while your attention is occupied by those emergences that get the most ink. One pass of the seine on an early June afternoon on New York's Beaverkill garnered seven different spinner species ranging in size from number 14 to number 22 (hook sizes) and in colors from rusty brown and olive to lemon yellow and cream. The test, incidentally, was made at an hour when not a single spinner was to be spotted over the river.

Many times, then, when your pet high-riding dun pattern isn't getting a look although trout are rising within range, your problem may prove to be profile. Switch to a spinner pattern that floats prone on the water and you're apt to find things will begin to click.

To fish spinners well, it's critical to understand that drag-free dead drift, while important, should represent but one aspect of a comprehensive spinner strategy. Unlike emerging duns that may drift idly along with the current, spinners seldom linger on the surface until they've breathed their last. Thus, ironic though it may seem, a skillful spinner fisherman must frequently engender more "life" into his fly presentations than an angler fishing emergers or duns.

Note how spinners behave during mating flights, for example, dipping , diving, hovering as if to cool their *derrières* against the skin of the surface, how trout respond with violent rises more commonly associated with the taking of stoneflies. No angler, of course, can hover an artificial over the water, but here are a couple of hints that may do until we master the mystery of levitation:

• Try using a fully hackled, standard dry to which a tiny bit of yellow, pea green or orange has been tied in as a tag to represent an egg sac. Shoot the fly right on the nose of a rising fish you've spotted and allow the fly to remain on the surface just two or three seconds before picking it up and casting

All those specks in the sky over the angler's head are mating spinners. Spinners seem to come in waves, and although the photo shows many spinners in the air, many more have already mated and dropped to the surface by this time. Trout begin to rise to spinners, however, even before they fall, that is, while they are still depositing their eggs. So, whether to use an upright or spent imitation in the early stages of a fall is a matter of observation.

A lucky and unusual photo: a live Hendrickson spinner and an imitation with egg sac as dressed by Galen Mercer. Note the long tails and hackle wings of the imitation. The wings, in particular, are important, since they give a translucent look to the fly when it is floating on the surface. When this natural falls later, chances are her wings will be splayed as are those of her bogus sister.

again. Should the trout fail to respond after at most six repetitions, rest the fish for a minute, then have at it with perhaps a five-second float. Normally, that is all it will take.

• On breezy days, replace your standard-length tippet with one five-, six-, even eight-feet long. Use the finest tippet material that will accommodate a skater or variant. Choose an ample fly but not one absurdly larger than the natural spinners in the air. Stopping the power stroke of your cast at high-rod, present the fly either across or across and slightly downstream and encourage the breeze to skitter your offering over all the likely trout lies. The exacting thing here is to be certain that your fly never rests. If it stalls, start it moving again by turning your wrist gently in an upstream direction, thus making small mends in your line.

Unquestionably the most important discovery I've made about fishing spent spinners issued from learning to handle earlier spinner stages as living insects, to crib a phrase from my good friend Len Wright. Presenting the flies across and downstream—as I do most dries—I was surprised by the number of trout that would sock spinners at the tail of the drift after drag had set in. Because I normally pick up a fly as quickly as possible with the onset of drag, I may have been slow to realize that by permitting drag to continue, I would catch one passel of fish, especially when adding tiny mends and twitches to further soup up my fly's action. Today, however, particularly in failing light as I have fits trying to monitor a dry fly's drift, this unorthodox technique has become my principal hedge against a skunking.

Why a trout would nail a dragging spent spinner while ignoring a standard dry fished the same way or snubbing even a wet presented in the conventional downstream manner, may be understood fully only should we come back as fish. But the upshot of my observation on the water, as briefly noted in an earlier chapter, is that dragging spinners bring out the worst in a trout's character.

When spinners fall, few simply die and drift away without putting up a fuss, trying, I suppose, to get back to the fun upstairs. Their "last gasp," to repeat what I said earlier to underscore its importance, generally takes the form of fluttering and kicking in small arcs—from a few inches to several feet—across a stream's surface. This frantic, if futile, action triggers in trout an irresistible urge to attack, most notably among those fish that haven't yet established regular feeding rhythms.

Given trout that are really nailing these struggling spinners, I sometimes forgo the dead drift presentation altogether, opting instead to fish my spent imitation much as I would a wet fly, that is, three-quartered downstream on a tight line. To do it right, though, demands that your fly be well greased, since a fish will seldom take one that is submerged, even an inch. Maintaining a high rod pitch over the water also helps assure that your spinner continues to float throughout this swing.

Nor does an uninterrupted drift work as well as one to which you add mends and twitches, thus making the float somewhat erratic. However, these adjustments must be accomplished so that only your fly's direction is altered, while its speed remains constant. Should your mends and twitches, about which I wrote in depth in *Fishing Dry Flies for Trout on Rivers and Streams*, become too heavy-handed, causing your fly to streak across the surface, most trout will pass it up in favor of one that behaves as a natural ought to.

All other wrinkles aside, there is no question but that on a day-to-day basis the most effective, if most exacting, way to fish spent spinners remains the traditional dead drift technique. Note I stress the word *exacting*, because to get it right is truly a game of instants and inches.

When a spinner fall gets under way, trout generally feed on the downed bugs along uniform lanes and at regular intervals. While the intervals, or rhythms, may vary considerably from fish to fish, experience teaches that once established, each trout will stick to its own until spooked by a bad presentation, for instance, or forced to alter it by a change in the number of natural flies that are present. It is essential, therefore, that you note each fish's feeding rhythm and seek to put your fly over the trout at the instant the trout is ready to take a natural. Being a tad too early or too late is what leads to that oft-heard exclamation: "He took a fly right next to mine."

Nor can you afford to be a whisker too long or too short

This lovely brown clobbered a dragging spent spinner after all light was gone. Had I not used this skittering technique, no way would I have been able to get my fly to fish, even if I was pretty certain where it was rising. Reason? It was a Delaware River trout and the Delaware is a wide river. My problem would have been putting the spent fly *exactly* on the fish's feeding lane, not an inch or two one way or the other.

Every sort of spinner imitation you'll ever need and probably one or two more. And yet each and every one may get the job done at some time when nothing else works. There are upright and spent wing dippers and divers, skitterers, and most important of all, spent wings that lie flush to the water and thus represent the spinner that's breathed its last—to the trout a sure thing. But even among spents you have, for instance, hackle wings and poly wings, the former being far better on calmer waters when trout are prone to be skittish, the latter more floatable and so fine for pockets where trout tend to get a briefer look at a fly. My advice: if you have to skimp, skimp somewhere else, not on spinners.

with your presentations, because trout will seldom alter feeding lanes to take artificials. Each spinner presentation should begin far enough upstream to ensure that your fly floats into a trout's window in the manner of a natural. Then it must drift without drag precisely over the spot where the fish's mouth breaks the surface tension as the fish feeds. Such an accurate presentation, when coupled with exact timing to intercept the rise, virtually guarantees trout for you during most spinner falls.

Finally, when it comes to tying or buying spinners, it's helpful to remember that natural spinners tend to be more dainty and fragile than their dun counterparts. Thus I recommend sparse dressings in most cases. Upright patterns should have considerably longer tails than dun imitations, slimmer bodies and no more hackle than necessary to achieve a good float. While egg sacs and wings tied spent constitute nice touches—especially egg sacs that can turn the trick during the heaviest flights, as pointed out earlier—neither are usually really necessary if a fly is fished optimally. I have seen no evidence, by the way, that splitting tails enhances this type of dressing.

Similarly, spent spinner dressings ought to appear as delicate as possible. Yet, for spents I confess I'm partial to split tails, since on the one hand they seem to support the impression of helplessness I'm trying to convey when I fish them dead drift, while on the other they assist in planing flies up when you intentionally drag them across the surface, as described earlier. Given my druthers, I prefer spent imitations to have wings of stiff hackle to either burnt-wing or poly-winged styles. Burnt-wings are likely to be opaque and therefore not lifelike, while poly-wings are frequently dressed too heavily by commercial tyers. Dressed lightly, though, poly-winged spinners are very durable and have worked for me just fine—unless the trout are being awfully fussy.

Ultimately, however, the trick is to make a spinner pattern work for you by making your artificial fly do what the naturals do. I've had trout forgive all manner of mistakes made at the fly tyer's vise, but I've seldom known one to forgive a fly that misbehaves when being fished.

CHAPTER 16

The Eggs and I

The evening is perfect, kinda muggy and very calm. A few thunderheads building to the west, but for now no threat of a storm. The barometer is high, but the fishing during the afternoon was unaccountably slow, so you have every reason to suspect the trout are "ready." You know there are lots of good fish. In fact, the water is flat and the level is such that from time to time you can see trout flashing hither, thither and yon, adjusting their lies, you assume, in anticipation of a big feed to come. And what is more, the air all around you is an orgy of, let's say, mating Sulphur spinners, flitting and floating, the females dipping to deposit their eggs by the thousands, tens of thousands, on the surface of the stream. Some of the spinners, spent after their brief *liaisons d'amore*, are beginning to fall and to drift downstream on the oily surface. In other words, all the elements of an angling dream are there.

Then the spinner fall begins in earnest and the surface becomes a carpet of dead and dying Sulphurs. And yes, there are *some* rises, but not nearly the number you'd been hoping for or expecting. So you begin fishing to what rising trout there are and perhaps you take a fish or two. But something's not right and you know it. You ought to be bangin' 'em.

Gotta be that the poly-wings on your store-bought spinner are too coarse, or maybe too dense. So you hurriedly snip off the poly-wing and yoke up a delicately dressed hackle-winged spinner, certain it'll do the trick. Another couple of trout, but no great shakes. But now the light is failing fast and you're wondering what the hell's going on and what the hell to do about it. Your dream is turning into a nightmare.

Frantic, you wrack your brain, seeking to draw upon every iota of experience in search of the key. Your tippet's too heavy. Why didn't you think of that before? So you go down from 5X or 6X to 7X. No difference. Okay, then there must be too many spinners on the water, so yours is "lost in the crowd." Now, what the

Galen Mercer "sights" with the onset of a spinner fall on the Upper Main Stem of the Delaware River. Problem is, he's finding, that although there are lots of flies on and over the surface, there are very few trout rising. He's already learned, too, that those that are rising are a piece of cake to catch. So, what's going on? At the time this photo was taken, neither of us knew.

dickens did that "guru" you were reading last winter suggest? A fly one size larger than the prevailing naturals? Or was it one size smaller? Can't remember, so you go both ways. Same result. *Nada*.

What else could it be? You do notice there aren't many fish rising and you're hooking those that are, suggesting in turn that your presentations are on the feeding lanes and you have the rise rhythms wired. Maybe you should sink your spinner? Fish it like a wet? You try it and catch a trout, but there's really no noticeable improvement over what you'd been doing on top. There's still a piece missing, you're certain, but as twilight becomes total darkness, you know you'll not put it in place this time out.

I've seen this scenario played out countless times, in fact have played the lead role in it more often than I like to admit—*until* I did what every angler ought to do more often. I put my rod aside and really *observed*. And what I discovered not only blew my mind, but has changed the way I've approached spinner falls— especially spinner falls on flat waters where sight-fishing is possible—ever since.

The answer? I'll get to it—but not before sallying briefly through the fruits of keen observation, too often underrated even by experienced anglers.

First, you should know that there is virtually no angling problem that can't be resolved, even if after painstaking observation and consequent trial and error the solution turns out to be that a given fish in a given place at a given time simply cannot be caught by you or anyone else. Frequently, however, angling problems turn out to be Trojan horses. So, metaphorically speaking, "beware of gifts," no matter in what guise they are borne. Or in purely practical terms, learn not to rely too much on the obvious. Sometimes you simply must delve deeper—climb inside the problem—to learn what you're really up against.

Remember those trout described earlier as "flashing hither, thither and yon," for instance? Nothing wrong with that observation as far as it went. And in many cases the *assumption* that this behavior would represent nothing more than a routine adjustment of feeding stations might have been valid enough. Where assumption became *presumption*, though, was when you concluded that this was the only likely implication of the behavior—that the trout would necessarily rise to the spent spinners out of those new lies you imagined they were taking up—and so you failed to observe, and thus even to see, much less perceive, what was really occurring. In other words, had you noticed that the trout had ceased neither the flashing nor the moving about with the onset of the heavy spinner fall, you might have been moved to another, more penetrating look-see. And that further observation *might* have taken you where you really needed to go.

Fly fishing for trout, especially after sunset, is usually an exercise in time-efficiency. Stop and think; there are scores of tricks one can turn to when things aren't going one's way, but only limited time to exercise the options. The greater your skill, the more tricks you likely know. And so while there was certainly nothing "wrong" with tippet fiddling or fly changes in the above-described situation, since both are proven problem solvers, you should have been quicker about it. Then, when you didn't fare any better after sinking your fly, you should have recognized that it was time to race back to the roots of the observation process from which you probably learned the lion's share of your technique tricks in the first place.

Let's say you'd done just that. Given you observed that most of the trout continued to move about, as opposed to holding to specific stations as you'd expect them to during such a spinner fall, you might have homed on several individual fish and monitored their every move. You would

I net a good Beaverkill brown hooked on an egg fly on Barnhart's Pool on the Beaverkill. As it happened, this was the first of several large fish I hooked that evening, all working close together on the shallow side of the pool. It wasn't easy, though, as I had to stalk close to the fish to see them well, then "feed" each one my egg fly in turn.

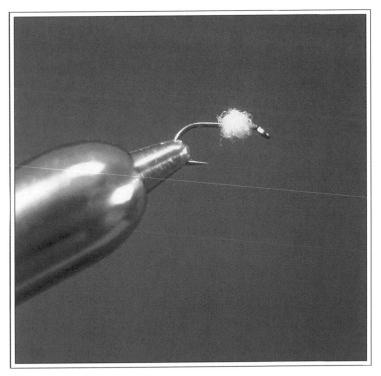

In the vise, you can see that an egg fly is quite small, however not as small as the eggs carried by natural spinners as they dip toward the surface. Go ahead and tie them larger than natural, because when the natural eggs enter the water, they expand in size, and by the time they reach the bottom (if they make it that far), they are pretty good sized.

want to see, for instance, whether their mouths were opening and closing, and if so at what intervals. A "yes" would suggest the trout were "on" something other than what was represented by your spinner imitations and that whatever that "something else" was, the fish were "locked into" it.

Then, since you normally can't see underwater insects, even large nymphs, your first question would logically be whether there was perhaps a "masking hatch" going on and whether it was into some subsurface stage of this emergence that the trout were locked. (Catskills anglers know, for example, that trout often ignore flotillas of meaty Hendrickson duns in favor of relatively small, but helpless, Paralep spinners.) So your next step would be to scan the surface and skies around you for anything to suggest that these trout were feeding not on the Sulphur spinners at all, but on something entirely different.

A "no," on the other hand, might have suggested either that the roaming trout weren't feeding at all, or that if they did eventually begin to feed, it would most likely involve the spinner fall. Reexamining the trout's *behavior*, then, or in this case their uncharacteristic shifting of positions in light of conditions, could have led you, as it eventually did me, to solving a problem, even one such as this, which ranks among the most elusive I've ever encountered astream.

Now for that "answer," after which permit me to work backwards sort of the way it's done by Columbo on television.

During heavy Sulphur spinner falls, as well as those of numerous other mayfly and caddis species, many trout feed exclusively on the *eggs deposited by the spinners or ovaposited by the caddis.* Think Art's lost it? So would have I, not to mention my fishing partner, Galen Mercer, had we not confirmed the phenomenon beyond all doubt the following evening.

Next day Galen fashioned a fistful of tiny Sulphur egg imitations in sizes 22 and 24, and as the afternoon waned, we headed for the same water—a Beaverkill flat. Fortunately, the evening proved a virtual carbon copy of the previous one, and to make a long story short, I found myself moving from trout to trout, hooking (if not necessarily landing) virtually every one to which I was able to make a respectable presentation of one of the new egg flies. Meantime, Galen, acting as the "control" in the experiment, tried every trick he knew while fishing conventionally, that is, with floating and sunken spinner imitations, with virtually the same results he had experienced the previous evening.

Not that it was simple. You (1) had to first spot a roving fish; (2) anticipate where it was going to be rather than where it was the last time it consumed an egg; (3) place your tiny "fly" right on the money, that is, virtually "feed" it to the trout; (4) avoid drag like the plague, which involved fishing a long, limp 7X tippet; and (5) see or sense precisely when a fish had taken your fly, as it was eminently clear that use of a strike indicator was out of the question. But the payoff was spectacular, since not only did I take more trout than I ever could have hoped for using conventional spinners, regardless of strategy and technique, but it also turned out that the pool's bigger fish preferred eggs while its smaller ones tended to be the risers, as evidenced by a comparison later between Galen's and my catches.

I remember, too, discussing how the hell we were going to get anybody to believe what we had learned, much less how to get anglers to add the discovery to their repertoire of tactics.

(Unbeknownst to us, one credible believer already existed—Lou Rossi, angler-conservationist who entirely on his own had made the same discovery after countless hours probing the nuances of trout behavior on the Beaverkill and elsewhere, and who subsequently published, I'm told [although I've never seen it], a piece on the trick in *Theodore Gordon Fly Fishers*, the New York–based conservation group publication.)

Make no mistake, though. Having fit this single piece into the trout tactics puzzle was and remains a mixed blessing, as it sometimes proves at least as limiting as it is helpful. In fact, there are occasions when I look back wistfully at ignorance as bliss and dearly wish either that trout didn't eat insect eggs at all or that I had never discovered it. First of all, to be effective really demands a dense spinner fall and that you see your target fish, which unless your eyes, with or without Polaroids, are better than mine, generally precludes any work in broken water, even relatively gentle pockets. Then, high or colored water is also usually out, even on flats, and "prospecting" in this manner is really futile.

But it's also true that once you develop the precision essential to mastering the technique, all other subsurface angling methods, such as upstream nymphing, become relative pieces of cake. Moreover, the flies couldn't be simpler to tie, and so to keep some eggs in your basket is no big thing.

Mayfly or caddis egg flies truly fall into that category of flies that do not take longer to tie than to lose, a favorite saying of my old and much missed pal, Ken Miyata, who tragically drowned in Montana's Big Horn River some years ago. The colors of these flies are yellow, orange and green, some more strident than others. Note, too, the heavy hooks so the flies will sink quickly. (For more egg flies see color insert, figure 4.)

We tie ours on size 22-26 hooks, using extremely absorbent materials, such as dyed rabbit underfur dubbed very lightly so the flies will sink. Colors should approximate those of prevailing natural eggs, but experience also teaches that enhanced, or somewhat more strident, colors than those of the real things, tend to work in your favor. A bit of hot orange mixed into the dubbing of a Sulphur egg, for instance, usually outfishes the warm yellow of the natural.

Nor does size seem to be particularly critical, meaning that within reasonable limits egg flies somewhat larger than prevailing naturals doesn't matter a whit. I don't know how to explain this, except I suspect it involves the tendency of natural mayfly and caddis eggs to expand somewhat after being deposited and beginning to sink. Take note sometime of the eggs stuck to your waders upon leaving the water after fishing a spinner fall, and you'll see what I mean.

Angler, artist, fly dresser *extraordinaire* Galen Mercer with a nice brown taken on an egg fly after he ceased to be the "control" in our experiment. Although Galen uses a 2-weight rod as his daily "gamer," he has remarkable skill for putting his egg fly right on the trout at just the right time. Extraordinary and essential.

I'm sure there must be scores of insect species to which the technique could apply, but in that regard I fear I can't be very helpful. On the Catskills streams near my home, I know it's useful during Hendrickson, Shad Fly, Sulphur, and Cornuta (olive) hatches, for example, but as to Midwestern, Rocky Mountain or Far Western species, I haven't a clue. Then, too, the abundance of the hatch and consequent spinner fall are also critical, meaning that while the technique might be ideal for, say, a Beaverkill Sulphur hatch, it might prove useless during Sulphur time on a stream, or even a stretch of stream, in the same region where hatches of the species are naturally sparse or perhaps have been degraded by pollution.

Among the joys of fly fishing is that you can make as much or as little of it as you wish. For some, the essential pleasure derives from relaxing days astream, free of the pressures of problem solving which plague their daily lives. For others— myself included—the more problems and the more complex the problems, the better. However, since governments don't rise or fall based on one's ability to catch fish, what one likes to do and how one goes about doing it should be seen not as an "issue," but as a simple matter of personal preference. In other words, it is not my intention here to yet again appear to be seeking to create chaos out of order and suggest that you swallow it.

By all means, those anglers who wish to, should continue to fish spinner falls by entirely conventional means, usually take their share of trout and wrap up most of their outings satisfied, if occasionally somewhat mystified by what happened, or rather didn't happen. Indeed, the potential for frustration really ought to be mitigated, and thus the experience enhanced, with the knowledge that limited catches on occasion are beyond the control of the conventional angler. On the other hand, for those to whom the essence of fly fishing is a continuing quest for answers, and particularly those for whom the problem is *the thing*, to become an "egghead" is right up your alley.

CHAPTER 17

Go Wet, Young Man

The first fly rod magician I ever encountered on a trout stream was fishing wet flies. Just a big-eyed kid then, I was plopped on a rock wrestling with a tangled leader provoked by my own artlessness and an overly-bushy dry. A retired schoolteacher, as it turned out, this magician approached me methodically, cast-step, cast-step, from upstream. To watch him at work, I'll tell you, was both a humbling and inspirational sight.

Such grace I've seldom seen since, nor such economy. Time after time he shot his set, or cast, of wets and the silk line he'd collected after his last retrieve without ever troubling himself to a false cast. Each cast, which was three-quartered downstream, was straight as a die and yet so gentle that even my young eyes could barely discern the reunion of line, leader and flies with water.

While his wets swam, he was clearly their lord and master. Even now I can see him adjust his rod's pitch to each element of each drift, jig its tip and rotate his wrist upstream and down to delay or hurry his flies. Meanwhile, his left hand kept busy stripping or drawing line at intervals or weaving it with a seemingly effortless hand-twist retrieve. All the time his vigilance was constant, his concentration absolute.

I never did get his name, but his likes are seldom found on streams today. Today, notwithstanding their usefulness for everything from pure attractors to imitations of emergers, drowned duns and spinners, traditional wets have lost favor. It has happened gradually over the last 30 years and whether the slide will continue remains to be seen. If so, it's our loss, for fact is that few recent innovations are any more effective than wet flies skillfully handled.

Four in one cast strategy. I cast a wet to the opposite bank from which I may pull a trout away, then crossing the white water I show my fly to any fish lying there, next it comes to the "edge" between fast and slow water where feeding trout often station themselves, and finally I retrieve the fly for the benefit of any fish either cruising or lying in the slack.

Moreover, wet fly fishing is still the simplest way for novice anglers to gain experience while hooking plenty of fish. A rudimentary presentation demands no more than casting a single fly across and downstream, plus an upstream line mend to prevent drag. That accomplished, your attention is free to monitor each swing without need to affect it. And since trout normally hook themselves against the tension of the line, you can relax until the time arrives to play your fish. Thus you are spared the frustration of seeking to master too much at once.

Proceeding at your own pace, you enhance this technique by adding wrinkles. You impart action, for instance, by introducing some form of retrieve and thus manipulating the line directly, or by utilizing your rod as a lever, as in jigging or twitching its tip, or by making multiple line mends. Or you may even opt to try fishing multiple wets by adding one or more "droppers" to your tippet.

Fundamental wet fly techniques shouldn't be dismissed out of hand by experienced fly fisherman either, of course. Sometimes the most elementary forms have turned the trick for me on challenging streams when much more sophisticated techniques have failed. A couple of examples: troublesome browns of Pennsylvania's Letort are relatively easy to snooker by using small Blue-winged Olive wets (sizes 18-20) in the spring and fall; the largest trout I've managed from Willowemoc Creek near my home tore into a trailing size 14 Alder fished wet.

Traditional wets can be divided roughly into two categories: *imitators* and *attractors*. Although their uses may dovetail—as with the Greenwell's Glory that serves as both an attractor and a caddis imitation—generally speaking, to provoke strikes, imitators represent natural insects that appeal to a trout's appetite, while attractors depend largely on a fish's disposition at a given time. However, in either event the classic wet's silhouette bears a striking resemblance both to a drowned or emerging aquatic insect, as noted, and hence traditional presentation techniques were developed by our forebears to suggest one or the other—or even both in the course of a single drift.

Essentially, wets tumbling along at the whim of prevailing currents imply naturals that didn't make it, or drowned spinners. Those that appear to swim in spite of the currents are consistent with emergers. Therefore, by beginning a presentation on a loose line in an upstream direction and completing it on a taut line downstream, it's entirely practical to create both impressions with a single cast. This alone ranks the wet as among the most *efficient* fly designs ever conceived.

Why, then, the wet's diminished popularity? The answer may be as simple as the legacy of Gordon's dries, plus the introduction of a generation of artificials known as nymphs. More likely, though, numerous elements conspired against the wet, not the least of which was that the wet didn't conform neatly to a growing passion for entomology and its preoccupation with verification. Small wonder wet fly diehards are seldom bewitched by quasi-biology.

By the time dries and nymphs came along, thousands of wet fly patterns already existed, some hundreds of years

Primarily known as a dry fly fisherman, Ed Van Put is a master of anything involving the long rod. Here he works a wet fly to a brush pile on upper Willowemoc Creek, challenging, if you will, the brookies and browns that live under the pile to come out and snatch it. Just seconds after this photo was taken, of course one did.

old. Most were developed for specific jobs, that is, to appeal to trout under certain conditions. That end is accomplished just as when fishing dries or nymphs: by combining pattern with technique so each trout sees your fly as the trout wants to see it. Given the number of patterns available, plus the potential to refine wet fly technique, you'd have thought the options were limitless and so the wet's continued use guaranteed.

The characteristics of effective wets are like those of any fly: size, shape (silhouette) and color. Additionally, the components of each fly, including the hook, properties of materials used and the manner of dressing, influence a fly's potency. Compare wets typically shown in today's catalogs with those of 50 years ago and you'll notice minimum attention is paid to these points, except perhaps for color. This isn't the case for dries or nymphs where hook size and silhouette, for instance, are perceived as critical. Thus, if today's wets seem less effective, maybe it's because too few alternative patterns have remained on the market.

A wet that works one day may not work the next because it fails to create the right *impression*. In this, wets are exactly like dries. We accept that high-floating dries with minimum wing silhouette knock 'em dead one day but bomb the next because the fish really want low-floaters with pronounced wings. Thus, if we acknowledge the fly as the trigger, why should wet flies be different?

Refining presentation skills works miracles. (Given the option, I prefer to fish the wrong fly well than the right one badly.) Nevertheless, wet or dry, there's only so much any angler can do. Hence, to unite the right technique with the right fly should be your ultimate goal.

During recent seasons, angling partner Galen Mercer and I have taken a new look at wets—with some very interesting (and productive) results. Our aim was to give *purpose* to each wet we fished by reconciling fly design and technique to the interaction between natural insects and feeding trout. The upshot is that wets proved even more versatile than we'd imagined they would.

Most of our work was done on nearby Catskills waters where we could apply trial and error on a sustained basis. Although largely unproven elsewhere, our success suggests that the essential principles should relate to most streams.

Beginning with the premise that if trout could be caught, they would take wets somewhere between streambed and surface, we homed on specific hatches, including caddis, and adapted fly patterns and techniques to given conditions. As best we could, though, we did so without losing track of the roots of wet fly fishing.

The March Brown (*Stenonema vicarium*) proved an excellent test case.

By varying only leader length and hook size during March Brown emergences, traditional dressings and techniques handled most pocket water situations nicely. We did especially well by positioning ourselves so individual or multiple wets drifted or swung inboard toward the shallower shore in keeping with March Brown nymphal migrations.

However, flats presented other problems, particularly slow-moving "thin waters" at their tails where March Browns, and thus feeding fish, tend to congregate. Here trout rooted nymphs from under and around stones, but true to their opportunistic natures, preferred to nail imminent emergers drifting or swimming by their noses in water just inches deep.

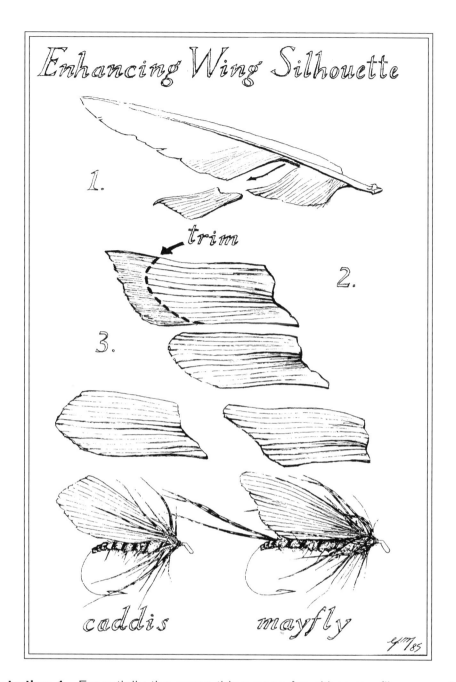

Illustration 1 Essentially the same thing goes for either mayflies or caddis. (1) Cut sections from matched pairs of wing quills; (2) trim them to shape with a sharp pair of scissors to remove the flimsy quill section tips; and (3) tie the wings in what has often been called the "Catskills" style, that is, low to the body (although there's no reason they can't be tied in higher if desired). Note, the wings must be set far enough back from the hook eye to allow room for a fur and feather collar. Note, too, there is a distinct difference in shape between enhanced wings for mayflies and those for caddis.

Given these waters, traditional patterns fished conventionally failed us for numerous reasons: (1) the low, swept-back silhouette looked too stiff and hence unnatural for such settings; (2) tippets were sometimes too heavy; (3) our flies created some commotion dropping into the water; and (4) hooks regularly snagged on stones before our wets had reached the fish. So, at this point we were obliged to build a better mousetrap.

We began by dressing traditional March Brown wets on dry fly hooks (1X stout-4X fine). They performed passably when fished dead drift or with tiny "bonefish strips" upstream, three-quarters upstream or three-quarters downstream. However, we were troubled by last-instant rejections and fish that spooked in the process of imparting fly action, regardless of tippet size. So we decided to incorporate as much visibility and action as possible *into* our flies.

Our goal was to create *impressionistic*, not representational, dressings. To enhance visibility, we abandoned conventional strip-wings in favor of fuller, more well-defined and sturdier quill wings shaped with scissors. (Resist lacquering your wings before trimming, for while facilitating dressing, resultant rigidity causes flies to keel and thus to behave unnaturally. Instead, shape wings from fibers closer to the quill stems and discard flimsy tips normally associated with tying wets.) Response to the altered wings was immediate, sparking more interest not only from trout in entrenched feeding stations, but from fish that highballed it considerable distances to take our flies.

One drawback remained, however. Our experience showed that, whereas slow, thin stretches bear infinitely more live insects than dead ones, until their wings broke up, our new flies were taken, we were sure, primarily for drowned bugs. In fact, an accidental twitch or suggestion of drag actually spooked some trout. So, next we sought to reconcile the visibility we'd achieved with the vitality that trout naturally associate with emergers.

In other words, we wanted our flies to appear to "breathe" without stimulation from behind the rod. This we accomplished by discarding the stiff throat hackle

Here's the March Brown wet illustrated on the previous page as it appears "in the flesh." You should readily see not only how the trout can home, or key, on the substantial wing, but also how the fur collar when wet makes the fly "breathe," and imbues it with life. Wets such as this can be dressed for virtually all mayflies, which in every case I've tried, anyway, enhances effectiveness. (Fore more March Brown wets see color insert, figure 5.)

of traditional wets in favor of a collar of spun hare's mask with guard hairs left in—or for even more *action*, a fur collar fronted by a turn or two of mottled partridge. Then, by dressing the flies on hooks ranging from light to heavy, we could effectively show an impressive imitation to even the spookiest or dourest trout at any depth we deemed appropriate.

We applied the concept, in turn, to a host of mayfly species, the Hendrickson, Sulphurs, Baetis, Potamanthus and Isonychia, to name but a few. Our interpretations outperformed conventional patterns in each instance. Of course the flies worked best when we factored into our presentations the relationships between trout and specific insects. Overall, however, our renderings demanded less manipulation, and so proved easier to fish, than standard wets, particularly on dicey waters.

All of a sudden wets seemed to become more versatile than ever. A single caddis pattern, such as a modified Leadwing Coachman or Alder, for instance, could be shown to one trout as an emerger, ovapositor or drowned adult, trebling the bases covered. By adding droppers and employing the three-quarters upstream or three-quarters downstream dead drift technique, we could handle multiple emergers effectively, even in the surface film. What is more, we sacrificed nothing when fishing the flies as wets have been fished for generations.

This lovely brown was working among the rocks near the tail of a Beaverkill eddy where it succumbed to one of our newly designed March Brown dries. The traces of rubbing on the trout's "snout" suggest that it had been rooting for migrating March Brown nymphs for several days before the hatch started in earnest.

Modern equipment has made specialized wet fly tackle unnecessary. The shock-absorbing stretch of monofilament, for instance, has rendered the legendary "noodle" rod obsolete. A long graphite rod (9-9 1/2 feet) helps by enabling you to minimize false casting. But I tend to use the same rods for wet and dry fly fishing, changing now and then only as dictated by water conditions rather than by technique.

Among the miracles of graphite rods is that most of them permit you to alter the character of your presentations simply by adjusting your casting rhythm. To keep a wet fly wet without fear of losing delivery potential, just open your loop by slowing down and lengthening your power stroke slightly. Then, to fish a wet in the film, or even as a dry on the surface, speed up, that is, tighten your loop, and keep your power stroke short. Excess water will be snapped from your fly at the tail of each false cast.

No other aspect of fly fishing dictates that your fly be quite so *organic* as wet fly fishing. Therefore, choosing the right line does remain critical. I use full-sinking lines, for example, only as a last resort—the "evil of two lessers" when using lead is the alternative. The trouble with sinking lines is that with so much line buried, you lose vital control and drag is actually encouraged.

Continuous control of your fly's behavior is the key to most wet fly techniques, including by inference those involving drag-free drift. For maximum control, the more limber your line the better. Silk lines are still ideal, although difficult to find at affordable prices. Next best are tired weight-forward floaters with more cracks in them than a Henny Youngman routine. Coupled with braided-butt leaders, they are extremely supple and sink just enough not to be influenced by surface chop. They don't, however, limit you to fishing flies beneath the surface.

Intermediate lines aren't too bad either. Although somewhat stiff, they sink slowly and are finer in diameter than floating weight-forwards in the same weight classes. Greased, they float just well enough to allow fishing wets as dries in a pinch. Because I like the resurrected floaters, though, I use intermediates mostly when committed to fishing wets three-quarters downstream against a taut line.

Sinking-tip lines are another matter. Combined with short leaders, they are the best means to maintain control of presentation while assuring that your wets get down to deep-feeding fish. The function of weight, or density, of the line's sinking portion speaks for itself. However, their practicality really hinges on the floating line trailing behind: it assures you control of each drift or swing that depends on mending, twitching, jigging, lifting or other delicate working line ministrations.

My trust in the versatility of wets has grown to a point today that I can fish them with confidence almost anytime or anywhere. At the two extremes, they represent an excellent alternative to fragile, no-hackle dries when fished on the surface during mayfly hatches, and fished deep, they're sometimes more effective than floating patterns during some spinner falls. And to imitate all but fluttering caddis, wets have become my favorite catch-all imitations.

Success with wets depends not on learning new and particularly complex techniques, but on mastering presentations already commonplace. Fish wets as dries just as you'd fish no-hackle duns, wets as spinners about as you'd fish nymphs on a slack line upstream. Likely you have the mechanics down pat already. So, all that's left is to muster some faith.

WET FLIES BY THE CAST

Whenever practical, for convenience's sake I like to make up a bunch of wet fly sets, or casts, in advance of every fishing trip. The same goes for when I anticipate fishing two or more nymphs, for example, or when I expect to be using, say, single nymphs and multiple wets or multiple nymphs and wet fly attractors.

Just so this doesn't read like the worst kind of jabberwocky to anybody, I'd better explain that a "cast" or "set" is a tapered leader made with one or more droppers tied into its tippet section. You can design it to accommodate as few as two hook points, that is, 2 flies, or as many as 15, as some British anglers have been known to do. The most efficient

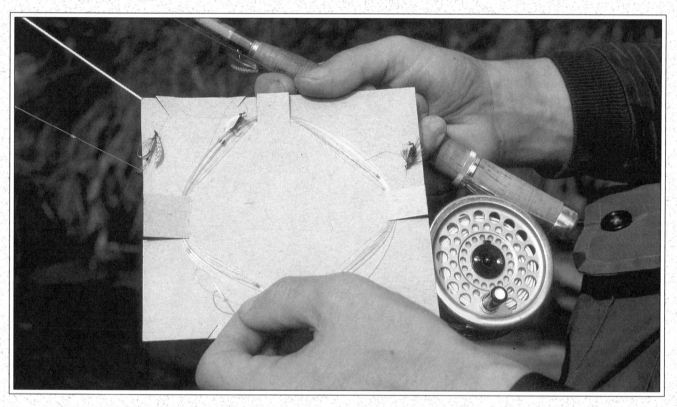

A marriage of the truly fine and the practical, my Bogdan trout reel and cardboard cast carrier made in minutes from the back of the very legal pad which I used to make notes for this chapter. I learned the trick, incidentally, from the late Walt Dette, master fly dresser and fly fishing innovator of truly remarkable vision and skill. Before Walt came up with this carrier, and especially when fishing at night, he used to wrap extra casts around the *band of his fedora hat.*

and effective way to make a cast is to tie a series of blood knots at intervals along the tippet, leaving one tag from each knot about four inches long. (Dropper tags longer than four inches are prone to snarl around the leader.)

Tying casts in advance encourages us to fuss a bit, to make each dropper just the right length to minimize tangling, and to affix each fly more meticulously than most of us would be likely to do on the water. Then there's always the advantage of being able to change casts in seconds when we might otherwise waste a lot of time untangling the occasional, but inevitable, snarl.

The only problem with preparing casts in advance recently has been that it has played hell finding a way to store them until you're ready to put them to work. Years ago when fishing multiple wets was S.O.P., this wasn't a problem. Numerous firms, notably Hardy Brothers of Alnwick, England, manufactured casts carriers. But, alas, these things have gone the way of so much of Hardy's truly neat stuff.

Although lacking the aesthetic appeal of a fine Hardy cast carrier, for certain, here's how you can make one with almost nothing, not even very much skill.

First, cut some squares of cardboard of the kind that comes as the backing of legal pads. The squares should be of uniform size that will fit in your fishing vest pocket. Next, use a pair of sharp scissors to cut a half-inch wide tab into each side to one of the cardboard squares. Each tab requires two cuts and should be located approximately midway between the outside corners of the square. The tabs should be about a half-inch deep.

Now, cut a single tab into one side of the square and hook the loop at the butt of your leader into it. Next, wind your leader around the cardboard, being careful to catch it on each tab it passes. Then, when you come to your first dropper fly, continue winding until the dropper is taut, and then while holding it in place with a thumb and forefinger, cut a slice in the cardboard about a half-inch deep and slide the fly into it. Repeat this step as you reach each additional dropper fly and when you come to the lead fly.

Finally, when you have prepared as many casts in this manner as you'll need for an outing or trip, simply stack them and slide them into a zip-lock plastic bag, which in turn you will slide directly into your vest or into your duffle bag for travel.

CHAPTER 18

Taking the Curse Out of Wind

Virtually all major works on fly fishing to date have included some line like: "Wind is the curse of the flyrodder." Yet, across the years precious little has been written about how fly fishermen should cope with uncooperative air currents, nor more important still, how they might learn to turn fickle winds to their advantage and thus get the most from otherwise potentially undermined outings.

The presence of breezy-to-windy conditions on most trout streams during a high percentage of angling days is one of those statements by nature which my brother George so aptly calls "givens." We can curse the wind just as surely as we can seek to spit into it—with much the same results. Even the most colorful vocabulary, though, won't alter the reality that winds have always been with fly fishermen and will remain with us for as long as the spirits have a sense of humor.

So why not save our collective breath and get down to the business of showing up the spirits, or at least try to get even?

Fact is that while wind is seldom a blessing, neither is it generally the disaster some fly fishing sages might have us believe. I like to think of wind as one of those ripples that keep trout fishing interesting. The capacity to encounter problems and to work them out is the standard by which fly fishing skill should really be measured. Thus, perhaps my share of problems and some of their solutions will assist in keeping you from wrapping your leader around your neck quite as often as I have around mine during the course of a misspent youth (and adulthood) of fly fishing.

First, certain winds ought to be identified as not for fly fishing whatsoever. "Ship sinkers," winds of gale force, for instance, just aren't worth the effort, not

Ah, the rewards of the zephyr—a joy forever, even for us, I suppose, it is often supposed are immune to such things. It happens to everybody. The important thing to remember is not to lose your temper and try to "cast" your fly out of the branches. If you do, sooner or later you're sure to break a rod tip. Rather, if you must break your fly off, do so with a *straight pull*. Oh, and one last thing: If you see your fly fall and you're perched on a boulder such as I am in this photo, don't try to catch the fly as it falls or you're likely to go swimming, the ultimate "joy" on a chilly spring day.

when so many "old trout" remain to be recaught over the mahogany at your favorite watering hole. Also, with the first gust of wind attendant to an approaching thunderstorm anglers should make tracks away from the water, no matter how many new fish continue to rise right under their noses. To stay anchored to trout pools, graphite rods waving overhead, during electrical storms is a frighteningly common practice along streams near my home. Like Russian roulette, to do so tempts fate and is a game you'll likely lose but once.

Otherwise, though, windy days are fair game not to be avoided or unnecessarily written off for lost.

To simply try to adapt tackle to wind is a common concession made to the condition by many fly fishermen. While fly rods with guts, or lots of backbone, and those for heavy lines may take some of the sting out of a tempest, forsaking your everyday favorite rod for the sake of additional power won't necessarily enhance either your enjoyment of the day's angling—my top priority—or your ability to make fly presentations with sufficient deftness to handle the water you're fishing at peak effectiveness. So, instead of becoming bogged down with alternative gear, why not reconsider your intended objective stream and seek instead to home on a river or stretch of river uncompromised by wind on that day.

Each season I receive dozens of phone calls seeking scoops about conditions current along Catskills trout streams. While prevailing fly hatches, water levels and water temperatures, even barometric pressures, are regularly regarded as critical by my callers, relatively few seem concerned with the potential for unfavorable winds on a given day. Such information, however, should always be brought to bear when deciding what river or stream to fish with a fly rod. To choose the wrong water during a blow is a surefire way to go down in flames.

Learning to read weather is all but as important to effective fly fishing as learning to read water. A composite of wind direction and its velocity as that composite relates to the chorography, or layout, of a stream can determine the optimum strategy for that fishery each day. Wind direction has particular relevance, since it directs you to the side of the stream from which it should fish best and to stretches or pools that are most likely to lie in the lee of the wind. Calculating wind velocity helps you ascertain whether or not such lees will exist.

The principal adjustments that fly fishermen ought to make for wind are tactical. By introducing something new to your repertoire on the one hand, or forgoing some device from your characteristic treatment of windless periods on the other, depending on circumstances astream, few pranks of wind cannot be parried, and once parried, then neutralized. In some instances, they may even be turned to the angler's advantage.

Not many fly fishing situations, regardless of weather conditions, bar a range of alternative tactics, and to choose those best to compensate for troublesome wind seldom requires more than common sense and experience. Common sense reinforced by experience, for example, dictates that a fly fisherman plying big water *use* a trailing wind, or a wind from his back, to extend his fly presentations. Conversely, it makes little sense, given viable options, to worry a streamer fly or wet fly three-quarters downstream into the teeth of a strong upstream wind. Then, too, whenever feasible, a fly fisherman should position himself in a stream so that his line, leader and fly are blown away from his body as he casts, thus negating the need to cast backhanded, the traditional defense against decorating your body with wandering flies.

A wind howling straight into your face, such as pictured here on a normally lovely stretch of Idaho's Silver Creek, makes the direct overhead cast, usually desirable, virtually impossible to pull off. So strong was this blow, indeed, that by trying to cast as shown here, the fly ended up literally no more than two or three feet in front of me in a snarl of line and leader. You'll note, too, that given where the trout were lying, I had no viable alternative to the spot from which I was trying to cast since the water of the entire pool was too deep for crossing.

Easy as flipping a page to see the best, if not ideal, solution to my gale-in-the-face problem, taught to me, by the way, by the late Joe Brooks, one of the nicest guys in the history of outdoor writing. The answer, keep your rod low but as vertical as possible to avoid friction, your line speed as fast as possible, shoot line into the backcast, and double-hauling, drive the line *under* the wind. It works as Joe learned from the Argentine legend Bebe Anchorena during the trip to windy Patagonia that spawned the television show *The American Sportsman*.

A head wind can prove handy to the savvy angler, just as one can use a trailing wind, particularly when the head wind is gusty. Discovering that shooting line need not be reserved for the forward cast, but can be applied to the backcast as well, the trick lies then in making your backcasts when the wind peaks and your forward casts during the lulls between gusts.

All anglers ought to learn the economy of shooting line into the backcast, whether the end be to compensate for wind or not. The skill requires no more than building additional line speed by means of a single haul on the pickup and an identifiable power stroke, or punch, when initiating the backcast. Assuming you are right-handed, then, line is released from your left hand as the rearward power stroke is made, exactly as you characteristically release line during the forward power stroke when shooting line ahead in the traditional fashion. Mastering this trick is integral to virtually all fly presentation techniques that suggest that your fly spend maximum time on or in the water and minimum time in the air. Prospecting with dry flies and downstream wet fly fishing are excellent examples that come quickly to mind.

Generally speaking, upstream winds typical of rivers and streams everywhere unquestionably subvert more fly presentation techniques than all other windy conditions combined. Although anglers sometimes conclude that light to moderate upstream breezes enhance, for instance, dry fly presentation, my experience shows quite the contrary to be true. Here's why.

Simplistically, it might seem that an upstream blow would straighten out a fly caster's leader and tippet and thus prove beneficial to him. In fact, the last thing a dry fly fisherman really wants or needs is a chalk-line-straight leader on the water except perhaps in rare and specialized instances. The curse of the straight leader is demon tippet and fly drag, which in turn, as I've pointed out over and over, is the most common cause of last-instant dry fly rejection by rising trout.

Wind or no wind, most effective upstream and three-quarters upstream dry fly, emerger and nymph presentations are produced by line, leader and tippet slack sufficient to promote the drag-free float or drift of your fly. On calm days you accomplish this by using several techniques, including, for instance, kicking your leader back with a jolt as each cast is completed, or the stop-and-drop technique illustrated earlier and featured in my book, *Fishing Dry Flies for Trout on Rivers and Streams*, or by "dumping" the line and leader by underpowering the forward cast as adapted to steeple or puddle casts, which I mentioned earlier as being favorites among spring creek devotees.

During periods of stiff upstream wind, however, ensuring essential line and leader slack becomes infinitely more challenging, since the upstream punch of the wind tends to counteract your best efforts at downstream kickback and to undermine attempts to soften presentation by dumping your line and leader.

The best way to compensate for winds that drive a fly fisherman's terminal tackle too far upstream is to slow down the false casting rhythm, which in turn opens the casting loop in the fly line and reduces line speed. Soften the forward delivery of the line by increasing the length of the power stroke or forward punch of the cast, while dampening the power stroke's force from that of pounding a

If you hum Sinatra tunes even as you talk to your flies, you want to be sure, "I don't lose you to a trailing wind..." Note how low the butt of my rod is at the completion of this presentation after slowing down every other element of the cast. This so-called "dampening" ensures plenty of "S's" in your line and so a drag-free float. Without it, though, your line, leader and tippet take off as if shot out of a gun, your fly ending up at the end of a chalk line, the consequence of which is drag before your presentation has really even begun. In other words, "Nice'n easy does it every time."

nail to, say, that of patting your bird dog on the forehead. Then halt the forward cast's thrust at high-rod, that is, with the rod tip pitched steeply over the water, while dropping the hand with which you grip your rod from its normal casting position abreast of your shoulder to one as close as possible to your hip.

Thus the angle of incline which the shooting line must climb along your rod will inhibit the line's speed, usually sufficiently to produce adequate slack line and leader on the surface when the whole business finally lights. If more brake is needed, however, an additional governor can be put on your line by feathering it as you release the loops held in your free hand one by one during the course of the cast and shoot.

Whereas upstream wind is normally bothersome, more often than not a generally downstream wind will prove a boon to a fly fisherman. While most anglers realize that three-quartering a wet fly downstream, for example, is facilitated by the flight of downstream wind, relatively few dry fly fishermen readily recognize that, given the light touch that issues from plenty of practice, this wind will also assist you when you throw mends into your line, leader and tippet, each of which are crucial to attaining a drag-free float. For best results, you should present the dry fly either directly across stream or across and slightly downstream. In either event, your fly and tippet will light on the surface downstream of your leader and line, hence leaving the leader and line to trail along behind the fly and tippet, which in turn minimizes the influence of the leader and line on the drift of your fly.

This stated, it ought to be noted that particular phases of each annual fly fishing cycle are in fact enhanced by the presence of wind, and in some instances by wind with accompanying rain. Such conditions vary considerably, of course, from region to region, or even from stream to stream. Nevertheless, here are a few examples.

• Strong winds tend to shower rivers and streams with terrestrial insects, including ants and beetles swept from streambanks and inchworms and other bugs snatched from the branches of overhanging trees. Most interesting to fly fishermen, though, are probably so-called "hopper banks" where trout muster to feed when tides of grasshoppers and crickets are pitched onto the water by heavy crosswinds. A "hopper bank," incidentally, is generally the one toward which the wind is blowing, that is, the west banks of a stream during an east wind, the south bank during a north wind, and so forth.

• Protracted periods of high wind may suppress, or temporarily suspend, emergences of some species of aquatic insects, including mayflies, caddis and stoneflies. When such periods happen to coincide with stream conditions that dictate the trout consume maximum food, the fish, denied the staple of their diet, are likely to turn to feeding ravenously on minnows and other rough fish. This phenomenon represents a potential field day for the bucktail and streamer fisherman.

This handsome trout fell prey to a hopper against a hopper bank during the heat of mid-day, which often raises winds, especially in the mountainous West. No big trick, really, except to be sure that given the trailing wind discussed elsewhere in this chapter, I didn't overshoot my mark and end up with my fly on the bank instead of on the water in front of it. A nice thing about fishing hopper banks is that you seldom need to lead the fish more than a foot or two.

• Then, certain aquatic insect species—the eastern mayfly known as the *paraleptophlebia*, Paralep or Blue Quill, for instance—are prone to hatch most profusely when upstream winds are blowing like a banshee and icy rains will sting your face. The wind and rain cooperate to keep the emerging mayflies on the surface longer than they would remain during a calm, dry day. Thus, because the naturals are duck soup for surface feeding trout, anglers who imitate them can really clean up.

Observe your favorite trout water over an extended period and you're certain to recognize comparable situations, which you can put to good use while other anglers are accomplishing little more than bucking the breeze.

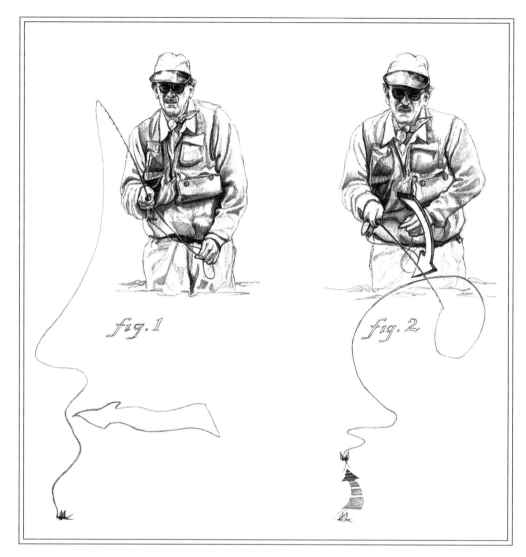

Illustration 1 The mend-and-twitch is an indispensable technique, wind or no wind, and is really quite easy to execute. Assuming a water flow from the angler's left to his right, as indicated by the arrow in front of figure 1, you make a fly presentation pretty much as normal, grasping the excess line in your free hand. Note the "S's" in the line, which permit a drag-free drift should you opt to go that way at the last moment. However, deciding you're going to try the mend-and-twitch, you simply rotate your wrist in an upstream direction (the mend) as indicated by the arrow in figure 2, which causes the fly to make a short skittering curve on the water, even as the distance between you and your fly is reduced slightly (the twitch). Meanwhile additional excess line is taken up by your free hand and formed into loops that are held in anticipation of your next presentation. This procedure can be repeated as often as you wish and at any interval you see fit. Remember, though, that if you wait very long between mends, since your line has straightened out somewhat, your fly is likely to begin dragging and thus offset at least some of the value of the specialized presentation you've really set out to perform. When the water is flowing from your right to your left, just reverse everything. The important thing to remember is that mends are usually made in an upstream direction, *except* when the water flow is very slow and you want to speed your fly up—a different matter altogether and really not worth going into here unless we want to create chaos out of order.

Numerous fly presentation techniques are also bolstered by wind. A skater dry fly ahead of a long tippet, for instance, is more easily skittered across a stream's surface with the assistance of a blustery wind than when fished on a mirrorlike surface on a dead calm day. Ditto, gusty cross winds are dandy for pulling off the *mend-and-twitch* dry fly technique shown opposite, a favorite of mine (also featured in *Fishing Dry Flies for Trout on Rivers and Streams*) which as its name implies, is used to impart lifelike "action" to caddis and stonefly imitations. Remember, too, that a wind is likely to ruffle a stream, hence enabling fly fishermen to utilize large flies and heavier tippets over skittish trout where use of such gear would be unthinkable when the air is still.

Perhaps the most timely technique of all for coping with wind, however, is the stalking of bank-feeders (see Chapter 14) during hard upstream blows. Since the technique involves creeping up behind fish rising tight to banks and presenting flies delicately directly upstream so the flies are visible to the fish but the leader and tippet are draped over the fish's "blind spot," or directly over a trout's back, what could be better than to use the trailing wind to facilitate your presentations? But be careful to keep your touch light. Since "bankers" tend to rank among a stream's most eclectic, or random, feeders, given a consistently light touch, you'll usually take a reliable quota by combining a well-chosen fly and your old pal the wind.

CHAPTER 19

Young-of-the-Year Streamers

A big trout tearing into a shoal of tiny minnows is an awesome spectacle, especially when such an eruption occurs within a confined area of stream just inches deep. To do more than observe, say, a brown "herding" or "corralling" bait fish, though, is but to bear witness to a predator at work. To pit your skill against that predator under such trying conditions, however, is something worthy of being called a trout fisherman's *ultimate rush*.

Trout are opportunistic feeders, as already noted, meaning that their feeding behavior is linked to those sources of food either most abundant or easiest to harvest during given periods of the year. (Hence, regarding aquatic insects, for instance, the phenomenon we presume to be "selective feeding.") Trout are programmed to net maximum nourishment for minimum energy expended, which in my experience anyway, suggests why a feeding fish may prefer, for example, helpless spinners to active emergers, or more apropos here, why it'll tear into a streamer at the height of a hatch.

Nor is it a secret that trout, particularly browns and rainbows, are cannibalistic, a trait typically intensified as the fish grows. It has even been said of some trout that by the time they've attained certain dimensions, they live almost entirely on "seafood." A trout's cannibalism, however, is normally less than obvious even to the observant angler, since unlike showy insect feeding activity, minnowing usually occurs underwater out of sight. Conventional streamer fishing techniques, then, are by necessity somewhat analogous to reading braille.

Episodes of "herding" and "corralling" fry and fingerling minnows are notable exceptions to this covert behavior. Along streams I fish day after day, I've

An absolutely ideal illustration of a good trout working the shallows of a Beaverkill flat in search of young-of-the-year minnows, among other tidbits. Although the fish will typically wake around and thus face in virtually every direction at one time or another, positioning yourself below the dead water in which the trout is working typically offers you your best shot and least chance of being spotted. Two other important rules are to stay low and not to present your fly until you know *precisely* where the trout is.

found such shenanigans more common than I once supposed, particularly during intervals when the dynamics of feeding on fry are readily reconciled with the priorities of a trout's opportunistic nature. Specifically, there are periods during which small minnows are especially plentiful, while insects, though present as always, are less numerous than some trout would have them.

The most abundant, and vulnerable, of baitfish are usually offspring from the most recent spawning period. By happy coincidence for trout and angler, incredible numbers begin to venture recklessly into areas where they are easy prey at the very time they're needed most as trout food. Usually as water levels recede, you'll observe school after school, a half inch to one and a half inches long, circling in side eddies, picking at minutiae around exposed stones or filing up and down adjacent to banks and along beaches and shores.

Just look down when you're wading sometime and see how many of these naive little fish have gathered to check out your boots. Then try to recall so many nymphs, for instance, of comparable size congregated in one place at one time. If you can't, as is likely, you should begin to appreciate what a windfall these minnows are for trout.

Frankly, I know precious little about the taxonomy of minnows beyond the fact that New York alone has some 48 species of chubs, dace, fallfish and shiners, a significant number of which would seem to inhabit the streams near my home. I'm given to understand that such is the case elsewhere on American streams, except perhaps in the Rockies where fewer species exist. All minnows with which I'm familiar spawn from early through late spring, meaning that stocks of the various strains begin showing up as fry and fingerlings at regular intervals from late spring through early fall. Where I live, for instance, broods are in evidence from early summer through late fall.

These little fish are imitated effectively by flies I call *Young-of-the-Year Streamers*—which is really just a reference to conventional streamer patterns that are dressed unusually sparsely and/ or small for this specific purpose. Sparse streamers as large as size 12 will occasionally do the trick as a consequence of rapid growth exhibited by a few minnow species. However, when I say small, I mean sizes 14-20, or flies that represent all the species we lump together as "pinheads" in my neck of the woods. Additionally, it's worth mentioning that these small patterns should be

Here is Galen Mercer's dressing of a "typical" Gray Ghost streamer, a size 4, as juxtaposed to his renditions of what I call young-of-the-year streamers so effective in the shallows of many rivers and streams. Most, you'll note, aren't particularly "natural" in that they don't look that much like the real things, which swim around in the hundreds or thousands along the edges of trout pools and runs. This difference in appearance, however, as long as the size approximates, actually seems to excite feeding trout and so works in your favor. (See also color insert, figure 6.)

tied on hooks lighter than usual for streamers, since they must be pitched into clear, still shallows with minimum commotion.

Appropriate patterns, of course, will vary from region to region, if not from stream to stream. My experience indicates, however, that pattern per se, or more precisely the exact color of your streamer, is generally less critical to its effectiveness than the fly's size and silhouette. Indeed, I've found that given a selection of patterns that approximate natural fry or fingerlings present in size and shape, I'm usually better off with one *decidedly different* in color from the prevailing naturals. The vast majority of trout, curiously enough, seem more inclined to home on small streamers somewhat more dramatic in overall appearance than drab patterns dressed to "match the minnow." Contrasting yellow with black and white, as in tying the old reliable Black Ghost, or simply putting a wee splash of red as found in the tail of Keith Fulsher's dandy Silver Tip, are good examples of the approach I take to stocking my boxes with young-of-the-year streamers.

Ol' reliable—the Black Ghost—even in such small sizes is the best streamer pattern I've found for browns working on tiny minnows anywhere in the world. For this purpose, I carry them in sizes 12-20. Judging by its relationship with the tip of the vise, this one, I think, is about a size 14, perfectly proportioned, as always, by the dexterous hands of Galen Mercer. (For more Black Ghosts see color insert, figure 3.)

Tying functional streamers in this style isn't especially difficult when you bear in mind a few fundamental principles and learn a couple of tricks. Essentially, you must endeavor to create a slim silhouette by (1) putting minimum material into each body, i.e., a single layer of tinsel or floss; (2) using throat hackle only to enhance a pattern's effectiveness, i.e., the yellow throat of the Black Ghost; (3) utilizing a sparing amount of curl-free winging material, such as bucktail or squirrel, or two hackle tips only, picked from a dry fly quality neck; (4) being careful that the wing of each finished fly is low to the shank of the hook.

To avoid discoloration of single-layered floss bodies when streamers are wet, try enameling your hook shanks white prior to dressing the flies. (I like enamel for its quick-drying property and matte finish.) White (for silver) or yellow (for gold) undercoating will also mask multitudes of sins when tying single-layered, tinsel bodies. To maintain a low wing profile, take care that the tie-in point is lump- and slope-free, or that it is flush to the level of the rest of the body on top of the hook. Winging material, including hackle tips, should be measured and clipped prior to being tied in. Then, also lacquer sparingly all wing butts of hair and synthetics to compress their overall bulk, as well as to guarantee that the wing stays in place once it's tied on the hook.

The length of wings on these streamers really isn't critical, except regarding how a wing's relative dimensions influence a pattern's appearance in the eyes of the quarry. The problem of short-striking seldom applies to streamers so small and thus probably shouldn't concern either tyer or angler. As a rule, however, I'm inclined to like wings that extend no farther back than to the tip of the tail when a tail is dictated by the dressing, or to the bend of the hook when I'm tying or buying tailless patterns.

Note the grass, which indicates how close to shore this brown trout, and ambusher, was lying when Kris and I happened on him. Except for a slight fanning of its tail, the fish was motionless *until* an unsuspecting school of pinheads came into range. Then the speed and accuracy, not to mention deadliness, of its attack were astounding. As a matter of fact, it all happened so fast, it was impossible to record on film. Maybe next time.

Whereas conventional streamer strategy is largely methodical prospecting for random feeders, to fish young-of-the-year imitations effectively obliges that little or nothing be left to chance. This is the most refined form of streamer work I know, with tactics at least as involved as those normally associated with the delicate presentation of terrestrials or midges to visible trout. Your ultimate goal—to turn the tables on a wary predator—is, in effect, a test of your own predatory attributes, as well as your fly fishing skills.

The first essential is to tailor your technique to the behavior of individual fish. For practical purposes, my experience suggests that these predators can be divided into two general categories: the *ambusher* and the *stalker*. Although a single trout may switch back and forth

This photo shows an excellent shore for minnowing trout to frequent. However, I found that the trout absolutely refused to hold on this day and so were impossible to stalk. What the fish did instead was to rush in from deeper water, make a quick pass at whatever minnows were in their paths, then return to deep water again. This left me no alternative but to "prospect" the entire stretch using a tiny Black Ghost. By doing so, I landed numerous good trout, some hooked in the shallows, others further out into the river.

between categories several times in the course of one hunt, simply put, the ambusher tends to lie in wait for minnows to pass within striking range, while the stalker cruises likely spots actively seeking fry or fingerlings to attack.

The difficulties and advantages presented by each category of predator trout are decidedly different. For instance, a well-camouflaged trout lying perfectly still is tough to spot in time to make a proper presentation before the fish spooks. Nevertheless, if spotted in time, the ambusher is usually quite easy to hook since the placement and course of your streamer should create the impression of playing right into the predator's hands. The stalker, on the other hand, is normally easier to see by wearing Polaroids and keeping the sun at your back, or by watching for the telltale wake a cruising fish makes while moving about in shallow water. Marking such a fish, however, offers no guarantee that you'll be able to anticipate its coming movements with sufficient accuracy to intersect its route with a streamer at the right instant, or indeed that you'll be able to introduce a streamer attractive enough to divert the trout's attention from natural minnows to which it's already committed.

Some minnowing trout can certainly be caught by simply rotating through stretches of stream, working potential hot spots with tiny streamers. There are many fundamental problems with this approach, however. Firstly, it diminishes the quality of sport, in my opinion, by increasing the ratio between presentations made and fish hooked to a point at which angling skill becomes largely irrelevant. As a purely practical matter, though, this chuck-and-chance-it technique is likely to attract but a minuscule percentage of potential takers, since where I fish anyway, most trout have proven disinclined to move far to intercept young-of-the-year streamers.

So what are the alternatives? One surprisingly effective tactic is to become an ambusher yourself by taking up a position in a proven spot, then bushwhacking trout that approach you. Another is to find an area with lots of minnows and to sit on the nearest bank that affords a good view, waiting for trout to find the minnows, too. Yet another option is to choose a particular school of fry, then to try to move with it in such a way that you're ready the instant a trout shows.

All such tactics, quite obviously, require considerable patience. Less so my personal favorite, which is to actively stalk minnowing trout in much the same fashion that trout stalk the minnows. During a typical outing, I enter the very tail of a pool and if possible wade to about midstream. Having thus divided the stream in two, I spend several minutes surveying the scene 360 degrees about me. I pay particular attention to shallows and water near banks and shores in hopes of picking up wakes or "V's," swirls or splashes, that tip off fry-feeding fish.

Seeing none, I proceed to move ever so slowly in a generally upstream direction, pausing with every four or five steps to reevaluate the situation. My wake must be minimal at all times, incidentally, and I try never to drag my feet over stones.

Upon spotting a trout, I spend as long as I dare estimating its size and monitoring its behavior in order to determine (1) whether this fish is worth perhaps spooking others to get to and (2) how I might seek to position myself most advantageously to present a fly when the time comes. At this point I may even opt to change fly patterns, or more likely still, to *grease* the little streamer I have on in hopes of convincing my opportunistic quarry that it has lucked into a disabled, and thus helpless, fingerling or fry.

Hard knocks have taught me that once committed to a fish, though, *nothing*—not even the sudden appearance of "My Moby Dick"—should divert me from my initial plan. I have to be deliberate and patient while trying always to anticipate the fish's next move before it is made. I decide in advance the precise point from which I'll present my fly, and once I've reached it, unless something unforeseen has occurred, I refuse to hear that little voice that keeps suggesting, "Why not risk just another few steps?"

Each presentation of a tiny streamer should be made from a position where pinpoint accuracy is assured. A long time back I learned that if I think about a second shot I'm almost sure to need one. I try to power each cast to the maximum compatible with delicacy, measuring line, leader and tippet precisely and well in advance of my fly touching down. When at all practical, I deposit my streamer within the trout's sight just ahead of its nose rather than the fish's left or right. If a cast to the side is the only alternative, however, I refrain from making it until I'm reassured that my tippet won't be detected. (In clear, shallow water, 5X is rarely fine enough.)

Finally, my method of retrieve—i.e., slow, fast, smooth or jerky— is virtually always determined in advance of a cast. Otherwise I may hesitate, when to appear natural, the retrieve ought to begin *the instant the fly makes contact with the surface*. To remember this is essential, since a streamer that moves laterally immediately upon hitting the water will frequently spark a strike, while even the smallest fly that hits and sinks with no lateral movement is likely to scare the same trout right out of its wits.

If you'd like to combine elements of both hunting and fishing into one exhilarating

So violent do trout often take young-of-the-year streamers that the fish, as is clear in this photo, are hooked much too deeply to retrieve the fly without danger of killing the trout by tearing a gill. In my book a trout is worth loss of a fly anytime, and so after netting the fish, I simply cut my tippet, leaving the fly in the trout's mouth and kiss the fish "goodbye," so to speak. Not to worry. Within days, enzymes secreted by the trout will disintergrate the hook, leaving the fish in excellent shape to fight another day.

sport, then young-of-the-year streamers just may be your meat. Though less contemplative than visceral in principle, perhaps, in practice such angling need be no less exacting or fulfilling than, say, fishing dry flies to free-rising rainbows or browns. And what's more, this purely primordial exercise offers no end of enlightening insights into the character of anglers and the nature of trout as worthy protagonists all.

CHAPTER 20

Long Winter's Hendrickson Into Spring

I wonder how many of you, like me, have presumed upon the Hendrickson to survive another winter. Even now, after jump-starting that damned old car, I'm confident I need do no more than to recall fishing the Hendrickson hatch last year and to anticipate how I might better fish those still ahead of me to endure. Without the faithful Hendrickson, though, I'm not quite sure what might become of me.

Fitting, isn't it, that during the seeming eternity imposed by winter the Hendrickson, or *Ephemerella Subvaria*, seems to dominate so many reflections, even among those who don't live near where the species hatches, as well as schemes for those who do? Nor should we really be surprised to discover that with the arrival of each spring, clouds of new, and often worthy, variations on the Hendrickson theme have winged off fly tying vises all over the country. For even those among us who protest most aggressively against preoccupation with fly pattern seldom want for a Hendrickson, as they say, "for each and every occasion." Such are the consequences born of cabin fever. At last tally I confess that no less than 60 Hendrickson patterns have found their way into my possession—remembrances, so to speak, of winters past. No doubt there'll be more come next May.

The Hendrickson hatch ushers in the annual rite of spring for many of us. While it may not be the first mayfly to show in the wake of ice-out and snow

To me there is no more beautiful sight than a Hendrickson dun perched on a budding branch in the early Northeastern springtime. How well I remember, many years ago now, how Jay "Fishy" Fullum, a fine angler, fly tyer and artist, said to me in the wake of the last Hendrickson hatch of that season, "You know Art, each time one of these ends, I can't help but subtract another year from my lifetime." It's that sort of emotion that this fragile bug imbues in us of "the quiet sport." (Also see color insert, figure 7.)

runoff, a lot of us are convinced that it is the first hatch that *matters*. A philosopher might argue that this is because we see something of ourselves in the character of this fragile yet hearty species of insect, something we must renew each season in order to be reassured that we, too, are survivors. Nevertheless, the Hendrickson is unquestionably the best-known and most-fished hatch east of the Rocky Mountains, which says, in effect, that it likely ranks as the number one hatch of American fly fishing.

My first-ever trout on a dry, I chose to believe, mistook somebody's hand-me-down for a Hendrickson and happened onto my hook. It was early May back in the years when a few gentlemen of taste had begun to predict that Art Flick's *Streamside Guide to Naturals and Their Imitations* would be a classic someday. The little brook babbled along over polished stones behind our home in the foothills of the Berkshire Mountains. Pussy willows were bursting and I remember measuring the buds of new leaves against the nail of my pinky, as counseled by a sort of adopted uncle who I lionized because he regularly fished Maine and was the one sparring partner who could go five rounds with my old man during the weekly bloodfests that took place Sundays in our converted basement. Pinky nail–sized buds mean good dry fly fishing, I reckoned then as I do now, having had more than 30 year's experience to bear witness to "Uncle" Harvey's thesis.

Today, I can't recall what stroke of luck managed to whack my fly over the little trout, nor whether the fly was dragging or not, nor the rise, nor setting the hook, nor even whether the fish was stripped, reeled or just hauled in. Funny, but I can recall only that I was wearing black rubber boots much too big for me and that I had dressed the fly very carefully with paste to be sure it would stay afloat. I don't even know whether or not my gut leader had been properly soaked. But I do remember most vividly standing looking over Grandma Lee's shoulder while she ate the trout and informing her emphatically that I had taken her breakfast on a *Hendrickson*.

Memory being convenient, the precise facts of that matter of so long ago are probably just as well lost in time. Whether partially apocryphal or not, however, the ultimate truth is that Art Flick's little book has indeed gone on to become a classic, while I have hounded Hendrickson hatches ever since, managing behind experience to learn a thing or two along the trail.

That which I pass along here issues mostly from my own doings astream, and as such, is thoroughly subjective, as well as perhaps a tad parochial. I've never fished the Au Sable in Michigan, for example, and thus can't vouch for how well or how badly my tune might play upon that storied stream. Nor have I troubled myself to extract all that I probably could have from those entomology texts which, although of value, I'm certain, to folks so inclined, do unto me that which I wouldn't dream of doing unto you.

Briefly, however, by way of background, it's valuable to note the following general information about the Hendrickson.

• The Hendrickson is a middlin'-sized mayfly of the same genus as numerous insects important to fly fishermen, including, for instance, the eastern Sulphurs.

• The Hendrickson is found on waters throughout the northeastern, middle Atlantic and southern states, ranging as far south, in significant numbers anyway, as the streams of western North Carolina and the mountains of Georgia. The

This is one of the prettiest days I can ever remember astream, here fishing the lower end of Cairn's Eddy on the Beaverkill during a Hendrickson hatch. The fish were tough, I recall, but that wasn't really important. The day was brisk and the freshness of the new grasses on the banks, emerging skunk cabbage and fiddlehead ferns and the young leaves on the maples and ashes and oaks, plus budding it seemed everywhere about me in every hue from pink and yellow to bright red, just made being there an experience of wonder, one of those unforgettable events given us by Mother Nature to make us fly fishermen even if we weren't really fly fishermen before.

species is also abundant throughout the upper Midwest, including on water in those states situated east of the Mississippi River. The Hendrickson is found, too, on many eastern Canadian streams, including some on which I fish salmon every year.

• The Hendrickson is unusual in that the female of the species, called the Light Hendrickson after one A.E. Hendrickson, an affluent New York angler whose ghost still wades the rivers and streams of the Catskills, resembles the male, or Red Quill as named by Art Flick, only in that both have dun-colored wings and three tails. Both male and female spinners, however, do look alike, varying (to the untrained eye) only in size. The best way to differentiate between the Hendrickson and Red Quill is by body color. Typically, the body of a Hendrickson is light tan with a decidedly pinkish cast, while that of a Red Quill is uniformly rusty brown. The bodies of both the male and female Hendrickson spinner are rusty in color.

• By mayfly standards, the Hendrickson is both adaptable and robust. The species is comfortable in waters large and small, slow and fast, including rich limestoners and relatively acid surface water streams. Within limits, too, the Hendrickson seems to tolerate pollution and other environmental strains exceptionally well, which contributes to its role as the principal insect along countless streams where mayfly hatches are considered at best to be marginal. This fortunate capacity, of course, has done nothing to hurt the Hendrickson's reputation.

• Hendrickson hatches are triggered by a consolidation of favorable climatic conditions, the most crucial of which is no doubt water temperature. When stream temperatures rise to approximately 54 degrees Fahrenheit, Hendrickson nymphs become very active and the first of numerous hatches occur. Daily or intermittent emergences can then extend for as long as several weeks, depending on region and fishery. Beginning at the southerly extreme of its range and progressing northward, your Hendrickson hatch should be expected to commence any time from early April until as late as mid-June. Here in the Catskills, old-timers would like to believe that the Hendrickson will show each season on the fourth of May—which is okay with me, since the fourth happens to be my birthday. In point of fact, though, in recent years in the northeast, most Hendrickson hatches have been over by May 1st. Hendrickson spinners are supposed to return to mate and fall from 24 to 48 hours after emerging as duns, although given weird weather conditions, I've seen them come back as much as two weeks later. So, who knows?

So much has already been written about fishing Hendrickson hatches that you, the reader, may be wondering why existing intelligence isn't sufficient without me padding it. Enough of the conventional wisdom is curiously inconsistent with, and sometimes contrary to, what I've learned on the water, though, that I feel obliged to let go my salvo.

The fruits of decades of engaging Hendrickson hatches, for instance, contradict the notion that the best period for prospecting with Hendrickson nymphs is but an hour or so before the day's emergence begins. My experience, in fact, indicates brief *dead periods* are likely immediately in advance of Hendrickson hatches, although such periods generally come in consequence of your intended quarry's behavior, that is, trout doing a bit of digesting and adjusting their lies, rather than the behavior of the nymphs themselves, which will hatch by and by.

Hendrickson nymphs are frisky critters that move about tirelessly from stream bed to surface during virtually all daylight hours except perhaps when the weather really fouls. So active is their behavior, indeed, that it's easy to fancy them as impatient to get the business of emerging over with well before the due time. Needless to say, all this energy isn't lost on hungry trout, which generally begin

I use my "gamer"—a nine-foot rod for a number-4 line—for fishing both Henrickson nymphs and dries and have found no reason to use anything else since The Orvis Company first came out with its Western series some years back. This brown was taken on a low-floating Henrickson emerger ahead of a 6X tippet. The latest in tippet materials make it possible to fish fine diameters yet still have plenty of breaking strength to land virtually any trout you hook.

gorging themselves on Hendrickson nymphs while anglers who accept the traditional portrayal of Hendrickson time as "bankers' hours" are still fast asleep.

I've learned that the early-morning hours of Hendrickson time offer the season's premier opportunity to indulge the old greased-line technique for taking lots of trout, especially if the weather is mild. Try three-quartering a cast of two Hendrickson nymphs or a nymph as point fly and Hendrickson wet as a dropper and don't be surprised when you bank many more fish between 7 A.M. and 9 A.M. than you do at those more "civilized hours" farther along in the day.

Nor am I inclined to accept Hendricksons as creatures of broken water, although trout are normally easiest to take *on* Hendrickson dries where the stream surface covers errors of fly presentation. Hendrickson hatches no less respectable than those along adjacent pocket water stretches occur daily on the long eddies of the Beaverkill, for instance, near my home. Moreover, a glassy surface over clear water and a rocky bottom are among the chief elements of sight-fishing, which profits you as an angler by enhancing your knowledge of trout and insect behavior, while you get one heck of a kick out of the show.

Despite ample water levels typical of spring, to fish Hendrickson dries effectively on flats dictates the cautious approach normally associated with sight-fishing to midging trout when streams are low. (Here's where that "Spring Training" discussed earlier comes in handy.) After choosing a target and positioning yourself for a clean presentation, pause to observe the trout through several rises with an eye toward ascertaining, (1) if the trout prefers naturals that float motionless on the surface to those that are struggling to get off the water; (2) if the trout's feeding rhythm is measured and thus predictable; (3) whether your trout demonstrates any inclination to alter or vary its feeding station, or lie, between rises; and (4) whether the trout rises and takes naturals without hesitation or inspects each one suspiciously before committing itself. Only thusly prepared should you begin to cast.

Because flats tend to be relatively unforgiving, I always try to give myself an edge by using the longest, finest leader and smallest fly I deem consistent with a profitable presentation. On rivers such as the Beaverkill and Willowemoc, for example, I seldom risk a leader shorter than 15 feet, 5 feet of which is 5X or 6X tippet, preferably the latter. Fishing flats has fostered in me a penchant for Hendrickson patterns, including no-hackle dries and emergers, that float low on the water, as opposed to those classic Hendrickson dressings that are ideally suited for dancing over pockets, on riffs and other such places. Fly size, of course, is a variable thing, but my stream notes indicate that the most dependable choice for the flats is a dry or emerger one size smaller than the apparent size of the prevailing naturals.

Should you find yourself wanting a low-floating Hendrickson dry, by the way, one can be fashioned from a traditional Hendrickson by clipping the fly's hackle squarely across the bottom flush to the dubbing wound on the hook. Similarly, an emerger can be improvised by clipping all the hackle from around the fly close to the hook, then trimming the fly's wings to about one-third of their original length. Given only one traditional fly on which to operate, however, you'd better not set your heart on an emerger until you're entirely satisfied that a low-floating dun imitation ain't gonna turn the trick.

Over the years, much ado has also been made of the need for precise representation of Hendrickson naturals. (Who hasn't coveted a red fox vixen's urine-stained underbelly for Hendrickson bodies at one time or another?) Suitable Hendrickson renderings are, of course, valuable, although color, in my experience, is far less critical than fly size and silhouette being appropriate to prevailing conditions. Most important, though, regardless of pattern, is unquestionably how skillfully the fly is presented.

While I concede that I carry more Hendrickson patterns than anyone should have a right to, I fish but a few on a regular basis and of those surely *need* only one or two. The Flick Hendrickson Nymph (sizes 12-16), for example, remains a sentimental favorite, although I discovered long ago that simple all-fur nymphs made of dark hare's ear and soft hackle patterns perform just as well, perhaps better. Then, living in the Catskills as I do, I must confess, too, a soft spot for traditional Light Hendrickson and Red Quill dry flies, which I suggest serve to underscore my point of view, since neither bears much resemblance to the natural after which it was conceived long ago. Not uncharacteristically, though, I'm sure, my favorite "Hendrickson" dry fly pattern now turns out to be a Sidewinder (sizes 12-16) designed to imitate the *Callibaetis* of the Henry's Fork in Idaho.

On rivers flush with Hendrickson hatches, other mayfly emergences of significance are easy to neglect or to miss altogether. Near my home, for instance, hatches of Quill Gordons, Blue-winged Olives and Paraleps frequently dovetail with those of the Hendrickson. The job of coping successfully with such situations calls for one fly pattern that "looks like nothing but looks like everything," so to speak. My choice, without reservation, is the old reliable Adams (sizes 12-18), the best all-round dun imitation ever conceived.

Multiple hatches alone, or multiple hatches dovetailing with single or multiple species spinner falls, sometimes produce situations in which our beloved Hendrickson diminishes in status or is actually shunned by the main force of a stream's hungry trout. Time and again I've seen fish pass up emerging Hendrickson duns in

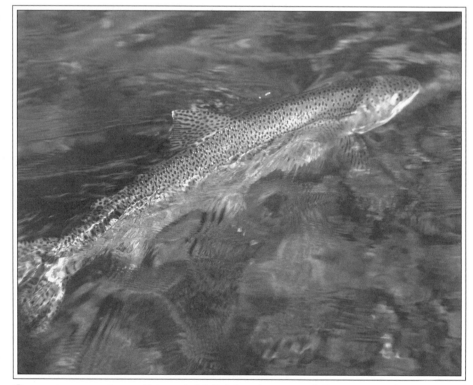

On waters such as this, sight-fishing is one of the great pleasures of Hendrickson time. With a practiced eye, you can spot the camouflaged trout lying over the bottom, present your fly carefully and watch a trout such as this one rise to take—or sometimes refuse—your offering. While I like to catch fish, so pretty is the overall picture that it doesn't break my heart when a trout makes me work over it a while before it finally latches 'hold.

favor of smaller Paralep spinners, for instance. The explanation, I'm certain, is that spent spinners constitute a "sure thing" to trout, while to feed on duns is at best a hit-or-miss proposition. Then, too, a crowd of anglers continuously putting mock Hendricksons over fish that inhabit a short stretch of water tends to put off those trout and redirect their interest to what we call "feeding selectively" on, say, the Paraleps, or if not, on some other insect species the fishermen have made no attempt to mimic. It's my rule, therefore, to fish a fly that covers as many bases as possible at once.

During concurrent emergences of Red Quills (males) and Hendricksons (females), for example, conventional strategy dictates that you use a Red Quill imitation one size larger than your bogus Hendrickson as you alternate back and forth between the two patterns. Since I've often observed Hendrickson males larger than females and females larger than males all coming off at the same hour of the same day on the same water, I have little faith in this strategy, which although neat and tidy for textbooks, perhaps, is in my view incompatible with stream ecology as it really is, while it limits an angler's capacity to get the most from his fly. Given the luxury of simultaneous Red Quill and Hendrickson hatches, normally I opt to fish a Red Quill *decidedly smaller* than the Hendrickson naturals on the water, since my experience has proven that by doing so, not only do I show an acceptable Red Quill to the fish, but I fool some trout with a taste for Paralep duns as well.

The first step toward matching a Hendrickson hatch is, of course, to catch a hatch, which unless you live on a trout stream, is usually more dodgey than you're led to believe by us writers. Emergence charts found in books and magazines ought to be perceived only as guidelines in the most general sense, not to be trusted when any firsthand source of intelligence is available. The fact is that no hatch is predictable. I have known Hendricksons to show two weeks early and two weeks late here on the Beaverkill and throughout the Catskills region. And the Catskills are no exception. One season to my surprise I found myself fishing a Hendrickson hatch on a balmy Easter Sunday. Another year I struck Hendricksons on Memorial Day. So there you have it. Not neat but true.

Nor should you rely on the Hendrickson to emerge according to a timetable once the annual hatches have gotten underway. While Hendricksons frequently do come off for a couple of hours each afternoon as customarily advertised, both morning and evening hatches are also normal in my experience, as are intermittent emergences that evolve at intervals throughout the day. Most common of all examples of unorthodox timing, though, has proven to be a midday hatch that is followed by a lengthy lull and another emergence that commences as late as 6 P.M. This evening emergence then proceeds without interruption until dusk and occasionally dark.

Ditto, Hendricksons have demonstrated themselves to be little more aware of clocks as spinners than they are as duns. Evening spinner falls predominate, of course, but I've also encountered falls of major proportions at all times of day, notably mornings in the wake of unseasonably cold nights. To underestimate the significance of the Hendrickson spinner is a terrible error in my opinion, particularly if you like to test yourself against the trout of flat water. Be that as it may, I've brought more *large trout* to steel over the years while using Hendrickson spinners than I've taken on dun and emerger imitations combined.

Now, I wonder if each reader might do me one favor and try to think of this chapter as a letter from a friend. You see, truth be known, I'm stuck as to how to end it, that old car won't turn over again, and I've got to come up with a way to get out of this artfully. So, for now please accept all my best wishes for your plots, your schemes, and yes, for all the new Hendrickson patterns you're sure to turn out between now and the next time we meet, either literally or figuratively, astream.

CHAPTER 21

The One, the Only Green Drake

The Green Drake (*Ephemera guttulata*) is the aristocrat of eastern mayflies. Throughout its life cycle fly fishermen view it as grand, elegant, even regal. Whereas other aquatic insects are routinely regarded in terms of numbers, the Green Drake somehow manages to maintain a distinct identity, even when it synchronizes its emergences with thousands, even millions, of other Green Drakes or later returns as the spinner we call the Coffin Fly.

As an individual, the Green Drake is uniquely impressive, evoking strong emotions in anglers and writers alike. We say a Green Drake "bursts through the surface" to emerge. Its wings "stir the air." It "arouses the best in trout." Even the demise of a Green Drake spinner after its unbridled lust in the air is perceived as some kind of tragic theater. And it is that Coffin Fly, lest we forget, that "brings up every fish in the river."

Objectively speaking, however, a case can be made that the Green Drake is just another aquatic insect of varying significance from region to region or stream to stream. The drake hatches and spinner falls of Pennsylvania's Penns Creek, for example, highlight the season, while those of Schoharie Creek, a Catskills stream, wouldn't have been missed at all by that river's once legendary dean Art Flick. I've never fished Penns Creek, but I remember a day on the Schoharie with Art when I declined one of the master's Gray Fox Variants in favor of banging around with a Coffin Fly. That Art knocked 'em dead, while this Art went down in flames.

Though that day clearly illustrated that "youth is wasted on the young," Green Drake hatches during intervening seasons have treated me respectably, especially once I'd learned to take some orthodox notions about the insect with a

179

grain of salt. For example, I learned never to hang my hat on a Green Drake hatch or Coffin Fly spinner fall. Both are singularly unpredictable from river to river and even pool to pool. Then, once hatches do commence, they are typically of short duration, seldom continuing for more than one week. Just to track Green Drake emergences in progress, therefore, obliges that you be a hound with a helluva sense of smell.

A stream's initial Green Drake emergences, in my experience, are fitful and scattered and thus easy to miss unless you diligently monitor trout feeding behavior as the appropriate period approaches. During the waning days of March Brown hatches on the Beaverkill one season, for example, I observed some explosive rises clearly out of keeping with the norm for that time. Stoneflies, of course, came to mind. Yet, those curious rises evoked a sort of *déjà vu* that gave me a hunch. The titanic Green Drake emerger prompted by the hunch turned out to be right on. Yet I didn't see a natural Green Drake emerge until *two days later*.

My slant on Green Drake hatches, Coffin Fly spinner falls and how to negotiate them successfully is decidedly unconventional and is likely to prove somewhat controversial.

Green Drake hatches and Coffin Fly spinner falls do, in fact, tend to bring up trout seldom if ever seen during any other time of the season. The reason, of course, is the size of the insect and how well it accommodates the natural programming of trout to obtain maximum nourishment for minimum energy expended. This big Beaverkill brown, taken on a Green Drake, had not a single hook scar although it lived smack in the middle of one of the river's two No Kill areas. This would suggest that except during Green Drake time, the fish was probably a nocturnal feeder.

First, my experience contradicts the tidy proposition that drakes generally emerge sporadically throughout the day while Coffin Flies mate and fall toward evening. By trucking myself from stretch to stretch, pool to pool, I've connected with concentrated hatches morning, noon and night, day after day. Once when thoroughly confused by insufficient hatches to account for the number of returning spinners, I tried sleeping by day and exploring by night until I caught the devils sneaking off between three and five in the morning.

Similarly, I've known Coffin Flies to fall in numbers at 4 A.M., just as at 8 P.M., a more conventional hour. The riddle of twilight flights that disappear for no apparent reason or those that are driven from the river by impending storms can

Beauty is certainly in the eye of the beholder, because to most eyes, I'm sure, this image would represent nothing more than an ugly scum full of flotsam (or is it jetsam?) along a riverbank, but to me and other experienced Eastern fly fishers, it is an astounding sight of the remnants of the previous night's Coffin Fly spinner fall—which sure was a *beauty*. After last light on rivers such as the Delaware River's Upper Main Stem, trout by the hundreds can be heard slurping these spread-eagled bugs in every backwater, and to say it's impressive is the ultimate understatement to be sure.

sometimes be reconciled by the falls that occur during the wee small hours. Nor should anglers neglect late morning to mid-afternoon falls, common in the Catskills anyway, on overcast days with a light drizzle falling.

It's also helpful to know that Green Drake hatches and spinner falls aren't isolated to the flat, silty stretches of most streams. Although the nymph is a burrower, it seems up to burrowing into any patch of fine gravel, the velocity and turbulence of flow notwithstanding. Time and again I've enjoyed fine drake fishing on pocket water where not only were naturals plentiful and other anglers seldom seen, but where trout tended to forgive my technical errors. Trout on flats, by contrast, exhibit a niggling ability to discriminate between naturals and imitations, particularly should the imitation be poorly presented.

Likewise, Coffin Flies are pleased to oviposit virtually anywhere handy, certainly when lots of them are in the air. One rainy afternoon I watched thousands deposit their eggs *on the road* that parallels the Beaverkill. Granted this phenomenon may be rare; but it is not unique. Thus to net your full measure of sport from each spinner fall, don't write off any stretch that harbors big trout, regardless of surface character.

My chief misgivings about traditional Green Drake angling strategy involve how flies should be fished during drake hatches, or indeed whether *hatching* Green

Green Drake dun. (For color markings, see color insert, figure 8).

Drakes should concern the practical fly fisherman much at all. Who first conceived the presumption that Green Drake emergers are of marginal interest to feeding trout, I haven't a clue, although I suspect he must have sided with the fish. I've found the theory that emerging Green Drake nymphs swim too fast to constitute a viable food source for hungry trout, to be so patently inaccurate as to be unworthy of any more ink.

Violent rises can be the tip-off to fish feeding on natural Green Drake emergers, a common, even daily, occurrence once the drake has begun to hatch with regularity. What's more, I've discovered that given the option, trout tend to *prefer* emerger patterns to all dun imitations with which I'm familiar.

And why shouldn't they? The Green Drake is a large insect, meaning that relatively few are required to make a meal. To chase Green Drake emergers, therefore, particularly in shallow water, is in keeping with a trout's instinct to obtain maximum food for minimum energy expended. An emerging Green Drake swims no faster than a fleeing sucker or minnow, and more pertinent still, the emerging drake swims to the surface with a predictable trajectory.

Trout are very fast swimmers, and given highly visible targets such as Green Drake emergers, aren't likely to miss so often that the exercise is rendered futile. Then, whereas floating duns may leave the surface instantly and thus be lost to risers, trout reap the benefit of the emerger's swim-up time, plus the time required for the insects to get off the water. Remember, most duns you observe on the surface were emergers just seconds ago.

This affinity for emergers works to your advantage as an angler, since the speed at which you can swim an imitation with confidence compromises a trout's capacity to inspect your pattern. Thus, while you may be limited to drag-free, dead drift floats when fishing duns, no such inhibition applies to presenting emergers. Similarly, I've found that to impart a little action to a Coffin Fly imitation—to mimic the futile effort of the natural to fly again before expiring as already discussed in previous chapters—tends to make your fly more attractive than one that floats dead drift.

With the annual appearance of the drake comes one of those rare periods during which you might have to be as particular about each fly you choose to present as you normally are about presentation technique. Most trout, notably big ones, are liable to ignore or reject Green Drake imitations not consistent with prevailing naturals, given time to look them over. Our worry no doubt derives from the size of the insect species, which makes suitable renderings difficult to turn out, even for proficient tyers.

The key is to forsake precise representation in favor of designs that create the *impression* of natural Green Drake nymphs, emergers, duns and spinners. Then, bearing in mind that the naturals vary in size from large to gigantic, your flies should be dressed on the small side in order to minimize obvious flaws in each pattern and thus to limit the fish's potential to scrutinize any shortcomings. Truth is, I've attracted many more trout to modest size 12 drake imitations than to hefty size 8s of the same or similar patterns.

Indeed, one of the curiosities of Green Drake emergences on my home waters is the eagerness with which some large trout take, for instance, small Adams even though the surface of the stream is cloaked with, say, helpless Coffin Flies. A five and a half-pound brown that jumped all over a size 16 Adams at the height of such a spinner fall on the Delaware is a perfect case in point. This trout disdained the best I could offer in a spinner, although I had observed the fish feeding on natural Coffin Flies at a remarkable rate. The "why" of this behavior frankly escapes me even now. But the upshot is that I'm as likely to try an Adams or Goddard Caddis (sizes 12-16) first during Green Drake time as to test the waters with a drake pattern I had a hand in originating.

The old saying that 90 percent of the trout are taken by 10 percent of the anglers could have been inspired by observing fish and fishermen during Green Drake emergences. Fact is that despite the mystique surrounding this mayfly species, few anglers do very well while drakes are abundant and fewer still connect regularly with the trout they're after—those real "tortugas" you seldom see at any other time during the season.

To take good trout on Green Drakes requires a *plan* carried out with meticulous attention. Don't let ravenous feeding behavior, for instance, dupe you into presuming that large fish aren't wary when the drake is on. The task is to approach each trout and to present each fly so as not to trigger selectivity likely to sabotage the pulling power of your best offering. Off-guard, a trout may climb all over, say, a White Wulff, a marginal Green

Leave it to the late Lee Wulff, the ultimate predator, to come up with one of the best Green Drake emerger imitations even when that wasn't first on his agenda while conceiving the fly. I refer to the yellow-bodied Lee Wulff Stonefly I used to catch this fish. Seems to make no difference whether the yellow, molded plastic body is topped with a brown, olive or white deer tail wing, there's something about this fly fished either dead drift or skimmed just beneath the surface that sparks strikes so hard by Green Drake-feeding trout that they almost pull the rod out of your hand.

Drake representation at best, while made suspicious, the same fish will refuse the most intricate drake pattern ever conceived though continuing to feed on the naturals.

For fishing Green Drake imitations, I like a powerful rod and fast line, i.e., a graphite 9-footer tapered so that the weight is back from the tip, and a WF5F line. This combination gives me not only the distance and line-driving potential I require, but also the capacity to turn over the long leaders and extremely long tippets (sometimes 15 feet-plus) sometimes integral to drake presentation techniques. The tippet, incidentally, should be soft but strong and of the finest diameter compatible with drake patterns you fish. Rarely do I use a tippet heavier than 5X, while 6X, though somewhat inclined to curl and twist, best performs when my chief concern is a dragless drift.

To extend your options for presentation technique, regardless of the stage of the prevailing naturals, I suggest you try to present to target trout in a generally across and downstream direction about 50 degrees below an imaginary point directly opposite your position. Such an approach will enable you to obtain a desired drag-free dead drift float—by casting an exaggerated mend into your line and leader or by inducing numerous "S's" into your line, leader and tippet, both devices entirely in keeping with conventional dry fly fishing strategy, or by "piling up" your leader and a long tippet so your fly is carried downstream to the target while the mess of monofilament behind it is being straightened out by the currents. This refinement is effective but requires plenty of practice.

The downstream presentation also permits you to swim or skitter your fly on a taut line, as typical of wet fly fishing, by twitching the rod tip or by initiating little line mends by rotating your wrist gently in an upstream direction. Then, too, when all else fails, you can even take advantage of this approach to flash your fly over or in front of a trout's nose by stripping line as for a retrieve.

The Green Drake is special for its capacity to show us big trout, and we shouldn't look such a gift horse in the mouth. All too briefly each season—beginning without apparent logic any time from the last week in May through the second week in June in the Catskills where I live—anglers lucky enough to hit it are best advised to ignore all small fish, no matter how tempting, in favor of "head-hunting." In other words, make each cast count. The commotion caused by hooking and playing but one small trout tends to increase the odds against fooling a big fish, if not by putting the big fish down, then by making it aware of your presence, more cautious and so much more difficult to catch. Remind yourself often that this is a Green Drake hatch you're fishing and small trout aren't what the Green Drake is about.

No doubt some readers have waded upstream through this chapter in hopes of reaching a comprehensive Green Drake emergence schedule for their region, if not for their favorite fishery. I regret that such a job is far beyond my experience, or inclination. That others have tried, I know. And yet, judging by the findings as they have related to the waters of my area, such undertakings have proven totally futile. Green Drake hatches are simply too fickle for a convenient timetable. Which leaves you with but one alternative—to wit, find a *reliable* on-the-scene source of extremely specific, day-to-day information and send him a bottle of 18-year-old single malt each Christmas.

FROM THE GRAVE TO THE CRADLE

Affixed in Walt Dette's own vise, Kris photographed this copy of the original Coffin Fly that Walter dressed for me some years ago (see color insert, figure 11). Note the hackle-tip wings that were later changed to tinted teal to more closely imitate the veins in the natural's wings. But otherwise the pattern has remained the same and has been used with great success since the day it was concocted. Mary Dette Clark, daughter of legends Walt and Winnie and one of the nicest and most gifted folks in the fly fishing field, continues to tie hundreds of these flies for customers each year in the little shop in the front room of the Dette house on Cottage Street in Roscoe, New York.

This yarn begins early one morning in June 1932 when a guy by the name of Ted Townsend, a game warden from Westchester County outside New York City, approached the late and great Walt Dette at the old Riverview Inn with a fly Ted had scooped off the surface of the Beaverkill during the previous evening's fishing. Could Walt, Ted wanted to know, concoct a suitable imitation? In his 20s then, Walter regarded the fly, a prodigious white spinner with wings etched with black veins, and suggested that they retire to his tying room one floor up to see what they could do.

These were the darkest days of the Great Depression and Walt and Winnie, his wife, were struggling against all odds to make a go of the Riverview, which in better times had belonged to Winnie's parents, Mr. and Mrs. Edwin Ferdon. They were enjoying very good fishing that year. It was to be the summer tourist season later that would kill them. But for now, there were lots of rising trout and good hatches and guests who fished hard—maybe to forget or to remember—and who buzzed late into the night about the newest flies and tackle as though reality didn't lie in wait for them when they got back to the city.

Townsend was an imposing figure with dark hair and a ruddy complexion. He spent a lot of time, on and off, at the inn during the season, and now he grabbed his usual chair and sidled it up alongside Walter behind Walt's tying table. He would have to break away shortly, Ted told Walt, because he had to go to a funeral. How he dreaded funerals, Ted surely grunted as we all do, and Walter surely nodded that he felt the same way. Walt had already chosen a large Allcock dry fly hook, had set it firmly in his vise, and now was scrutinizing the natural insect which they'd laid out in front of them on the table.

Ted chatted idly about things in general, while Walt thumbed carefully through materials in search of just the right makings. Maybe Ted reported that Cory Ford and Bill Shaldach had already gone out fishing. He certainly repeated that he wasn't looking forward to this funeral one bit. Walter no doubt sympathized again and told him not to worry, that once they'd agreed upon a pattern, he'd have a half-dozen for him to try when he got back from the village. A buck and a half, less cost of materials, of course, wasn't bad money for a half-dozen dries back in 1932. Soon enough Walt and Winnie would be turning out wholesale flies at $1.25 per dozen.

After considerable experimentation the new fly emerged. It was going to be, both men agreed, a legitimate "lulu." It had black hackle-tip wings, a lemon wood duck tail, a sleek body of cream seal's fur and ample badger hackle. Walter removed the brainchild from his vise and held it up for Ted's closer inspection. Now, together, they looked it over every which way—into the light, away from the light, and so on—from top to bottom. With some ceremony, they parked it on the table next to the natural. The natural was beginning to shrivel. They suspended their creation at a decent elevation and dropped it to the tabletop, once, twice, three times. What was a dry fly, for goodness' sake, if it wouldn't cock for you when it lit on the surface?

In short, I reckon it's fair to assume that those two were verily flushed with pride of invention. And I guess that on this morning they did about everything you can do indoors with a fly pattern, except that is, to *name it*.

At some point during the fandango, Ted Townsend must have plucked his watch from his pocket, suddenly recalling his obligation to the deceased and his survivors, and announced that he had to be off but would be back soon. After seeing him to the door, Walter returned to his tying table. He was alone and a budding ritual of tidiness that endured in Walt for his entire life then occupied him until his supply of unneeded materials was again properly reposed in their proper niches. Only then could he finally contemplate the new fly through his most critical eye—the best eye, by the way, I have ever known.

Perhaps there was something curiously unsettling about the new pattern. Not that Walter perceived anything wanting in it as a practical fishing fly. It would be some years yet before he would change the black hackle-tip wings to barred teal. No, this was something quite different, something to be sensed rather than seen, certainly not something to be recognized by a busy youth of 24 who had to turn to now and crank out a fast half-dozen. Walt Dette dressed Ted Townsend's flies.

Townsend returned to the Riverview in a couple of hours. No doubt he felt like he needed a drink or a nap, or both. Instead, however, he changed back into his well-worn fishing clothing as quickly as he could, leaving his dark suit, white shirt and black tie draped carelessly over a wooden hanger. Then he left his room and started down the hall.

The flies were received by Ted in a small cardboard box, the inside walls and bottom of which were gray, the shade of thin cloud masking the moon. Townsend lifted the lid, peered into the box and then looked up at Walt. There was a distant, almost haunted expression, in his eyes and he didn't smile. Walt glanced down into the box, too, thinking perhaps that something was wrong. The flies lay there in the bottom, waxy pale and still. It took Walt but an instant to understand.

It will never be established for certain who of these two in the moments that followed was first to commit the name *Coffin Fly* to the permanent history of American fly fishing. Walt, until his dying day, liked to think that it had to be Townsend who was so inspired. Ted, after all, had just come back from a funeral. Yet, anyone lucky enough to have known Walt Dette knows that absolute integrity was essential to his character. To defer rather than to doubt or be doubted was to Walter instinctive. Be that as it may, however, there remains one indisputable fact concerning the doings that day at the old Riverview Inn. To wit, Walter C. Dette conceived and dressed the first Coffin Fly ever to carry that handle.

Coffin Fly. (For color markings, see figure 10 in the color insert.)

A TRIO OF GREEN DRAKE EMERGERS

Each of the Green Drake emergers featured here was designed to create an *impression* of a hatching natural and thereby to enhance an angler's presentations to feeding trout. The flies are illustrated as dressed by Galen Mercer. As noted in the accompanying text, they were conceived by committee, so to speak, and were dressed intentionally scruffy in the best tradition of Mike Kimball of Ithaca, New York, the finest all-round fly fisherman I have ever known. In the instance of the high-wing pattern, the wing silhouette and breathing gills of philo plume are intended to serve much the same impressionist purpose as the overall scruffiness of the other two patterns.

Despite entomological assertions to the contrary, we, that is, Mercer, Kimball (educated in entomology at Cornell University), the late Ken Miyata, a professional biologist, and I, observed undeniable variations among individual insects during the daily Green Drake emergence process. Some naturals we found to literally burst from their shucks and so we imitated them with our snowshoe rabbit's fur pattern. The wings of other naturals we saw appear while the nymphs were still intact; hence our high-wing emerger. Then others still we watched emerge from their shucks and ride them awhile before finally trailing the shucks behind them still attached to their bodies. Our trailing shuck pattern covers that alternative nicely.

Each pattern has proven *extremely effective*, although in all candor we remain unable to predict accurately which among the three will perform best on a given day or, indeed, on a given fish. Therefore, I suggest that readers obtain a supply of each and not hesitate to switch regularly during days astream. Here's how they are tied.

High-Wing Green Drake Emerger (also see color insert, figure 9)

Hook: Number 4-10 (TDE, fine wire, 2X-4X long), i.e., Mustad 94831

Thread: Tan 6/0 pre-waxed nylon

Tail: A small bunch of lemon wood duck feathers tied extremely short

Overlay: Tannish poly-yarn pulled forward as a wing case but from the bend of the hook

Rib: Tan monocord

Gills: A single philo plume from a ringneck pheasant or ruffed grouse body feather pulled forward as in a wing case but from the bend of the hook

Abdomen: Cream fur dubbing

Wing Case: Section of grouse tail split down the middle after tying in (Note: the wing case is lacquered when the fly is completed)

Wing: Matched pair of thin lemon wood duck strips tinted pale olive and set back at a 45-degree angle over the hook shank

Thorax: Cream fur and hare's mask blend, either spun and clipped top and bottom or dubbed and picked out to represent legs

Trailing Shuck Green Drake Emerger (also see color insert, figure 9)

Hook: Number 10-12 (TDE, fine wire) i.e., Partridge Capt. Hamilton Dry Fly L3A

Thread: Tan 6/0 pre-waxed nylon

Trailing Shuck: Combed out creamish sparkle yarn 1 1/2 times the hook length topped with a few fibers of lemon wood duck and a small bunch of short, tannish marabou tied in at the bend of the hook

Abdomen:	Short section of dubbed cream fur (i.e., red fox)
Wing Case:	Light olive tinted barred teal or lemon wood duck, tied humped and prominent
Legs:	Medium dun hackle wound and clipped top and bottom
Thorax:	Dark hare's mask dubbed loosely and full
Head:	Cream fur dubbing (i.e., red fox) tapered forward toward the hook eye and affixed to the hook with tying thread

The wing case is formed by taking a barred teal or lemon wood duck feather and stripping off the downy material near its butt. The feather is then placed concave side down with the butt of the quill pointing toward the rear of the hook. The quill is then secured on top of the hook with two loose turns of tying thread. The length of feather required to form the wing case is then pulled carefully through these loose turns of thread toward the rear of the hook. When this is achieved, the feather is secured tightly with tying thread and the excess feather in front of the thread is clipped away.

Usual Green Drake Emerger

Hook:	Number 4-10 (TDE, fine wire, 2X-4X long), i.e., Mustad 94831
Thread:	Light olive 6/0 pre-waxed nylon
Shuck:	Large bunch of cream snowshoe rabbit's foot hair tied in as for a tail

Tail:	A few fibers of lemon wood duck tied long and over the shuck
Abdomen:	Light olive and cream fur blend dubbing tied slim
Wing Case:	Barred teal or lemon wood duck tinted light olive and tied in as for the Trailing Shuck Green Drake Emerger described above
Upper Thorax:	Cream snowshoe rabbit's foot hair tinted light olive and tied upright as for a Haystack pattern, then split and splayed by pulling the wing case over the top
Lower Thorax:	Light olive and cream fur blend dubbed loosely
Head:	Light olive and cream fur blend dubbing, tapered forward toward the hook eye and affixed to the hook with tying thread

Chapter header

CHAPTER 22

The Usual
With a Twist

What could be better than a fly that "looks like nothing but looks like everything?" The Usual, originated by Francis Betters, dean of New York's Ausable River, and named by the late Bill Phillips, a gadder from Ontario, is such a fly. The answer? A fly that "looks like anything and looks like everything." With minor modification, the Usual is also *that* fly .

The prototype Usual was a master stroke typical of Betters—as simple as a small tuft of wiry hair and underfur from a snowshoe rabbit's foot for the tail; a larger shock of same splayed for the wing, and some dubbed underbody for the body. To hear Francis tell it, he was inspired by a rabbit's foot that had "wiggled" to the top of the ubiquitous clutter on his tying table. But his remarkable sixth sense also had to divine that feet that hop around on Adirondack snow must be possessed of material consistent with dry flies that *float*.

I obtained my first Usual not from Francis, but from Phillips at streamside on the Ausable so long ago now I can't begin to recall just when it was. He and Francis had begun to vary the Usual's body colors by then. This was a size 16 Olive. I still have the fly and until quite recently when I retired it, fished it religiously once a year even though the scruffy thing had stung at least 50 trout. It never let me down.

Even without modification, the Usual is an impressionist's dream. To trout eyes it would appear to capture an instant of opportunity. Presentation notwithstanding, the pattern seems to suggest what a trout *wants to see*, alive or dead, i.e., a floating dun, a stillborn emerger, or if sunk, a struggling emerger, drowned dun or stillborn, or maybe a nymph. Moreover, the Usual's buoyancy permits you to dunk the fly, then to refloat it as an emerger, either slowly by relaxing line tension or suddenly by raising your rod tip or drawing line.

During my Henry's Fork baptismal years ago, I recall a hatch of some kind was expected. So, before fanning out, my hosts Jack Hemingway and Fred Arbona schooled me on what to expect. Then they gave me a fistful of nymph, emerger and dun patterns to use as the emergence progressed. Someplace I must still have those flies, too, for they never got wet. I fished a small Usual throughout the hatch and hooked more nice rainbows than any greenhorn had a right to. Usuals remain my best bet for the Henry's Fork and other western spring creeks to this day.

However, experience has also taught me that the basic Usual's effectiveness owes at least as much to ingredient as design. Conceptually, the pattern is an extension of the deer hair Haystack Betters conceived in 1949. Though Francis has never received credit commensurate with his achievements, his Haystack was really the precedent for all no-hackle dries evolved during the next 40 years. So the first Usuals were tied not really to herald a new idea, but to reconcile the pelage of the snowshoe rabbit's foot to an ideal already tried and true.

For a lot of years now, Galen Mercer and I have refined and expanded Better's initiative, much as Francis developed his Ausable Wulff using Lee Wulff's work as a point of departure. Specifically, we have sought to discover precisely what makes the Usual click, then to key our findings to characteristic angling situations by adjusting the basic pattern. We also wanted to square our principles to practical hatch-matching and thus provide impressionist means to take problem trout. Our results have surpassed expectations.

We quickly concluded that the Usual is a *better* fly than the Haystack and other hair-winged no-hackles. The Usual routinely takes fish when a Haystack won't, but a Haystack seldom takes fish when the Usual won't. Forgive the allusion, please: that's the "bottom line."

We've dressed Usuals in sizes 8-28 and found them uniformly effective. We've fished them throughout the East and West, as well as in Argentina and northern Iceland. Placing them with regulars on far-flung waters from the tarns of Tasmania to the chalkstreams of France and Great Britain drew ecstatic reviews. However, the acid test was passing them out to anglers stumped by tricky periods on

With the original Usual dressing as originated by Francis Betters at center, our adaptations (clockwise from top) are: the Hendrickson Usual, Red Quill Usual, March Brown Usual, Olive Usual and Sulphur Usual. Each has become the staple of our fishing strategy during these emergences on Catskills waters during the season. (Also see color insert, figure 12.)

nearby Catskills streams. Each subsequently solicited either the patterns or sources from which to obtain these (supply your own synonym for "incredible") flies.

The difference is clearly the rabbit's foot fur, a more responsive and expressive material than deer hair. Snowshoe rabbit's foot fur is translucent, while deer hair is decidedly opaque. Deer hair is straight and stiff; snowshoe rabbit is frizzy and supple. Coarseness, plus high oil content, makes snowshoe rabbit *far* more buoyant than deer hair. Thus it can retain considerable water without sinking. *How* retained water serves to enhance the Usual's appearance is most interesting, too.

A Usual's wing contains countless chambers and passages, each bounded by fibers that repel water naturally. Some water runs off, but that retained actually stretches within the chambers, approximating the principle of a bubble pipe. This water, then, becomes part of the wing, creating sparkle and sheen, often peaking a Usual's effectiveness only after it has been soaked or has taken several trout.

A deer hair wing, by contrast, is a victim of gravity. Being linear,

Just desserts for a guy as close to me as a brother, Jack Manes of North Salem, New York. The trout Jack is hefting is the largest (at 7 pounds) I've ever seen taken from the Beaverkill on a dry fly. It took a beautifully presented March Brown Usual curiously enough at midday. Another one of those trout, by the way, that although it was caught in a No Kill section, had no hook scars in evidence, meaning that until this day, it must have fed mostly at night. Of course, Jack released the trout, but we never saw it feeding on top again. Great guy, great fish.

water simply runs down the fibers to the body. What's more, because deer hair is hollow, permeating water is trapped inside, explaining the frustration of trying to float sodden deer hair flies. Deer hair, therefore, constrains you to tying with buoyant body materials, greasing your flies and changing flies regularly.

The Usual imposes no such constraints. Thus, dressing flies as true elements of strategy is unfettered by compromise. Body materials normally reserved for wets and nymphs can be employed with impunity, whether dubbed very loosely or very tightly. Wings can be tall or short, sparse or full, slim or wide, to meet specific angling problems. Options are limited only by insight.

So, "if it ain't broke, why fix it?" Our modifications presume to do no such thing. Rather, they affirm the Usual's potential by getting just a bit more from an already great thing.

Variations using snowshoe rabbit for buoyancy and to enhance a lifelike appearance. (From left, beginning at top) Trailing Shuck Caddis Emerger, Caddis Ovipositor with rabbit tied into the body and just behind the wing, a Brassy with a sprig of rabbit near the head, and a Griffith's Gnat-type midge with rabbit fore and aft. All have proven decidedly more effective than conventional dressings of similar patterns.

The modifications have taken three forms: (1) simple adjustments of color and silhouette though retaining the essential Usual dressing; (2) considerable structural alterations while preserving the Usual's character; (3) application of snowshoe rabbit's foot fur to unrelated pattern concepts.

At first we altered only body colors to correspond to specific hatches. Then we began tinting wings and tails so they too approximated prevailing insects. For example, a Hendrickson Usual was given a pinkish tan body, dun wing and tail, a Red Quill a dun wing and tail and rusty brown body. Thus we gained an edge, particularly where trout are pounded, without altering the Usual's form.

However, we still wanted to ascertain precisely what was triggering the response. Feeding behavior, including rise forms, suggested that our Usuals were perceived as emergers or stillborns when floating low, duns when floating high. So next we sought to reinforce those perceptions by fine-tuning profile.

With the work of Vince Marinaro in mind, duns got tall, slim wings, coupled with buoyant, poly-blend bodies. We also abandoned rabbit's foot tails now and then in favor of hackle fibers split in the manner of no-hackle dries. Our Sulphur Usual is a good example. Finally, sometimes we mixed a few fibers (e.g., wood duck) into our fur wings to further enhance the impression. Each new touch has paid off.

Emergers, by contrast, generally got low, full wings and short tails. Body silhouettes were more nymphlike than those of duns, approximating the appearance of natural species. For example, our Baetis Usual Emerger bodies were short and squat, while their Paralep counterpart was long and lean.

Results, though positive, raised another intriguing question. Why should wary trout feeding on, for instance, Sulphurs, like a yellow orange emerger pattern when the natural emerger was decidedly brown? Observation demonstrated more adult-colored stillborns than we had supposed. These lifeless forms in the film represented easy pickings and suggested the root appeal of our honey-toned Usuals. So we began alternating dead drift with subtle, swimming presentations and found that the former, consistent with the stillborns, far outperformed the latter, consistent with a true emerger.

True emergers came next. First we tried dark hare's ear bodies. The flies worked well. But why a wing? It functioned as a trigger, we know. However, that didn't explain what the trout sees. So we asked ourselves wouldn't it be more consistent with natural emergers if the "wing" wasn't being seen as a wing at all, but as a dun's head and thorax exiting the nymph's shuck? Pulling the trigger, then, proved as simple as tinting the wing the color of the emerging dun's head and body rather than of its wings. Or in the instance of our brown-bodied Sulphur Emerger, yellow orange instead of neutral tan.

Really smelling blood now, we contrived numerous impressionistic nymphal patterns, each punctuated by a tuft of tinted rabbit's foot bursting through a split wingcase. This represented our first appreciable departure from the pure Usual design. Though tied on dry fly hooks to ride higher, each silhouette featured a conspicuous abdomen and thorax consistent with a specific genus or species of natural nymph. Size and color also conformed to emerging naturals.

The natural color of snowshoe rabbit's foot ranges from off-white to dusky tan. Consequently, no tinting is required for Usuals imitating cream mayflies, such as Potamanthus, the Light Cahills and some Sulphurs. Occasionally we do find "freak" feet to cover the darker flies, i.e., the Hendrickson or March Brown. More often than not, however, tinting is needed to get the wing, tail or tuft colors just right.

We use indelible Pantone pens in black, gray, golden yellow, auburn and various shades of olive. These colors should suffice for the flies of most regions. We buy each color in both chisel-tip and fine points, the former for tinting on the foot, the latter for on-stream touch-up. For best results, tint the fur 24 hours before you plan to fish the flies. Even then colors will tend to fade, requiring touch-up after catching several fish. To do so, however, is preferable to dyeing the fur, as the dyeing process removes oils critical to float.

If the Usual strain has a drawback, it is difficulty in obtaining snowshoe rabbit feet. In part this issues from few anglers having recognized the material's value in the past and thus now is turning around as demand has increased. So far we've found no viable substitute, though, despite repeated tries. Western jackrabbit is fair. Flies look similar but lack essential buoyancy. Unfortunately, common cottontail is useless for Usuals: *it sinks like a rock*.

However, the range of the snowshoe rabbit, or varying hare, is vast and the species is widely hunted. Snowshoes are found throughout the Northeast, the highlands of the middle Atlantic states, the upper Midwest, the Rockies and the Far West, including the high country of northeastern California. The species also inhabits every province of Canada and most of Alaska. Most feet we've used have come from New York's Adirondacks, although the *best* were received from a friend in Colorado. My advice is to lobby tyers and materials distributors to obtain supplies from hunters and game clubs. Most people habitually discard feet when cleaning rabbits for the pot.

So effective were our Usual mutations that Galen and I ultimately decided to try adapting snowshoe rabbit to established fly concepts apart from the Usual form. On Wulff-like flies, wings of snowshoe rabbit proved more buoyant and translucent than those of traditional bucktail or kip. By either inserting a small tuft of snowshoe rabbit under a hare's ear collar or spinning a collar of snowshoe, trailing shuck caddis emergers required less dense strands of trailing poly to keep them up. (Filmy trailing shucks of reduced poly are most suggestive of life.) Similarly, sparsely dressed caddis ovipositors floated infinitely better with bodies of dubbed snowshoe underfur than with conventional dubbings, including poly blends.

Most significant, however, proved to be incorporating snowshoe rabbit into midge dressings. For instance, an excellent variation of the Griffith's Gnat can be tied with an underbody of snowshoe rabbit dubbing. Or a larval imitation such as the Brassy is improved by winding a few turns of snowshoe rabbit behind the hook eye. The buoyant material causes the forward end of the fly to float in the surface film while the rear hangs suspended in keeping with many *Chiromonidae* naturals.

There's nothing mysterious about techniques commonly employed for fishing Usuals. In fact, because such allure is invested *in* Usuals, they tend to be more forgiving of technical shortcomings than conventional patterns. In a nutshell, go with tactics that perform, given standard dressings and similar circumstances. Fish Hendrickson Usual duns, for example, as you'd fish classic or no-hackle dries during hatches. Ditto Usual emergers as other emergers—Usual stillborns as other stillborns, etc. Ultimately the edge will be manifest in the impression the Usual creates in the trout's eye.

But suppose one wanted to limit patterns to, say, basic Usuals in various sizes and body colors. (Despite all our work, my own inclination at times.) The trick is to know in advance of each presentation what stage of emergence your Usual is to represent at that time and to adjust your presentations accordingly. You may want a high float to imitate a dun, for instance, a low float for an emerger. Dead drift may suggest a dun or stillborn, while imparting action suggests an emerger. Or you may opt for complex offerings, like fishing the Usual as a dead drifting dun early in a presentation, then swimming it through the final stages as an emerger. Given the Usual, limits are imposed only by your skill.

Among essential advantages of all Usuals is that they seldom need greasing. (Exceptions might be the sparsest duns for the highest floats or to keep the soggiest emergers flush to the surface.) You command the level of float, drift or swim by adjusting casting mechanics.

Simply put, floating a Usual is a product of line speed and loop management. Most Usuals can be "snapped" dry with a single false cast by building maximum line speed, then driving the line fore or aft an instant *before* the leader straightens out. Galen, who usually fishes a number 2 weight rod, dries his Usual with an abbreviated power stroke followed by a snappy backcast, begun early. That way the fly is dried in front of him. Using a number 4 weight rod, I prefer a snubbed backcast and compact power stroke, thus drying my fly behind me. By maintaining a tight loop, multiple false casts also dry a Usual. The more false casts, the drier the fly. By contrast, lower floats are attained by opening the loop, retarding line speed and making certain the leader straightens out completely during each false cast. In this instance, fewer false casts mean more water retained by the fly.

Among the reasons that Galen Mercer is such an exceptional fly tier is that he is a tier who spends some time of most days fishing. Regardless of the species sought, there's nothing like experience "where the band plays" as carried to the bench and vise. This experience makes it possible for Galen to relate materials, for instance, to precisely how he wants his flies to behave on or in the water. To believe that a good fly is simply a fly that "looks good" is one of the biggest mistakes many anglers make.

The Usual wasn't exactly named for bar lingo, as many anglers have supposed. But the name is rooted in the answer to a question heard astream as often as "What'llya have?" comes across the mahogany. That question is, "What are you using?" Phillips' straight answer was as old as the best bottle of Scotch. All Galen and I had to add to "the Usual" was that we'd take ours *with a twist*.

THE USUAL AND UN-USUAL

Dressing basic or modified Usuals requires no special skills. Any tyer with a good sense of proportions and understanding of reconciling materials to fly function should find the Usual easy. Usuals are a "rough tie," practical, not pretty. So, if finished flies appear more suitable for frame than fish, better start again.

The key is control. Materials should be chosen and applied according to the specific job you want each Usual to do. Duns should suggest duns, emergers, emergers. High float and low float must also be considered. Pay particular attention to silhouette.

Since the Usual is as much about material as design, we begin by examining the snowshoe rabbit's foot like the one shown below. Feet are typically five to six inches long. The material of interest is located on the bottom of the foot, which for our purposes becomes the top, as feet are easier to work with upside down as shown. The ridge of useful fur has a dense, almost wiry, appearance as opposed to the straight, soft material found elsewhere on the foot.

Rabbit's foot pelage is composed of guard hair and underfur. This material changes in character and length gradually from toe to heel. (See illustration 1.) Typically, the shortest, most translucent material is found near the heel. It is longest about two-thirds of the way from heel to toe (b). The material at the

toe (a) is generally the coarsest and least translucent on a foot. Because it compresses poorly and lacks some luster and buoyancy, avoid it when dressing duns or other high-riding Usuals. It is okay, however, for scraggly, low-floating stillborns and emergers.

Generally, the material found at the toe (a) accommodates hook sizes 12-18, the mid-section (b) sizes 10-16 and the heel section (c) sizes 18-28. However, as the length and density of wings vary from pattern to pattern, e.g., dun to emerger, adjustments are sometimes necessary to match fur to hook size.

For example, how well the fur at the base of the wing compresses is critical to dressing a slender Usual dun. Therefore, the long, relatively fine fur of the middle section (b) is generally best for this purpose. However, given the same hook size, fur from the toe section (a) may do for an emerger with a lower wing if sparkle and high-float aren't essential. Or if translucence and sheen are your top priority, you may opt for the prime fur near the heel.

Snowshoe rabbits' feet are like rooster necks: ideally you keep as many good ones on hand as you can find or afford. Shade and fur length vary somewhat from foot to foot. Carefully utilized, you can get six or seven dozen Usuals from a foot. When buying, look for luster. A small, lustrous foot is bet-

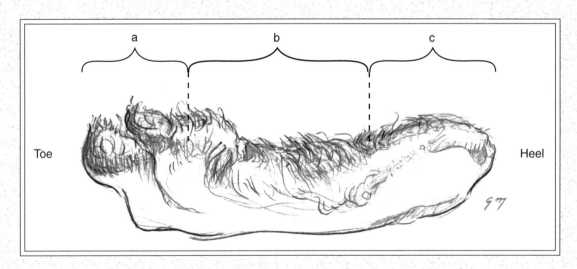

Toe

a b c

Heel

Illustration 1

ter than a large, relatively dull one. The greatest find is a dark, shiny foot, since it enables you to imitate dark wings and tails without tinting.

However, tinting *is* integral to dressing Usuals in a myriad of light and dark shades. *Do not dye snowshoe rabbit. Dyeing removes natural oils critical to float.*

Use Pantone indelible marking pens in the following numbers and colors: No. 583 M and F, greenish olive; No. 404 M and F, gray; No. 136 M and F, yellowish orange; No. 154 M and F, brown; and black M and F. (Black pens aren't designated by number.) The letters M and F designate medium (chisel) and fine points. Use chisel-tips for tinting on the foot, fine points for touch-up, especially astream.

Whenever possible we tint "on the foot" rather than "on the fly." Colors take best and thus hold better when Usuals are baptized. You also avoid discoloring fly bodies, either with stained hands or excess ink. This is particularly important with regard to dark wing light-bodied patterns, such as the Hendrickson dun.

To tint, hold a foot parallel to the floor and using a chisel-point marker, apply ink with a swirling, digging motion. Reverse the foot's direction several times to ensure uniform coverage of guard hairs and underfur.

We normally tint only small areas at a time so we're not restricted to one shade on a good foot. Because some ink always washes away, we tint slightly dark. We also carry fine-tip pens astream for touch-up as needed.

Whether tinted or untinted, the procedure for cutting snowshoe rabbit is the same.

❶ Hold the foot level in front of your face, and using thumbs and forefingers of both hands, separate slightly more fur than you'll need for a wing.

❷ Pinch the material at the base so you feel the bone of the foot.

❸ Using *curved-blade scissors* convex-side down, cut fur lengthwise, or parallel to the foot. (Curved scissors cut flush. Straight blades cut at an angle, causing wasteful, uneven ends.)

Also, don't cut across the foot or the cut will include unwanted, absorbent material from the side of the foot.

❹ Keeping your fingers firmly compressed, withdraw the material you've cut.

Material in hand, now it can be separated into three useful bunches. Pinch all you've cut about two-thirds of the way to the tips of the guard hairs, and relaxing your grip slightly, draw out some soft underfur and fine guard hair. Now, set what's left of the original bunch aside and repeat the procedure with the second bunch, that is, the bunch you've just drawn out. The resulting third bunch should be composed almost entirely of soft underfur. The first bunch, then, can be used as a wing, the second bunch a tail and the third either for winging and tailing tiny Usuals or for dubbing bodies of the original Usual design.

For wings and tails, the fine underfur of the third bunch is somewhat inferior to the short, translucent guard hair and underfur found at the heel. Consequently, it should be used only as a substitute when the real thing is in short supply. Store it in a shallow, flat box where a uniform direction of fur fibers can be maintained.

Now let's apply snowshoe rabbit to dressing Usuals. Following are illustrated tying instructions for three specific patterns: the original Usual, March Brown Usual Dun Emerger and March Brown Usual Emerging Nymph. They are featured, however, not because they are necessarily the most effective patterns with the widest applicability, but because they include *all* procedures essential to dressing an array of Usual variations. Think of them, then, more in terms of method and style than specific pattern.

To further demonstrate this interrelationship, I've listed the makings of an additional pattern in each style. Throughout the instructions, I also refer to adjustments useful when adapting the principles to other Usual patterns. Pattern potential is virtually limitless. However, to master just these three is essentially to master all.

Original Usual (also see color insert, figure 12)

Hook: Light wire dry fly, sizes 12-22 (i.e., Orvis Dry Fly, model 15098-00, or Partridge Capt. Hamilton Dry Fly, code L3A)

Thread: Gray, pre-waxed 6/0 nylon

Wing: Snowshoe rabbit's foot guard hair and underfur tied in as a clump

Tail: Snowshoe rabbit's foot underfur with some guard hair tied in as a clump

Body: Snowshoe rabbit's foot underfur dubbed on thread

Hendrickson Usual (also see color insert, figures 12 and 13)

(Alternative Example Related to the Original Usual)

Hook: Light wire dry fly, sizes 12-16 (i.e., Orvis Dry Fly, model 1509-00, or Partridge Capt. Hamilton Dry Fly, code L3A)

Thread: Tan, pre-waxed 6/0 nylon

Wing: Snowshoe rabbit's foot guard hair and underfur tinted gray and tied in as a clump

Tail: Snowshoe rabbit's foot underfur with some guard hairs tinted gray and tied in as a clump

Body: Pinkish tan underfur found near the shoulder of the red fox (or synthetic substitute) dubbed on thread

Tying the Original Usual

❶ Cut snowshoe rabbit from section of foot appropriate to fly size and separate into three bunches as described on page 201.

❷ With butts facing rearward, tie in first clump of guard hair and underfur you separated. Position as wing about two-thirds of the way from hook bend to eye. Trim butts to help taper body later. Now, pull wing back and make several tight turns of thread in front to spirit wing upright. Wind thread to tailing position. (See figure 1.)

❸ The second bunch of rabbit you separated becomes the tail. Tie in as short clump on top of and just ahead of bend of hook. Leave butts long enough to meet butts of wing. Then form tapered underbody by winding thread forward to envelop butts of both tail and wing. Wind thread back to base of tail. (See figure 2.)

❹ Using fingers, blend some underfur and fine guard hairs of third bunch into dubbing. Dub onto thread so body will be tapered. Wind dubbing forward to a position ahead of wing but far enough back from hook eye to permit easy access. Whip finish and lacquer to complete fly. (See figure 3.)

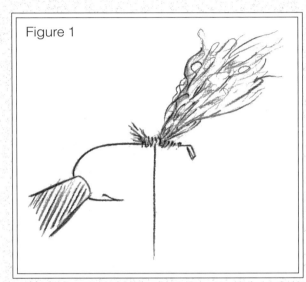

Figure 1

The original Usual is *scruffy*, with a short wing and tail and husky body. Both wing and tail are quite thick and dense, and the body is dubbed so stray fibers are encouraged to "break up" its silhouette. This character is maintained when tying many effective variations, including those as simple as tinting wings and tails or using alternative fur blends to vary body colors.

However, the character is also easily adjusted. A more dunlike impression can be created, for instance, by slimming down the entire fly. The wing is taller and less dense, the tail longer and sparser, with a higher proportion of guard hairs to underfur. The body is slim and precisely tapered.

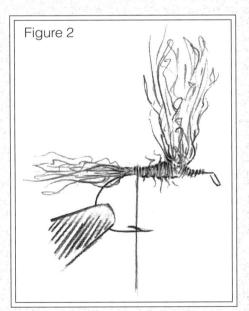

Figure 2

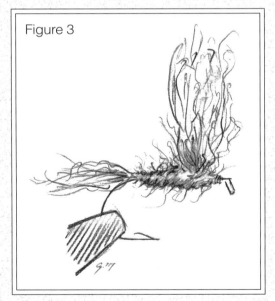

Figure 3

→

March Brown Usual Dun Emerger (also see color insert, figures 12 and 13)

Hook:	Light wire dry fly, sizes 10-12 (i.e., Orvis Dry Fly, model 1509-00, or Partridge Capt. Hamilton Dry Fly, code L3A)
Thread:	Orange, pre-waxed 6/0 nylon
Wing:	Snowshoe rabbit's foot guard hair and underfur tinted light brownish amber, variegated with indelible black or dark brown ink and faced with a sprig of well-marked, dark lemon wood duck fibers
Tail:	Snowshoe rabbit's foot guard hair and underfur tinted brownish amber, topped by wood duck guard hair fibers
Ribbing:	Black silk thread
Body:	Coarse blend of red fox underfur and seal's fur in pale brownish amber. Top of abdomen is dappled from base of tail to base of wing with dark brown ink

Sulphur Usual Dun Emerger (also see color insert, figures 12 and 13)

(Alternative Example Related to March Brown Usual Dun Emerger)

Hook:	Light wire dry fly, sizes 14-22 (i.e., Orvis Dry Fly, model 1509-00 or Partridge Capt. Hamilton Dry Fly, code L3A)
Thread:	Primrose, orange or hot orange, pre-waxed 6/0 nylon, depending on Sulphur species imitated

Wing: Snowshoe rabbit's foot guard hair and underfur, natural or tinted pale gray, tied in as a clump and faced with a sprig of lemon wood duck or gray mallard fibers, depending on insect

Tail: Snowshoe rabbit's foot guard hair and underfur, either natural or tinted pale gray, topped by a few wood duck fibers

Body: Pale yellow to yellow orange poly dubbing blend in keeping with natural insect imitated

Tying the March Brown Usual Dun Emerger

❶ Tint snowshoe rabbit pale brownish amber on foot as described above. Allow color to set. Cut guard hair and underfur and separate into three bunches. When cutting and separating, consider that this pattern has a longer and slimmer wing and tail than the original Usual in comparable sizes.

❷ Again the first clump of rabbit guard hair and underfur you separate becomes wing. Tie in as for original Usual but leave room for wood duck facing. Leave thread in front of wing and touch butts with drop of lacquer. (See figure 4.)

❸ Gather wing between thumb and forefinger and apply variegation markings on all sides with fine-tip black or brown pen. With wing compressed, markings should appear as horizontal bars. Release wing and allow ink to set. Although added work, variegations enhance the impression of movement in the finished fly. Colors can be varied according to naturals you imitate. (See figures 5 and 6.)

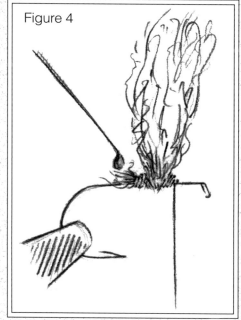

Figure 4

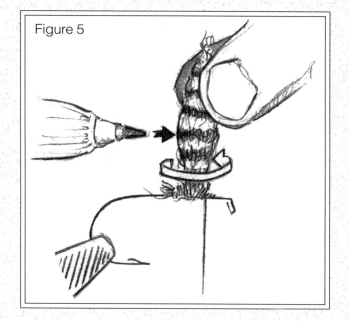

Figure 5

Figure 6

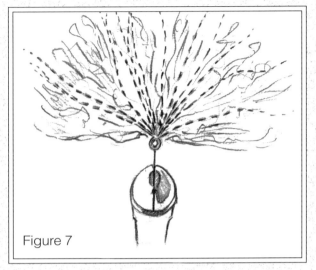

Figure 7

❹ Tie in sprig of wood duck flush to front of wing and splay both rabbit and wood duck until wing appears head-on as shown in drawing. Now wind thread back to tailing position, pausing to lash down wing butts on the way. (See figure 7.)

❺ Using the second bunch of tinted guard hair and underfur you separated, tie in tail on top of and just ahead of bend of hook. Tail should be longer and less dense than that of original Usual. Leave tail butts long enough to meet wing butts. Tie in a few wood duck fibers atop rabbit tail. Taper underbody by winding thread forward to base of wing and back to base of tail. Tie in several inches of black silk for rib. Dub abdomen material on tying thread. It should be quite smooth and tight. (Thorax dubbing later will be scruffy and loose. See figure 8.)

❻ Wind trim but tapered abdomen forward to base of wing. Rib to same point and secure. Dapple top of abdomen with dark brown pen. Dub thorax to permit easy access. Thorax should include stray fibers to represent legs and enhance illusion of movement. If too smooth, pick out dubbing with needle after whip finishing and lacquering head. (See figure 9.)

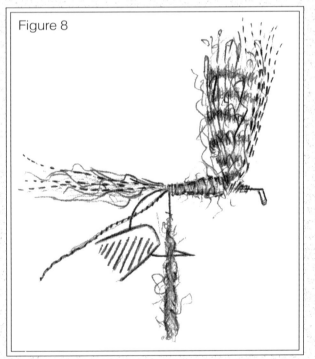

Figure 8

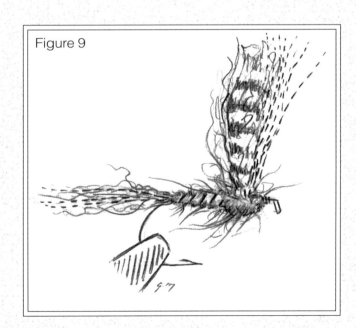

Figure 9

March Brown Usual Emerging Nymph

Hook:	Long shank dry fly, sizes 10-12 (i.e., Mustad No. 94831)
Thread:	Amber, pre-waxed 6/0 nylon
Tail:	Three long, reddish cock ring-necked pheasant tail fibers, split
Ribbing:	Black silk thread
Abdomen:	Coarse blend of red fox underfur and seal's fur in pale brownish amber. Top of abdomen is dappled from base of tail to rear of wing case with dark brown ink
Wing Case:	Section of ring-necked pheasant, ruffed grouse or brown turkey quill, pre-lacquered and split with a needle after being tied in
Emerging Wing:	Snowshoe rabbit's foot guard hair and underfur tinted light brownish amber (Optional—can be faced with a sprig of well-marked, dark lemon wood duck fibers)
Thorax:	Coarse blend of hare's mask and seal's fur in pale brownish amber, picked out after tying

Sulphur Usual Emerging Nymph (also see color insert, figure 14)

(Alternative Example Related to March Brown Usual Emerging Nymph)

Hook:	Light wire dry fly, sizes 14-22 (i.e., Orvis Dry Fly, model 1509-00, or Capt. Hamilton Dry Fly, code L3A)
Thread:	Amber, pre-waxed 6/0 nylon
Tail:	Tips of 3 or 4 reddish, cock ring-necked pheasant tail fibers, tied very short
Abdomen:	3 or 4 reddish brown, cock ring-necked pheasant tail fibers twisted on bright, golden yellow silk thread
Wing Case:	Section of cock ring-necked pheasant or ruffed grouse (red-phased bird) quill pre-lacquered and split with a needle after being tied in
Emerging Dun (might also be called wing):	Snowshoe rabbit's foot guard hair and underfur tinted yellowish orange and tied in as short clump
Thorax:	Coarse blend of hare's mask and seal's fur in orangy brown, picked out

Tying the March Brown Usual Emerging Nymph

❶ Tint snowshoe rabbit pale brownish amber on foot as described above. Set aside.

❷ Begin by tying tail and abdomen as for standard nymph dressing being careful to split tails, rib evenly and pick out abdomen on sides to suggest gills. Dapple top of abdomen with dark brown pen. To this point, fly should look from above as in accompanying drawing. (See figures 10 and 11.)

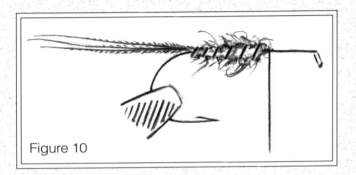

Figure 10

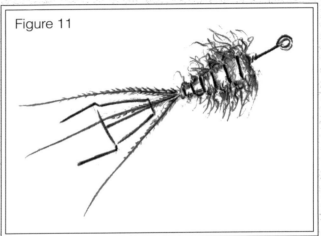

Figure 11

❸ Choose section of pheasant, grouse or turkey quill for wing case. Using sewing needle and tips of thumb and middle finger, lacquer section either while still on quill or after cut away. Allow time to set. Tie in wing case on top of hook immediately in front of abdomen, then split wing case carefully down middle with sewing needle. (See figure 12.)

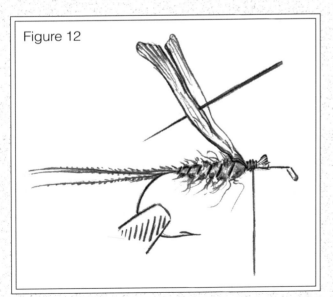

Figure 12

❹ Returning to tinted rabbit's foot, cut a relatively small amount of guard hair and underfur and separate into three bunches. (Depending on whether you want high or low silhouette, either first or second bunch will become wing. After deciding, put alternative bunches aside for use on other flies.) Tie in wing with butts facing rear about one-half distance between base of wing case and anticipated location of head. Secure well, clip butts as close as possible and taper butts with several turns of thread. Pull wing back and make several tight turns in front to spirit wing upright. If desired, tie in wood duck facing as described

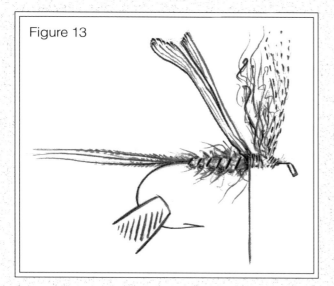

Figure 13

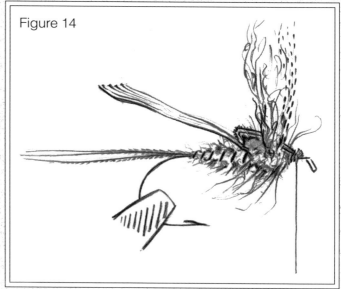

Figure 14

for March Brown Usual Dun Emerger. Wind thread back to base of wing case. (See figure 13.)

❺ Dub thread loosely with coarse thorax blend. Wind fulsome thorax to a position ahead of wing but far enough back from hook eye to permit easy access after wing case is also tied in. Using sewing needle, crease wing case across base. Bring rear (left) wing case strip forward over top of thorax and tie off as for nymph. (See figure 14.)

❻ Bring front (right) wingcase strip forward over top of thorax and tie off. (Be careful; two sections begin abutting as close as possible in front of wing.) Wind small, neat head, whip finish and lacquer. Remove fly from vise and pick out thorax with dubbing needle. Using thumbs and forefingers of both hands, stroke material from bottom of thorax out to sides to represent legs. To finish fly, trim stray fibers from bottom (only) of thorax. (See figure 15.)

For Usuals of this style, proportions and silhouette are *extremely important*. Note that wingcases of some large mayflies, e.g., Green Drake, are very short in relation to overall body length. To reduce bulk, choose the most compressible winging material from the rabbit's foot and use more guard hair than underfur when tying in.

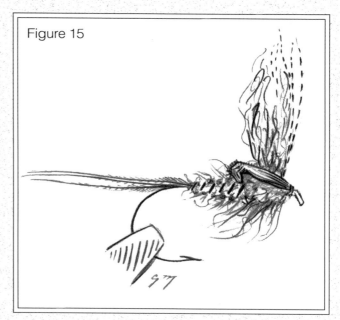

Figure 15

CHAPTER 23

The "Right" Foot Forward

Have you ever presented a floating fly to a rising trout, certain the fly is right *on* the fish's feeding lane, only to have the trout show no interest at all? We all have. Let's assume a suitable fly pattern and that you've "wired" the trout's rise rhythm—that is, your fly appears to be where it ought to be when the target trout is most likely to rise to a natural. But still no go. Then what about the old maxim: "Off by an inch, off by a mile." Herein may reside your problem and here are some whys, wherefores and what I've learned to do to compensate.

In the main, only two situations usually oblige dry fly fishermen to be "right on the money": (1) copious hatches or spinner falls when so many flies are on the surface, notwithstanding the size of the naturals, that trout needn't (so won't) move to gorge themselves; and (2) when naturals are both tiny and abundant, and so for trout to gain maximum nourishment for minimum energy expended dictates as little movement as possible.

Now, neither of these presentation challenges occur during all hatches, which means you've got to be on the ball to recognize them. Among the best ways to accomplish this is as simple as seeing how you do at the end of each outing. In other words, if you do well, you're either already "on," so to speak, or precise presentation isn't critical. However, if you keep coming up empty, you'd better be sure you're playing the "game of inches."

Also be mindful that the situation may change from day to day during any given insect emergence. During Hendrickson hatches here in the East, for example, I have days when it seems trout are willing to swim halfway across every pool to gobble my duns or emergers, others when they simply won't budge. Considerable movement to tiny flies is rare, however, which is unfortunate since the

The presentation style of each angler is somewhat different. But that doesn't diminish the need for absolute accuracy under certain situations. Note that Galen Mercer's stance, if you will, is slightly more upright than mine shown on the following page, in part, I guess, because I am much taller than he is. The critical thing, though, to be seen here clearly, is your ability to monitor your fly's progress *directly*, as Galen is doing correctly over his rod.

combination of small, hard-to-see imitations and absolute accuracy is no piece of cake even for the most skilled angler.

Over the years I've observed hundreds of dry fly fishermen, and if I've learned anything, it's that no two, even the best, go at it in exactly the same manner. Dry fly presentation, however, is fundamentally rooted in fly casting, and although perhaps it should go without saying, it follows that the better caster you become, the more accurate your presentations tend to be. But how good you are *doesn't* necessarily relate to how far, for instance, you can cast, nor to how "pretty" your style is. For example, how Lee Wulff with his unorthodox style managed to get flies within feet, much less inches, of where he wanted them is still something of a mystery to me. But then, Lee Wulff was Lee Wulff. What more need be said?

Each year thousands of new folks take up dry fly fishing, many of whom cut their teeth at fly fishing schools. Having audited several schools, I sometimes come away uneasy because of a seeming preoccupation with student priorities, most notably that ol' demon distance, rather than the need to convey a full and clear perception that fly casting is but one element of stream strategy that is comprised of a meticulously evolved index of tactics and techniques, cerebral as well as mechanical. Moreover, some instructors seem to overemphasize "just getting it out there," I suppose that is to minimize student frustration, although doing so comes at the expense of sufficient emphasis on what really ought to be the point from the outset: *exactly where on the water the fly ends up.*

Instructors argue, with justification, that teaching time is short, student expectations are ofttimes inordinately high and that the very survival of a school may depend at least as much on satisfied graduates as on competent ones. It's better, or so the inference goes, to turn out "happy casters" than to risk loss to the sport of "unhappy casters." No comment. But it does seem that as a result, all sorts of little "tricks" are taught—"drift" in casting mechanics notable among them—which, though serving perhaps to keep the beginner's backcasts off the water and thus him from looking bad to himself or others, can cost countless trout in years to come.

For the record, I believe the less "drift" incorporated into the mechanics of a precise dry fly presentation, the better.

Anyone who knows me knows I believe good baseball batting coaches can teach as much, or more, about fly casting as most fly casting instructors. Hitters learn by having it drummed into them via muscle memory that *keeping it simple* is the most likely route to Cooperstown. Nothing more than a hitch in your swing, for example, will ultimately "gitcha" as it did even the great Willie Mays when his lifelong swing-hitch eventually made it impossible for him to catch up with the fastball.

The ultimate bugaboo, though, is anything that takes a batter's eye off the ball, even for a microsecond, as it zooms toward the plate. Much the same is the case with regard to firing a rifle, shooting pool—or *fly casting*. Just try "drifting"

See the difference between my presentation style and Galen's on the previous page? But see, too, that essentially we end up "in the same place," that is, into the cast and in position to watch our flies directly rather than obliquely. I should also note that I, like Galen, do it the same way *every time*, with the hallmark being to "keep it simple."

next time you get yourself into a friendly dart game at the neighborhood saloon and see who ends up sporting beers all evening.

Let's look at an accurate dry fly presentation from the bottom up, and since there's probably greater crossover between anglers and shooters than anglers and baseball buffs, I'll trade metaphors from bats and balls to shootin' irons and targets for purposes of illustration. Also for convenience, I'm going to presume you're right-handed. (Southpaws need only reverse everything.)

First comes foot positioning. At almost every fly fishing school you'll notice that practice casters stand either (1) with their left feet in front of their right or (2) with feet parallel to each other, that is, square to the water in front of them.

The former is all right *if* the object is distance casting, for instance, or simply to get the fly, bit of red wool, or whatever, onto the water somewhere. But it's the kiss of death to accuracy unless you happen to be a master compensator, in which case it's unlikely you'd be taking the school in the first place. Positioning students thusly, however, is handy for instructors, for it expedites the turning of the students' heads to monitor backcast height and timing. Left-foot-in-front-of-right also boosts distance potential, by the way, because placing the bulk of your weight on your right foot during the backcast while maintaining balance with the toes and ball of your left, then transferring your weight smoothly in the course of the power stroke and follow-through, first from the back foot and toes of the front foot to the ball of the back foot and finally fully to the front foot, assists you in driving line. Throw in a double-haul, and you may make a helluva tarpon fisherman one day—if that's your goal.

The latter, the square-to stance, or planting your feet side-by-side, has *no* redeeming qualities in fly casting, or for that matter virtually any other aspect of sport I can think of with the possible exception of the hockey goalie's crouch. In fact, the stance is antithetical to the grace and coordination required of feet and legs intrinsic to almost any athletic endeavor. Specifically with regards to fly casting, it at once undermines distance potential while making pinpoint accuracy virtually impossible even for the most skillful practitioner.

So, where are you? You're flat-footed, that's where. Or equally awkward, you're rocking precariously back and forth from the balls to the heels of your feet in unison. Or just maybe you're rotating your hips alternately to the right and rearward, and vise versa, with each back and forward cast respectively, which at least demonstrates you're instinctively inclined, quite correctly, to want to get one foot (which one for the moment is not my concern) out in front of the other so you'll be using more than your arms with which to cast. For be aware that if you don't swivel, that's exactly what you're most likely doing—arm casting—which typically causes exaggeration of the power stroke, hence turning what you'd hope might be a respectable presentation into something more akin to a lob, the misadventure which prompts many novices to fly casting classes in the first place.

And as for accuracy, forget it. The square-to stance thwarts accuracy even more profoundly than the left-foot-in-front-of-right-foot stance does.

Which, for purposes of illustration, brings us to shooting.

Have a rifle handy? If not, use a broom, a yardstick, a closed umbrella—anything you can sight along as though you were aiming at a charging "buff" and your life depended on an accurate shot. Bring the "stock" to your shoulder, plant your feet side-by-side, and keeping *both eyes open*, aim at a small target. You should observe the terrifying reality that your chances of hitting that target are virtually nil. Then, close your right eye and sight again. Worse yet, no? Why? Because you're sighting down the "barrel," not directly but obliquely. But now close your left eye and open your right and repeat the exercise. Better? You bet. That's because, notwithstanding the multiple drawbacks of your stance, at least you're eyeballing the target directly.

Now place your left foot in front of your right and go through the entire process again. You should note marginal improvement in the first and second steps but certainly not enough to stake your life on. But when you close your left eye and open your right, you'll see that you're looking *directly* over the barrel of the "rifle," that is, sighting *directly* on your target. You need then only to fire to save your skin. If you still have doubts, try alternately opening and closing your right and left eyes and see what happens. You wouldn't want to stake your life on a left-eyed shot, now would you?

Next time you pick up a fly rod, take the same test—but this time actually place some small object—say a saucer—within reasonable dry fly presentation range. First, stand square-to and try to place your fly on the saucer, then put your left foot in front of your right and try again. No easy task, right? But now try reversing your feet so your right foot is in front of your left and have at it again. *Voilà.* The difference should be immediately apparent, as your fly will land pretty as you please on the saucer almost every time. But why?

Simple. When you attempt a dry fly presentation while standing square-to or with your left foot in front of your right, whether you know it or not, you're sighting on your target obliquely, that is, at an angle. However, by placing your right foot in front of your left, you're now sighting directly over your rod at the target and therefore what you're seeing is what is really happening, not some optical illusion that deceives you into believing your fly is where it isn't. Then for the ultimate revelation, try positioning yourself with your right foot in front of your left and making your presentation to the saucer with your left eye closed. *Wow.*

Although your body configuration is considerably different than when employing either the square-to or left-in-front-of-right casting stances, the transition to a right-in-front-of-left stance isn't difficult *if* you recognize that all fly presentation, notably precise dry fly presentation, involves not just hand-eye

Illustration 1 Not with this rifle—an old .32-.20 lever action from my collection—but with "enough gun" as Robert Rouark used to say, I'd bet my life against any charging lion or buff. (Given, of course, that I didn't spook and run off in search of my mommy's apron.) Reason? Stance is right, that is, solid, and most important, I'm sighting directly, not obliquely, on my target. Note my right eye is sighting over the barrel, my left tightly shut. That's the way it should be done, and the same applies to accurate presentation of flies.

Illustration 2   Catch the similarity between this and the rifle-aiming illustration on the previous page? As in that one, my form is right, that is, leaning *into* the cast, but most important is that I'm sighting directly *over* my rod to where my fly is. Any distortion of the image which might occur (it doesn't with me) can be overcome by closing your left eye, too, as one must do when sighting a rifle. Whichever way you opt to go, though, both eyes open or one eye closed, learn to focus absolutely on your target. Other chores, such as making casting loops in your left hand like the one I'm starting here as I retrieve line, should be done without looking down, and so away, from the principal job of fly monitoring.

coordination but harmonious interaction throughout your entire body. In other words—while keeping it simple—to pull off an accurate dry fly presentation, your feet, legs (especially knees), waist, abdomen, chest, lower and upper arms, shoulders, neck and eyes must be no less in sync than when undertaking to hit a precise golf shot. And just as with the golf shot, the more synchronous this interaction, the better, that is, the more accurate your presentation is likely to be.

Begin by standing, rod in hand, as you would to cast with your left foot in front of your right. In my case, at approximately six feet tall, the distance between

Illustration 3   This is what typically happens when an angler casts with his left foot forward. His profile is either more or less straight up and down or tilted somewhat rearward, as shown here. The consequence is that most of his weight is thrown backwards, too, and rests on his right foot (just where it shouldn't be). Posturally, then, virtually everything is already out of whack before you even begin to consider the angle at which he observes his fly once he has completed a fly presentation.

my left heel and a point exactly parallel to my right toes is about two to four inches, depending largely on the push of the current. Now note that your weight inclines to be concentrated on your back (right) foot and that your overall body profile is more or less straight up-and-down or even cocked slightly rearward.

Next, holding your rod and line in the ready-to-cast position, take one step forward with your back foot so it's now in front of and parallel to what formerly had been your front foot. For comfort and balance, you'll probably slide your left (rear now) foot slightly outboard, thus ending up with your feet spread somewhat farther apart than they were in the left-foot-forward stance. That's fine. The rectilinear distance between your front heel and rear toe, however, will most likely remain about the same, or in my case two to four inches.

You'll immediately note, too, a dramatic change in weight distribution and overall body posture, as most of your weight should shift to your right (front) foot. Most likely you'll find yourself bending somewhat at the knees and stabilizing your overall balance with the ball of your left foot. No doubt you'll also bend at the waist. Positioned thusly, or decidedly forward, you'll be leaning *into the cast* (as opposed to straight up-and-down or away from it) as it should be.

Your rod's pitch should be ahead of the vertical and your working line clasped in your left hand about three inches in front of you, an inch or so above and approximately four inches to the left of where a trousers' belt buckle is normally worn. Bear in mind, however, that these measurements will vary somewhat from angler to angler depending on height and build, so you'll have to make small adjustments to accommodate your physique.

Presuming you already have line on the water (or lawn) in front of you, initiate a backcast by lowering your rod tip, then drawing and lifting, driving the line behind you as though you were, as the late Joe Brooks used to teach, tossing a pebble over your shoulder. Keep the rod's plane as vertical and straight as possible, as opposed to oblique, your right elbow tucked in and as far forward as you can. Ideally, the right elbow should be three or so inches directly off your right side at the completion of the backcast—or about the width of a hardcover copy of *War and Peace.*

Using the old "clock" guide—no matter what anyone tells you to the contrary—*stop* your rod tip to complete the backcast at about 10 o'clock. Do not "drift" rearward, either with arm or rod tip. The only "drift" there ought to be will come from your left hand—the one holding your line—and left arm, both of which will quite naturally and comfortably slide from the position where you initiated the backcast to one about four inches above your belt buckle, four inches to its right and six or seven inches off your lower midriff.

Also note the dramatic redistribution of your weight and change in your posture in the course of making the backcast. As you rock gently backwards, the preponderance of your weight should shift from your right foot to your left, with your right heel now coming to perform the balance function the ball of your left foot had performed earlier on. Note, too, that while your left knee remains bent, as does your waist, your right leg will straighten, even lock, at the completion of the backcast.

Allow sufficient time for the backcast to straighten out completely. You won't be able to monitor your backcasts by turning your head as you can in the left-foot-in-front-of-right stance. So you'll have to learn to do this by "feel"—excellent

Illustration 4 From the first day I learned that at certain times of the season you had better know *exactly* where your fly is at all times, I have used the right-foot-forward technique. I think this illustration by my fishing partner Galen Mercer clearly demonstrates why. Note how I'm leaning *into* the cast, and although this is a side-view, you can just tell that my rod hand and right eye are perfectly coordinated to see my fly directly rather than obliquely. For a long time, though, I was more or less a voice crying in the wilderness. Of late, however, more and more anglers are converting, most notably *Fly Fisherman Magazine* Editor and Publisher John Randolph, who spends one heck of a lot of time "doing research" astream, gets to fish with the best just about everywhere and so knows the game as well as anyone.

Illustration 5   Couldn't be simpler, as our forefathers in their wisdom understood, than the old clock system. My aim here is for a tight loop, and therefore I've stopped my rod a 11 o'clock on the back cast and brought it to a point just a tick ahead of 1 o'clock on the forward cast. See how short the power stroke really need be? In fact, the shorter the power stroke, within reason, the greater the speed you can build into a cast. By lengthening the power stoke, you open the loop and thus slow down the cast. By adding a single, much less double, haul, a 10-inch power stroke makes casting a full fly line a piece of cake—not that you should really want to do so if trout fishing and accuracy are the game you are playing.

training. (In time, deprived of the visual crutch, you'll even learn to shoot line into the backcast, an important tool when both distance and accuracy are called for.) At the precise instant your line straightens out behind you, then, it's time to begin either a forward false cast or the forward cast designed to place your fly on the water precisely where it ought to be.

First, let's look briefly at a forward false cast, then move on to the "moment of truth," actually presenting and monitoring a dry fly. Before doing either, however, I really should note that additional backcasts in essence will be repetitions of the mechanics I've just described, except that since you'll presumably have more line in the air with each subsequent backcast, you'll have to adjust, particularly your timing, accordingly.

Reverse line direction for a forward false cast by flicking your right forearm ahead while keeping your right elbow tucked in and as stationary as you can. In other words, don't "reach" or otherwise roll your arm, or you'll alter (for the worse) your line's course in the air. Nor should the straight plane of your rod change one iota.

With this in mind, and again using the ol' "clock" as a guide (refer to illustration 5), propel your line forward until your rod tip is situated between one and two o'clock. Notice how, as your line glides to the front, your body's weight will gradually shift once more to your right foot and ball of your left, how your knees and waist will bend *into the cast* again and that your left hand, even while releasing some line into the air, will retreat either smoothly and gradually or with a pronounced tug—depending on how much line speed you seek to build—down and away until it comes to a point about two inches off and three inches in front of your left hip. Maintain this posture until the line straightens out before you and it's time to undertake another backcast.

Now, having completed the desired number of false casts, fore and aft, it's time to place your dry fly exactly where you want it on the surface. Neither the mechanics nor optics alone of doing so should prove difficult, even given your revised, that is, right-foot-in-front-of-left-foot, stance. However, you will have to be sure you end up shooting, that is, casting, the right length of line, one element of this transition you'll master only with considerable practice.

Two hints, though. (1) If you make a mistake, make it short, not long, because by overshooting the mark, you'll "leader" your target trout and likely put it down. (2) *Do not*, as instructors commonly suggest, seek to measure line length "in the air," that is, by false casting until your fly passes over your target trout's feeding lane. A trout is only marginally less likely to spot a fly and/or leader whizzing over its head or principal focus of its attention in or on the water upstream than a bit of tippet on the surface between its narrow feeding lane and a drifting dry fly.

Now, to make an accurate presentation, begin with a backcast as described above, but as your line, leader and fly straighten out behind you, drive, rather than flick, the line forward, or as though hammering a nail, to borrow again from Joe Brooks. Keep the power stroke *short*, or between 9 and 10 inches (as shown in illustration 5), measuring from the point of the tip of your thumb extended along the top of the cork grip at the start and finish of this compact movement. A longer power stroke, like "going to sea in a sieve," opens your casting loop, causing your line to arc in the air, which diminishes line speed instead of maintaining or increasing it, and consequently sabotages line control in terms of both distance and accuracy.

Remember, *keep it simple*. If you do so, when you begin the power stroke, your torso, legs (including your knees), and feet should be positioned and balanced just as when culminating a backcast, as should your left arm and hand. Likewise, as described above, your weight distribution and overall posture should shift forward while in the midst of your power stroke. But now, as your left arm and hand move downward and to the left, you'll release either all (if called for) or the portion of line needed to reach your target, as well as to compensate for, say, intervening currents that cause drag.

Line release timing is *critical*, since if you let go too soon, the cast will literally fall apart; too late and you'll either hustle your line downward onto the water,

Here it is, a no-miss presentation—if I do say so myself. All the elements are there, and besides, I know what occurred next. I once wrote that "the biggest mistake many anglers make is to give trout too much credit." True enough. But even at that, 90-percent of all trout caught each season are still caught by 10-percent of the anglers. Why? Simple. Too many anglers also fail to recognize that to be good at it, you simply have to master the fundamental skills that give you the advantage, the edge if you will, over your not-too-bright quarry.

which causes it to collide with, rather than light on, the surface, or to just unfold in a manner a friend of mine delicately likens to "a cow running and pooping."

Because your goal is absolute accuracy, right elbow tuck also remains crucial at this juncture, as your rod—its plane sweeping through the air maintained as always straight as possible—should pass as close to your right cheek as the combined width your right shoulder and bicep will permit. Indeed, if you're very broad shouldered or have been pumping *mucho* iron, you may actually have to reposition your head somewhat to the right—say, to a point over your right collarbone. In doing this, however, be careful not to distort your square-to perspective of the surface and your target trout's feeding lane.

Regardless of the angle of rod pitch eventually involved in a given fly presentation, you should always seek to complete a cast with your rod virtually in front of your right eye, or so you're looking *directly* over it at your drifting fly. In the simplest situations this requires only that you spirit your rod smoothly butt to tip a few inches to your left, that is, inboard, during the brief follow-though period that begins immediately in the wake of the power stroke.

In many instances, though, you'll find that during the follow-through, you'll also be required to execute one or more of the scores of dry fly presentation refinements you learn over the years. Examples: given a left-to-right direction of flow, bringing your rod across your body while your line is still in the air in order to create an upstream bow of line on the surface; wiggling your rod tip to create "S's" in your line; or maybe kicking your line backwards abruptly, then lowering your rod tip dramatically, the "stop-and-drop," illustrated earlier, an excellent means by which to coax drag-preventing slack into your leader and tippet.

No matter how many niceties you introduce into a presentation, though, you want to end up monitoring your fly directly over your rod. Otherwise, your view of both fly and line of drift will be oblique and thus distorted sufficiently to cause your dry to miss the trout's feeding lane by that inch which, as every dry fly fisherman must learn sooner or later, can prove to be the proverbial mile.

The upshot of that right-foot-forward presentation on the previous page—this lovely brown that was rising in a tricky spot close to the far bank. Moreover, it was one of those fish that had I been off by an inch, I might as well have been off by a mile. Ultimately, each angler must measure his or her own success by a multitude of personal criteria. To some, catching fish isn't of much importance. Fine. But if catching fish *is* important to you, it should go without saying that you're far better off doing it right. Then, ultimately, you'll know that you've got it made when the time comes that you are more surprised when a trout doesn't take your fly than when one does.

The Center of Solitude

It had rained for three days, the kind of light rain that seems to descend upon Maine rather than fall. The front that had drawn the weather in had come with a mean force that had whipped both ponds into whitecaps. But just as suddenly as it had materialized in the notch between the mountains to the west, it had pushed on, leaving a chill sullenness that softened all your images, of the ponds, the bog, the spruce forest and the mountainside, into shades of putty, gray, bronze and black. The rounded summits of the mountains dissolved into the low-hung clouds, and standing there on the porch of the cabin, there was no shaking a feeling that the whole world lay under a mantle of semi-darkness and brooding silence.

Inside the cabin it was warm. We had stood a fire three days back when the front had driven up off the big pond and had maintained it faithfully by turns around the clock, even during the first day or so when we had ventured out slickered down to troll fruitlessly for landlocks. The cabin rested in a clearing surrounded by spruce on a narrow bridge of high ground between the two ponds. Vince had bought it—stolen it, we liked to tell him—from the guy who had built it, a plumbing contractor from downstate, Bangor, I think. The outside walls were of logs, but the guts of it the builder had trucked in about seven miles along a tangle of narrow lanes cut by the paper company that owned most of the surrounding wilderness.

It was a good cabin, tight and laid out not so much to make you comfortable in the Winnebago sense as to impress you instantly with the degree to which man has neglected his soul in his infatuation with convenience. There were four rooms, two small ones for stacked sleeping, a big living room dominated by a stone fireplace and a kitchen from which—Vince confided after one too many pops—all women had been strictly barred under the jurisdiction of the previous owner. Each piece of furniture was a treasure of tramp art, whacked out of local wood and nailed or glued together by a man who obviously recognized the transience of his future intentions. Vince's wife, Adele, had made some changes to be sure, but although they were not intended to be obtrusive—a gas range to go with the old gas refrigerator, paisley curtains for the living room windows, a tired braided rug and cushions for the chairs and davenport—each one seemed somehow to stick out in this setting, to compromise an unstated determination that had begun when the plumbing contractor resolved to put in no plumbing.

Before the rain came, trolling on the big pond had been good. Alternating stations on two old wooden boats powered by 10-horse motors, each of the five of us—Vince, Rick and me, all out-of-staters, and Parker and Wes, both downeasters—had hung at least two silvery salmon that whaled into tandem streamers skipping through the chop. With the change, though, the breeze had died, flattening out the surface, but more disastrous still, the barometer had crashed, putting all the salmon, or so it seemed, into the sort of sulk that invariably sticks until the weather breaks. Even being out on the pond under such conditions is a sloppy, discouraging affair, and so when after a day and a half of it Parker declared, "If 10 people tell you you're drunk, by Jeezus, you better know enough to lie down," it didn't take a lot more palaver to adjourn us to the orange glow of kerosene lamps playing off our wooden walls, bubbling baked beans and tin cups socked with smoky Scotch and, of course, poker.

Marathon poker is an ideal opiate for waiting out stinkers, and at first at least an apparently inexhaustible repertoire of one-liners, played to the house by Parker and Wes with emphasis on the downeastern twang, made losing your nickels, dimes and quarters almost as much fun as fishing. But unconsciously, as night and day began merging into indefinite periods of disoriented retreat, a pervasive sense of confinement and its inescapable consequence, mute hostility among the squeezed, started to occupy each of us in turn until it mingled with the aura of amber light and cigar smoke into an impossible atmosphere of stagnation approaching physical pain.

"Interest you in another drink?" Parker coaxed Wes sometime deep in the third night.

"Not likely, by Jeezus, unless you happen to be packin' an auxiliary liver," Wes replied, his deadpan expression screened by the cards he had gathered up to shuffle.

"Somebody's light," Vince said abruptly around his cigar.

Parker looked at Wes, and Wes looked at Parker. "I'm in," they announced in unison.

"Me, too," I echoed mechanically.

"Don't look at me," Ricky told his brother-in-law a little defensively.

"Whatcha goin' to do, Ricky, jap us for a quarter?" Vince challenged derisively, brandishing his tin cup in front of Rick's nose.

"Wouldn't put it past ol' Wes," Parker tried.

"Hey, Vince, why don't you have another fifth for the road," Rich cut him off. His youthful face all at once seemed etched by 10,000 years of primordial competition always there, I guess, within families imposed on one another through marriage. "I told you I was in . . ."

"Well, I'm out," I declared, pushing my chair away from the table, standing up and striding toward the room where I'd been sleeping. "Why don't you donate my ante to the cause of world peace," I added irritably over my shoulder, still at the time wondering, *had it been me?*

I was aware the weather had cleared even before I awakened. Something in the night must have told me, perhaps a change in barometric pressure, and cast me into the deepest sleep where the immediate past can no longer touch you. Nor can I be entirely certain of the precise instant at which my woolly consciousness arrived at the decision, but by the time I awoke to the still darkened clockshop of masculine breathing, every part of my person except my body had already fled this place for the day.

I left a note, something akin to, *All—Have hightailed it for awhile. Fill the boats, willya*, grabbed an apple, a couple of slices of bread, a hunk of butter wrapped in foil and my miniature hot dog grill, and wearing hip boots and my fly vest and carrying a light fly rod, left the cabin by the door that fronts on the small pond.

To hear Vince talk, you'd hardly know the small pond existed. Partly filled in and silty, it held no landlocks, he complained, as if this trifle was symptomatic of disease or intentional transgression. Besides, to Vince's eyes the small pond was ugly, bordered as it was at its lower end by a broad swath of perennially yellow bluepoint grass that gave way near its head, just below the mouth of a little feeder stream, to a bog bristling with the skeletons of downed spruce trees. Vince could see beauty in none of this, not in the dense islands of loosestrife clinging to the defeated spruces nor in the tea-colored water that caused the islands to heave and bow when the wind blew hard. And failing to mark this beauty, he was blind, too, to the great bull moose that parted the islands as he ambled out to feed and to the coppery reflection of the mountains and the sky with its changing cloud formations on the rippled surface, deaf to the yodeling of the loons, the tapping of working woodpeckers and the breath of a simple breeze pushing the leaves of yellow birch and mountain ash and bending the grasses away from the water.

Above a bend at the head of the pond the feeder wandered through a wide meadow. Halfway up the meadow, I could see a bulge in the stream where a small beaver dam impounded the water. The sun was well up now, and I felt hungry. Finding a fallen spruce, I settled on its trunk and set my rod aside. The apple I'd decided to eat was cold and sugary and snapped smartly when I bit into it, and so I chewed slowly, savoring its sweetness while the taste was gently appropriated by my mind to mingle deliciously with the warmth of the sun and the fragrance of clean air.

From somewhere across the meadow a raven called, two quick *cr-r-rucking* sounds that I interpreted to mean, "Howya doing?"

"Just fine now, and you?" I answered with crisp whistles.

"Never better," the raven replied, repeating its call.

"Come closer," I whistled.

"Thought you'd never ask," it answered, soaring suddenly from out of the darkness behind the woodline and lighting at the pinnacle of a wind-bleached spruce.

"I'm going fishing," I whistled. "Had to get away."

"So I see," the big black bird replied.

"Right up there." I indicated the beaver dam.

"Okay by me," the raven cr-r-rucked.

"Good spot?" I wondered.

"Ought to be," the bird answered with a shrug. "Not a fisherman myself."

"Thought I'd try using a Parmachene Belle," I called.

"A Maine fly?" inquired the raven.

"A Maine fly," I whistled.

"Is there any other kind?" the raven replied.

"Want some apple?" I asked. "You see, we don't eat the cores."

"Don't know what you're missing," answered the big bird. "That's where all the vitamins are and the seeds we carry around with us until we drop them somewhere where another tree might grow."

"Why don't you drop over and pick it up?" I suggested.

"Should stop and tell the beavers you're coming first," was the bird's reply. "Just leave it on the stump there if you don't mind."

"Right you are," I assured the raven.

"Bye, now," the raven crucked.

"Bye, now," I whistled to my departing visitor.

"*Cr-r-ruck, cr-r-ruck, cr-r-ruck,*" it answered back to me.

"You, too," I whistled. "Maybe see you again . . ."

The blackened skin of three small brookies sizzled between the jaws of my grill, absorbing the smoke and heat of the campfire I'd made from twigs sprung from branches the beavers had scooted along en route to their damsite. I had laid the fire of twigs over a fistful of chips I'd found scattered near the pointed stump of a downed poplar, and now it snapped and flared with the touch and go of a fondling breeze. The sky was clear, not a cloud, and against it, the mountains from base to summit exhibited for me their true, unobstructed colors, looking almost one-dimensional the way Van Gogh and Cezanne painted them, close yet far away, hung by one of those artists with a genius for seeing country. The pool, ruffled only by the circling breeze, betrayed none of the fuss that had disturbed it just a few minutes earlier when the three little brook trout had wriggled on the surface until I could slide each of them into the grass on the streambank.

I had taken only three—one, two, three—on consecutive casts, but with them lying in the grass at my feet, their red spots haloed by incandescent blue, a part of me was tempted to take more, to keep taking for no more complicated reason than the little trout were so easy to take. But there was another part of me, the part, I'm sure, that could hear a chain saw working a ways off yet, perhaps beyond the next ridge, that could recall the whine of our outboard motors on the big pond, remember the honking of horns in Manhattan, the clatter of factories in the heartland, the hollow cries from men in despair pleading, "No, no more," and so instead I had rested my rod against a tuft of grass growing from a lump of black turf and had set about cleaning the three trout quickly and neatly and certainly lovingly. Now they were almost ready, swelling and glistening with butter, to flake in my fingers; the firm, golden meat I would lift to my mouth to savor and swallow, to make part of me forever, there where the stream bulged about halfway up the meadow around the bend above the head of the small pond, in Maine, at the center of solitude.

Index

Note: Page numbers followed by c refer to the caption/picture on that page.

About
the Author

Art Lee, the editor-at-large for *Fly Fisherman* Magazine, has been writing for that bible of the sport since the mid-1970s, longer than any other contributor. His 40-plus years of experience have earned Lee the reputation of being the consummate writer and angler.

Lee takes pride in being a fishing writer who actually fishes. The words from his pen flow from his line as he fishes at home and abroad, where he has caught nearly every species of sport fish from bluegill to blue marlin. He has fished the most storied fresh and salt waters of the United States, Canada, South America, Africa, Europe, the Caribbean, and the Pacific.

He has recorded his vast experience in an impressive body of work that includes hundreds of articles for a wide range of publications. He is the editor-at-large of *The Atlantic Salmon Journal* and *Wild Steelhead & Salmon* Magazine. He has also written two other books for Human Kinetics, *Fishing Dry Flies for Trout on Rivers and Streams* and *Tying and Fishing the Riffling Hitch*.

Lee is the only three-time winner of the Orvis Writing Award for excellence in the fields of outdoor and conservation journalism. Through his appearances on ESPN's *Fly Fishing the World* and ABC's *The American Sportsman*, he has become the most recognizable face in American fly fishing. Lee and his wife, Kris, live and work in the Catskill Mountains of New York.

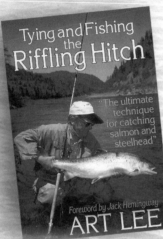
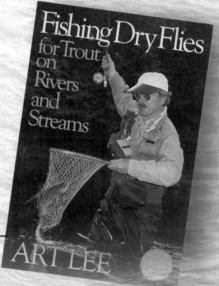